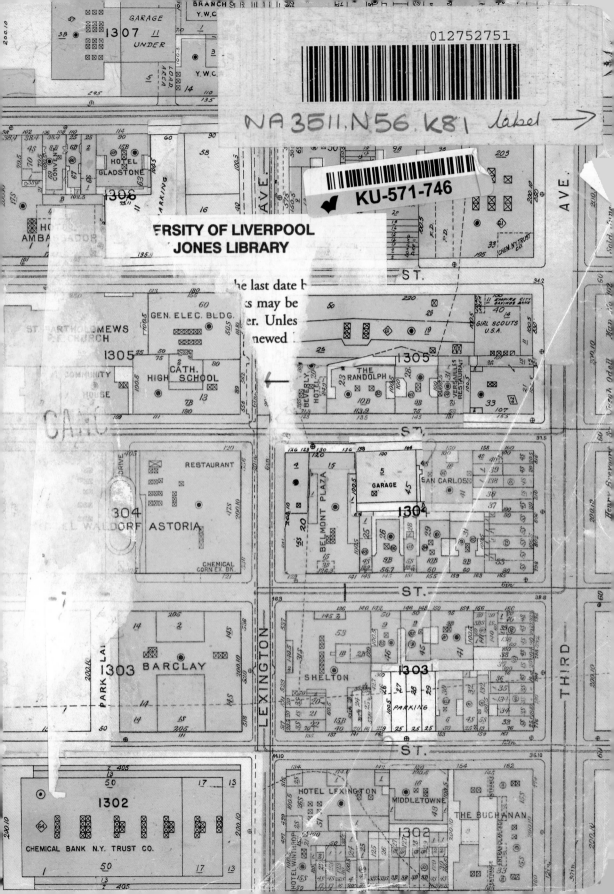

Delirious New York

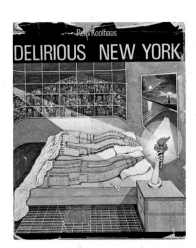

Delirious New York, 1978.

Delirious New York
A Retroactive Manifesto
for Manhattan

Rem Koolhaas

010 Publishers, Rotterdam

New edition first published in the English language in all countries of
Europe, Japan, Korea, Taiwan and the U.K. and Commonwealth
(except Canada) in 1994 by
010 Publishers,
Watertorenweg 180, 3063 HA Rotterdam, The Netherlands.

New edition first published in all other countries by
The Monacelli Press, Inc.
10 East 92nd Street, New York, NY 10128.

CIP/ISBN 90·6450·211·0

Printed and bound in Italy

Contents

9   **Introduction**

13   **Prehistory**

29   **Coney Island: The Technology of the Fantastic**

81   **The Double Life of Utopia: The Skyscraper**
82   The Frontier in the Sky
110   The Skyscraper Theorists
132   The Lives of a Block:
       The Waldorf-Astoria Hotel and the Empire State Building
152   Definitive Instability: The Downtown Athletic Club

161   **How Perfect Perfection Can Be: The Creation of Rockefeller Center**
162   The Talents of Raymond Hood
178   All the Rockefeller Centers
208   Radio City Music Hall: The Fun Never Sets
220   Kremlin on Fifth Avenue
230   2 Postscripts

235   **Europeans: Biuer! Dalí and Le Corbusier Conquer New York**

283   **Postmortem**

293   **Appendix: A Fictional Conclusion**

313   Notes

317   Acknowledgments

318   Credits

Introduction

Philosophers and philologists should be concerned in the first place with poetic metaphysics; that is, the science that looks for proof not in the external world, but in the very modifications of the mind that meditates on it. Since the world of nations is made by men, it is inside their minds that its principles should be sought.
— Giambattista Vico, *Principles of a New Science*, 1759

Why do we have a mind if not to get our way?
— Fyodor Dostoyevski

MANIFESTO

How to write a manifesto — on a form of urbanism for what remains of the 20th century — in an age disgusted with them? The fatal weakness of manifestos is their inherent lack of evidence.

Manhattan's problem is the opposite: it is a mountain range of evidence without manifesto.

This book was conceived at the intersection of these two observations: it is a *retroactive manifesto* for Manhattan.

Manhattan is the 20th century's Rosetta Stone.

Not only are large parts of its surface occupied by architectural mutations (Central Park, the Skyscraper), utopian fragments (Rockefeller Center, the UN Building) and irrational phenomena (Radio City Music Hall), but in addition each block is covered with several layers of phantom architecture in the form of past occupancies, aborted projects and popular fantasies that provide alternative images to the New York that exists.

Especially between 1890 and 1940 a new culture (the Machine Age?) selected Manhattan as laboratory: a mythical island where the invention and testing of a metropolitan lifestyle and its attendant architecture could be pursued as a collective experiment in which the entire city became a factory of man-made experience, where the real and the natural ceased to exist.

This book is an interpretation of that Manhattan which gives its seemingly discontinuous — even irreconcilable — episodes a degree of consistency and coherence, an interpretation that intends to establish Manhattan as the product of an unformulated theory, *Manhattanism,* whose program — to exist in a world totally fabricated by man, i.e., to live *inside* fantasy — was so ambitious that to be realized, it could never be openly stated.

ECSTASY

If Manhattan is still in search of a theory, then this theory, once identified, should yield a formula for an architecture that is at once ambitious *and* popular.

Manhattan has generated a shameless architecture that has been loved in direct proportion to its defiant lack of self-hatred, respected exactly to the degree that it went too far.

Manhattan has consistently inspired in its beholders *ecstasy about architecture.*

In spite — or perhaps because — of this, its performance and implications have been consistently ignored and even suppressed by the architectural profession.

DENSITY

Manhattanism is the one urbanistic ideology that has fed, from its conception, on the splendors and miseries of the metropolitan condition — hyper-density — without once losing faith in it as the basis for a desirable modern culture. *Manhattan's architecture is a paradigm for the exploitation of congestion.*

The retroactive formulation of Manhattan's program is a polemical operation.

It reveals a number of strategies, theorems and breakthroughs that not only give logic and pattern to the city's past performance, but whose continuing validity is itself an argument for a second coming of Manhattanism, this time as an explicit doctrine that can transcend the island of its origins to claim its place among contemporary urbanisms. With Manhattan as example, this book is a blueprint for a "Culture of Congestion."

BLUEPRINT

A blueprint does not predict the cracks that will develop in the future; it describes an ideal state that can only be approximated. In the same way this book describes a *theoretical* Manhattan, a *Manhattan as conjecture,* of which the present city is the compromised and imperfect realization. From all the episodes of Manhattan's urbanism this book isolates only those moments where the blueprint is most visible and most convincing. It should, and inevitably will, be read against the torrent of negative analyses that emanates from Manhattan about Manhattan and that has firmly established Manhattan as the *Capital of Perpetual Crisis.*

Only through the speculative reconstruction of a perfect Manhattan can its monumental successes and failures be read.

BLOCKS

In terms of structure, this book is a simulacrum of Manhattan's Grid: a collection of blocks whose proximity and juxtaposition reinforce their separate meanings.

The first four blocks — "Coney Island," "The Skyscraper," "Rockefeller Center" and "Europeans" — chronicle the permutations of Manhattanism as an implied rather than explicit doctrine.

They show the progression (and subsequent decline) of Manhattan's determination to remove its territory as far from the natural as humanly possible.

The fifth block — the Appendix — is a sequence of architectural projects that solidifies Manhattanism into an explicit doctrine and negotiates the transition from Manhattanism's unconscious architectural production to a conscious phase.

GHOSTWRITER

Movie stars who have led adventure-packed lives are often too egocentric to discover patterns, too inarticulate to express intentions, too restless to record or remember events. Ghostwriters do it for them.

In the same way *I was Manhattan's ghostwriter.*

(With the added complication that my source and subject passed into premature senility before its "life" was completed. That is why I had to provide my own ending.)

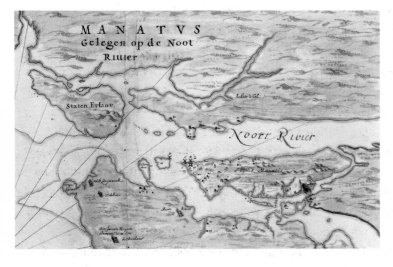

Manhattan: a theater of progress (small appendage near entrance to New York Harbor will later develop into Coney Island).

Prehistory

PROGRAM

"What race first peopled the island of Manhatta?

"They were, but are not.

"Sixteen centuries of the Christian era rolled away, and no trace of civilization was left on the spot where now stands a city renowned for commerce, intelligence and wealth.

"The wild children of nature, unmolested by the white man, roamed through its forests, and impelled their light canoes along its tranquil waters. But the time was near at hand when these domains of the savage were to be invaded by strangers who would lay the humble foundations of a mighty state, and scatter everywhere in their path exterminating principles which, with constantly augmenting force, would never cease to act until the whole aboriginal race should be extirpated and their memory ... be almost blotted out from under heaven. Civilization, originating in the east, had reached the western confines of the old world. It was now to cross the barrier that had arrested its progress, and penetrate the forest of a continent that had just appeared to the astonished gaze of the millions of Christendom.

"North American barbarism was to give place to European refinement."[1]

In the middle of the 19th century — more than 200 years into the experiment which is Manhattan — a sudden self-consciousness about its uniqueness erupts. The need to mythologize its past and rewrite a history that can serve its future becomes urgent.

The quotation above — from 1848 — describes Manhattan's program with disregard for the facts, but precisely identifies its intentions. Manhattan is a *theater of progress.*

Its protagonists are the "exterminating principles which, with constantly

Jollain, "bird's-eye view of New Amsterdam," 1672.

augmenting force, would never cease to act." Its plot is: barbarism giving way to refinement.

From these givens, its future can be extrapolated forever: since the exterminating principles never cease to act, it follows that what is refine-ment one moment will be barbarism the next.

Therefore, the performance can never end or even progress in the con-ventional sense of dramatic plotting; it can only be the cyclic restatement of a single theme: creation and destruction irrevocably interlocked, endlessly reenacted.

The only suspense in the spectacle comes from the constantly escalating intensity of the performance.

PROJECT

"To many people in Europe, of course, facts about New Amsterdam were of no importance. A completely fictitious view would do, if it matched their idea of what a city was...."[2]

In 1672 a French engraver, Jollain, sends into the world a bird's-eye view of New Amsterdam.

It is completely false; none of the information it communicates is based on reality. Yet it is a depiction — perhaps accidental — of the *project* Manhattan: an urban science fiction.

At the center of the image appears a distinctly European walled city, whose reason for being, like that of the original Amsterdam, seems to be a linear port along the length of the city that allows direct access.

A church, a stock market, a city hall, a palace of justice, a prison and, outside the wall, a hospital complete the apparatus of the mother civiliza-tion. Only the large number of facilities for the treatment and storage of animal skins in the city testifies to its location in the New World.

Outside the walls on the left is an extension that seems to promise — after barely 50 years of existence — a new beginning, in the form of a structured system of more or less identical blocks that can extend, if the need arises, all over the island, their rhythm interrupted by a Broadway-like diagonal.

The island's landscape ranges from the flat to the mountainous, from the wild to the placid; the climate seems to alternate between Mediterranean summers (outside the walls is a sugarcane field) and severe (pelt-producing) winters.

All the components of the map are European; but, kidnapped from their context and transplanted to a mythical island, they are reassembled into an unrecognizable — yet ultimately accurate — new whole: a utopian

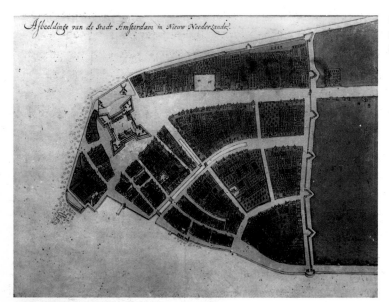

Bird's-eye view of New Amsterdam as built — "North American barbarism" gives way to "European refinement."

Phantom sale of Manhattan, 1626.

Europe, the product of compression and density. Already, adds the engraver, "the city is famous for its enormous number of inhabitants...." The city is a catalogue of models and precedents: all the desirable elements that exist scattered through the Old World finally assembled in a single place.

COLONY

Apart from the Indians, who have always been there — Weckquaesgecks in the south, Reckgawawacks in the north, both part of the Mohican tribe — Manhattan is discovered in 1609 by Henry Hudson in his search for "a new route to the Indies by way of the north" on behalf of the Dutch East India Company.

Four years later, Manhattan accommodates four houses (i.e., recognizable as such to Western eyes) among the Indian huts.

In 1623 30 families sail from Holland to Manhattan to plant a colony. With them is Cryn Fredericksz, an engineer, who carries written instructions on how the town should be laid out.

Since their whole country is man-made, there are no "accidents" for the Dutch. They plan the settlement of Manhattan as if it is part of their fabricated motherland.

The core of the new city is to be a pentagonal fort. Fredericksz is "to survey a ditch 24 feet wide and 4 feet deep enclosing a rectangle extending back 1,600 feet from the water and 2,000 feet wide....

"The outside of the surrounding ditch having been staked out as above, 200 feet shall be staked out at the inside along all three sides A, B, C, for the purpose of locating therein the dwellings of the farmers and their gardens, and what is left shall remain vacant for the erection of more houses in the future...."[3]

Outside the fort, on the other side of the ditch, there are to be 12 farms laid out in a system of rectangular plots separated by ditches.

But "this neat symmetrical pattern, conceived in the security and comfort of the company's offices in Amsterdam, proved unsuitable to the site on the tip of Manhattan...."

A smaller fort is built; the rest of the town laid out in a relatively disorderly manner.

Only once more does the Dutch instinct for order assert itself: when the settlers carve, out of the bedrock, a canal that runs to the center of the city. On either side is a collection of traditional Dutch houses with gabled roofs that maintains the illusion that the transplantation of Amsterdam into the New World has been a success.

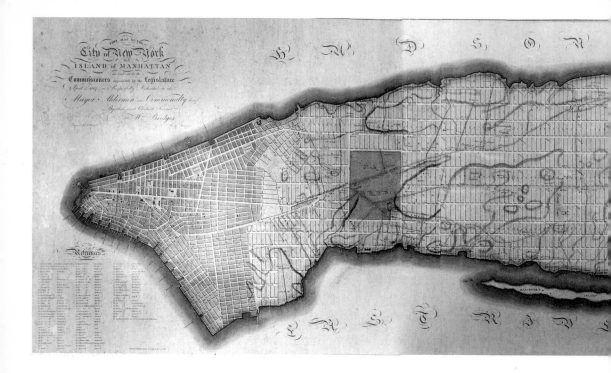

In 1626 Peter Minuit buys the island Manhattan for 24 dollars from "the Indians." But the transaction is a falsehood; the sellers do not own the property. They do not even live there. They are just visiting.

PREDICTION

In 1807 Simeon deWitt, Gouverneur Morris and John Rutherford are commissioned to design the model that will regulate the "final and con-clusive" occupancy of Manhattan. Four years later they propose — above the demarcation that separates the known from the unknowable part of the city — 12 avenues running north-south and 155 streets running east-west.

With that simple action they describe a city of 13 x 156 = 2,028 blocks (excluding topographical accidents): a matrix that captures, at the same time, all remaining territory and all future activity on the island. The Manhattan Grid.

Advocated by its authors as facilitating the "buying, selling and improving of real estate," this "Apotheosis of the gridiron" — "with its simple appeal to unsophisticated minds"[4] — is, 150 years after its super-imposition on the island, still a negative symbol of the shortsightedness of commercial interests.

In fact, it is the most courageous act of prediction in Western civilization:

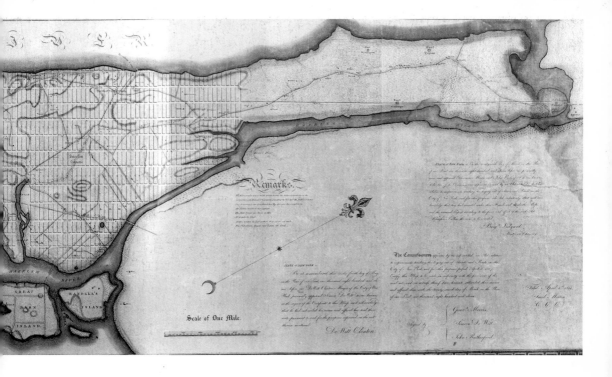

the land it divides, unoccupied; the population it describes, conjectural; the buildings it locates, phantoms; the activities it frames, nonexistent.

REPORT

The argumentation of the Commissioners' report introduces what will become the key strategy of Manhattan's performance: the drastic disconnection between actual and stated intentions, the formula that creates the critical no-man's-land where Manhattanism can exercise its ambitions.

"One of the first objects that claimed their attention was the form and manner in which business should be conducted; that is to say, whether they should confine themselves to rectilinear streets or whether they should adopt some of these supposed improvements, by circles, ovals and stars, which certainly embellish a plan, whatever may be their effects as to convenience and utility. In considering that subject, they could not but bear in mind that a city is composed principally of the habitations of men, and that strait sided, and right angled houses are the most cheap to build, and the most convenient to live in. The effect of these plain and simple reflections was decisive...."

Manhattan is a utilitarian polemic.

"It may, to many, be a matter of surprise, that so few vacant spaces have

been left, and those so small, for the benefit of fresh air, and consequent observation of health. Certainly, if the city of New York were destined
to stand on the side of a small stream such as the Seine or Thames, a
great number of ample spaces might be needful; but those large arms of
the sea which embrace Manhattan island, render its situation, in regard
to health and pleasure, as well as to convenience and commerce,
peculiarly felicitous; when, therefore, from the same causes the price of
land is so uncommonly great, it seemed proper to admit the principles
of economy of greater influence than might, under circumstances of
a different kind, have consisted with the dictates of prudence and the
sense of duty...."

Manhattan is a counter-Paris, an anti-London.

"To some it may be a matter of surprise, that the whole island has not
been laid out as a city; to others, it may be a subject of merriment that the
Commissioners have provided space for a greater population than is
collected at any spot this side of China. They have been governed in this
respect by the shape of the ground.... To have come short of the extent
laid out might have defeated just expectation and to have gone further
might have furnished materials to the pernicious spirit of speculation...."[5]

The Grid is, above all, a conceptual speculation.

In spite of its apparent neutrality, it implies an intellectual program for
the island: in its indifference to topography, to what exists, it claims the
superiority of mental construction over reality.

The plotting of its streets and blocks announces that the subjugation, if
not obliteration, of nature is its true ambition.

All blocks are the same; their equivalence invalidates, at once, all the
systems of articulation and differentiation that have guided the design
of traditional cities. The Grid makes the history of architecture and all
previous lessons of urbanism irrelevant. It forces Manhattan's builders to
develop a new system of formal values, to invent strategies for the
distinction of one block from another.

The Grid's two-dimensional discipline also creates undreamt-of freedom
for three-dimensional anarchy. The Grid defines a new balance
between control and de-control in which the city can be at the same
time ordered and fluid, a metropolis of rigid chaos.

With its imposition, Manhattan is forever immunized against any (further)
totalitarian intervention. In the single block — the largest possible area
that can fall under architectural control — it develops a maximum unit of
urbanistic Ego.

Since there is no hope that larger parts of the island can ever be dominated by a single client or architect, each intention — each architectural ideology — has to be realized fully within the limitations of the block. Since Manhattan is finite and the number of its blocks forever fixed, the city cannot grow in any conventional manner.

Its planning therefore can never describe a specific built configuration that is to remain static through the ages; it can only predict that whatever happens, it will have to happen somewhere within the 2,028 blocks of the Grid.

It follows that one form of human occupancy can only be established at the expense of another. The city becomes a mosaic of episodes, each with its own particular life span, that contest each other through the medium of the Grid.

IDOL

In 1845 a model of the city is exhibited, first in the city itself, then as a traveling object to substantiate Manhattan's growing self-idolatry.

The "counterpart to the great Metropolis" is "a perfect *fac-simile* of New York, representing every street, land, building, shed, park, fence, tree, and every other object in the city.... Over the model is a canopy of carved ornamental woodwork in Gothic architecture representing in the finest oil-painting the leading business establishments of the city...."[6]

The icons of religion are replaced by those of building.

Architecture is Manhattan's new religion.

CARPET

By 1850, the possibility that New York's exploding population could engulf the remaining space in the Grid like a freak wave seems real. Urgent plans are made to reserve sites that are still available for parks, but "while we are discussing the subject the advancing population of the city is sweeping over them and covering them for our reach...."[7]

In 1853 this danger is averted with the appointment of the Commissioners of Estimate and Assessment, who are to acquire and survey land for a park in a designated area between Fifth and Eighth avenues and 59th and 104th (later 110th) streets.

Central Park is not only the major recreational facility of Manhattan but also the record of its progress: a taxidermic preservation of nature that exhibits forever the drama of culture outdistancing nature. Like the Grid, it is a colossal leap of faith; the contrast it describes — between the built and the unbuilt — hardly exists at the time of its creation.

"The time will come when New York will be built up, when all the grading

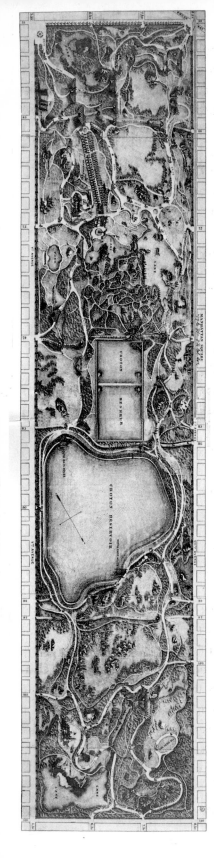

Manipulation of nature: "Tree moving Machine ... larger trees could be transplanted and the lag between planting and finished appearance reduced...."

Central Park, synthetic Arcadian Carpet grafted onto the Grid (plan c. 1870).

and filling will be done, and the picturesquely-varied, rocky formation of the island will have been converted into formations of rows and rows of monotonous straight streets, and piles of erect buildings. There will be no suggestion left of its present varied surface, with the exception of a few acres contained in the park.

"Then the priceless value of the present picturesque outlines of the ground will be distinctly perceived, and its adaptability for its purpose more fully recognized. It therefore seems desirable to interfere with its easy, undulating outlines, and picturesque, rocky scenery as little as possible, and, on the other hand, to endeavor rapidly, and by every legitimate means, to increase and judiciously develop these particularly individual and characteristic sources of landscape effects...."[8]

"To interfere as little as possible," but on the other hand *"to increase and develop landscape effects"*: if Central Park can be read as an operation of preservation, it is, even more, a series of manipulations and transformations performed on the nature "saved" by its designers. Its lakes are artificial, its trees (trans)planted, its accidents engineered, its incidents supported by an invisible infrastructure that controls their assembly. A catalogue of natural elements is taken from its original context, reconstituted and compressed into *a system of nature* that makes the rectilinearity of the Mall no more formal than the planned informality of the Ramble.

Central Park is a synthetic Arcadian Carpet.

TOWER

The inspiring example of London's International Exhibition, held in 1851 in the Crystal Palace, triggers Manhattan's ambition. Two years later, it has organized its own fair, staking a claim for its superiority, in almost every respect, over all other American cities. At this time, the city hardly extends north of 42nd Street — apart from the omnipresent Grid. Except near Wall Street it looks almost rural: single houses scattered on the grass-covered blocks. The fair, implanted on what will become Bryant Park, is marked by two colossal structures that completely overwhelm their surroundings, introducing a new scale into the island's skyline, which they dominate easily. The first is a version of London's Crystal Palace; but since the division into blocks precludes structures beyond a certain length, it is a cruciform whose intersection is topped by an enormous dome: "Its slender ribs seem inadequate to sustain its vast size and it presents the appearance of a balloon expanded and impatient for a flight into the far-off sky...."[9]

Latting Observatory.

Elisha Otis presents the elevator — anticlimax as denouement.

The second, complementary structure is a tower on the other side
of 42nd Street: the Latting Observatory, 350 feet high. "If we except the
Tower of Babel, this may perhaps be called the World's first
Skyscraper...."[10]

It is built of iron-braced timber, and its base accommodates shops. A
steam elevator gives access to the first- and second-floor landings, where
telescopes are installed.

For the first time, Manhattan's inhabitants can inspect their domain. To
have a sense of the island as a whole is also to be aware of its limitations,
the irrevocability of its containment.

If this new consciousness limits the field of their ambition, it can only
increase its intensity.

Such inspections from above become a recurrent theme under
Manhattanism; the geographical self-consciousness they generate is
translated into spurts of collective energy, shared megalomaniac goals.

SPHERE

Manhattan's Crystal Palace contains, like all early Exhibitions, an
implausible juxtaposition of the demented production of useless Victorian
items celebrating (now that machines can mimic the techniques of
uniqueness) the democratization of the object; at the same time it is a
Pandora's box of genuinely new and revolutionary techniques and
inventions, all of which eventually will be turned loose on the island even
though they are strictly incompatible.

For new modes of mass transportation alone, there are proposals for
underground, on-grade and elevated systems, which — though in
themselves rational — would, if applied simultaneously, utterly destroy
each other's logic.

As yet contained in the colossal cage of the dome, they will turn
Manhattan into a Galapagos Island of new technologies, where a new
chapter in the survival of the fittest, this time a battle among species of
machines, is imminent.

Among the exhibits in the sphere is one invention that above all others
will change the face of Manhattan (and, to a lesser degree, of the world):
the elevator.

It is presented to the public as a theatrical spectacle.

Elisha Otis, the inventor, mounts a platform that ascends — the major
part, it seems, of the demonstration. But when it has reached its highest
level, an assistant presents Otis with a dagger on a velvet cushion.

The inventor takes the knife, seemingly to attack the crucial element of

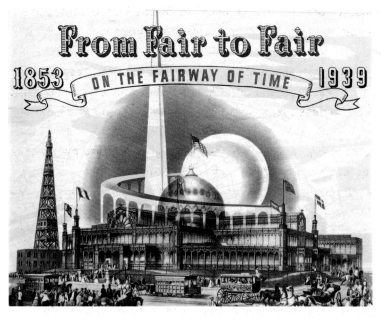

Crystal Palace and Latting Observatory at first New York World's Fair, 1853. Double image appearing in background: Trylon and Perisphere, theme exhibit of 1939 World's Fair. At the beginning and the end of Manhattanism: *needle* and *globe*.

his own invention: the cable that has hoisted the platform upward and that now prevents its fall. Otis cuts the cable; it snaps.

Nothing happens, to platform or inventor.

Invisible safety catches — the essence of Otis' brilliance — prevent the platform from rejoining the surface of the earth.

Thus Otis introduces an invention in urban theatricality: the anticlimax as denouement, the non-event as triumph.

Like the elevator, each technological invention is pregnant with a double image: contained in its success is the specter of its possible failure.

The means of averting that phantom disaster are almost as important as the original invention itself.

Otis has introduced a theme that will be a leitmotiv of the island's future development: Manhattan is an accumulation of possible disasters that never happen.

CONTRAST

The Latting Observatory and the dome of the Crystal Palace introduce an archetypal contrast that will appear and reappear throughout Manhattan's history in ever-new incarnations.

The *needle* and the *globe* represent the two extremes of Manhattan's formal vocabulary and describe the outer limits of its architectural choices.

The needle is the thinnest, least voluminous structure to mark a location within the Grid.

It combines maximum physical impact with a negligible consumption of ground. It is, essentially, a building without an interior.

The globe is, mathematically, the form that encloses the maximum interior volume with the least external skin. It has a promiscuous capacity to absorb objects, people, iconographies, symbolisms; it relates them through the mere fact of their coexistence in its interior. In many ways, the history of Manhattanism as a separate, identifiable architecture is a dialectic between these two forms, with the needle wanting to become a globe and the globe trying, from time to time, to turn into a needle — a cross-fertilization that results in a series of successful hybrids in which the needle's capacity for attracting attention and its territorial modesty are matched with the consummate receptivity of the sphere.

Location of Coney Island *vis à vis* Manhattan.
Toward the end of the 19th century, Manhattan's
new bridges and modern transportation technologies made Coney Island accessible to the
masses. Visible on Coney: on the left, Sandy

Hook, refuge for the criminal element of the
Greater New York area; at right, the Synthetic
Arcadia of the Grand Hotels; between them,
the "middle zone" of the three great parks—
an embryonic Manhattan.

Coney Island: The Technology of the Fantastic

The glare is everywhere, and nowhere a shadow.
— Maxim Gorky, "Boredom"

What a sight the poor make in the moonlight.
— James Huneker, *The New Cosmopolis*

Hell is very badly done.
— Maxim Gorky, "Boredom"

MODEL

"Now, where the waste was ... rise to the sky a thousand glittering towers and minarets, graceful, stately and imposing. The morning sun looks down on these as it might upon the magically realized dream of a poet or painter.

"At night, the radiance of the millions of electric lights which glow at every point and line and curve of the great play city's outlines lights up the sky and welcomes the home coming mariner thirty miles from the shore."[1]

Or:

"With the advent of night a fantastic city of fire suddenly rises from the ocean into the sky. Thousands of ruddy sparks glimmer in the darkness, limning in fine, sensitive outline on the black background of the sky shapely towers of miraculous castles, palaces and temples.

"Golden gossamer threads tremble in the air. They intertwine in transparent flaming patterns, which flutter and melt away, in love with their own beauty mirrored in the waters.

"Fabulous beyond conceiving, ineffably beautiful, is this fiery scintillation."[2]

Coney Island around 1905: it is no coincidence that the countless
"impressions of Coney Island" — products of a hopelessly obstinate
desire to record and preserve a mirage — can all be substituted not only
for each other but also for the flood of later descriptions of Manhattan.
At the junction of the 19th and 20th centuries, Coney Island is the
incubator for Manhattan's incipient themes and infant mythology. The
strategies and mechanisms that later shape Manhattan are tested
in the laboratory of Coney Island before they finally leap toward the
larger island.
Coney Island is a fetal Manhattan.

STRIP

Coney Island is discovered one day before Manhattan — in 1609, by
Hudson — a clitoral appendage at the mouth of New York's natural harbor,
a "strip of glistening sand, with the blue waves curling over its
outer edge and the marsh creeks lazily lying at its back, tufted in summer by green sedge grass, frosted in winter by the pure white snow...."
The Canarsie Indians, the original inhabitants of the peninsula, have
named it Narrioch — "Place Without Shadows" — an early recognition that
it is to be a stage for certain unnatural phenomena.
In 1654 the Indian Guilaouch trades the peninsula, which he claims is
his, for guns, gunpowder and beads in a scaled-down version of the
"sale" of Manhattan. It then assumes a long sequence of names, none of
which stick until it becomes famous for the unexplained density of
konijnen (Dutch for "rabbits").
Between 1600 and 1800 the actual physical shape of Coney Island
changes under the combined impact of human use and shifting sands,
turning it, as if by design, into a miniature Manhattan.
In 1750 a canal cutting the peninsula loose from the mainland is "the
last touch in fashioning what is now Coney Island ...."

CONNECTION

In 1823 the Coney Island Bridge Company constructs "the first artificial
connection between the mainland and the island,"[3] allowing it to consummate its relationship with Manhattan, where humans have by now
congregated in densities as unprecedented as that of Coney's rabbits.
Coney is the logical choice for Manhattan's resort: the nearest zone of
virgin nature that can counteract the enervations of urban civilization.
A resort implies the presence, not too far away, of a reservoir of people
existing under conditions that require them to escape occasionally

LUNA PARK AT NIGHT, CONEY ISLAND, N. Y.

"Where the waste was ..."

Coney Island: a clitoral appendage at the entrance to New York Harbor.

to recover their equilibrium.

Access must be carefully calculated: the channels from reservoir to resort must be wide enough to feed the resort with a continuous flow of visitors, yet narrow enough to keep a majority of urban inmates in place. Otherwise the reservoir will engulf the resort. Coney Island can be reached by an increasing number of artificial connections, but not too easily; at least two consecutive modes of transport are required.

Between 1823 and around 1860, as Manhattan changes from a city into a metropolis, the need for escape becomes more urgent. The cosmopolites who love Coney's scenery and its isolation construct, on its eastern end — the part furthest from Manhattan — a civilized Arcadia of large resort hotels full of brand-new 19th-century comforts, planted on unspoiled grounds that restore them to their senses.

At the opposite end of the island, that same isolation attracts another community of fugitives: criminals, misfits, corrupt politicians, united by their common dislike for law and order. For them the island is unspoiled by the law.

These two parties are now locked in an unspoken battle for the island — the threat of more corruption emanating from the western end competes with the puritanism of good taste in the east.

TRACKS

The battle becomes critical when the first railroad reaches the middle of the island in 1865, its tracks stopping dead at the surf line. The trains put the oceanfront finally within the reach of the new metropolitan masses; the beach becomes the finish line for a weekly exodus that has the urgency of a jailbreak.

Like an army, the new visitors bring a parasitic infrastructure in their wake: bath houses (where the largest number can change in the smallest possible space in the shortest possible time), food supplies (1871: the hot dog is invented on Coney Island) and primitive accommodation (Peter Tilyou builds Surf House, a tavern/hot dog stand, next to the railroad's abrupt terminus).

But the need for pleasure dominates; the middle zone develops its own magnetism, attracting a range of special facilities to provide entertainment on a scale commensurate with the demand of the masses.

In a laughing mirror-image of the seriousness with which the rest of the world is obsessed with Progress, Coney Island attacks the problem of Pleasure, often with the same technological means.

TOWER

The campaign to step up the production of pleasure generates its own instruments.

In 1876 a 300-foot tower — centerpiece of the Centennial Celebration in Philadelphia — is dismantled in anticipation of re-erection elsewhere.

Sites all over the States are considered and rejected; suddenly, after two years of disassembly, it stands reassembled in the middle zone of Coney.

From its top the whole island is visible and telescopes can be focused on Manhattan. Like the Latting Observatory, the Centennial Tower is an architectural device that provokes self-consciousness, offering that bird's-eye inspection of a common domain that can trigger a sudden spurt of collective energy and ambition.

It also offers an additional direction of escape: mass ascension.

FLOTSAM

The journey of the vagrant tower from Philadelphia to Coney Island establishes a precedent for the subsequent journeys to Coney of other remnants of Exhibitions and World's Fairs.

The island becomes the final resting place of futuristic fragments, mechanical flotsam and technological litter whose migration across the United States toward Coney coincides with the trek of tribes from Africa, Asia and Micronesia to the same destination. They too have been on display at the fairs, as a new form of educational entertainment.

This totemic machinery, a small army of midgets and other freaks who retire to Coney after a life of hectic traveling, some residual Red Indians who have nowhere else to go and the foreign tribes constitute the permanent population of this narrow beach.

BRIDGE

In 1883 the Brooklyn Bridge removes the last obstacle that has kept the new masses on Manhattan: on summer Sundays Coney Island's beach becomes the most densely occupied place in the world.

This invasion finally invalidates whatever remains of the original formula for Coney Island's performance as a resort, the provision of Nature to the citizens of the Artificial.

To survive as a resort — a place offering *contrast* — Coney Island is forced to mutate: it must turn itself into the total opposite of Nature, it has no choice but to counteract the artificiality of the new metropolis with its own Super-Natural.

Instead of suspension of urban pressure, it offers intensification.

TRAJECTORY

The reconstituted Centennial Tower is the first manifestation of an obsession that will eventually turn the entire island into a launching pad of the proletariat.

In 1883 the antigravitational theme it has initiated is elaborated in the Loop-the-Loop, a railroad that loops around itself so that a small vehicle will cling to an upside-down surface, provided it travels at a certain speed. As a piece of research, it is costly; it claims several lives each season. Only four customers at a time can experience the momentary weightlessness it affords, and only a limited number of vehicles can complete the inverted trajectory in an hour. These constraints alone doom the Loop-the-Loop as an instrument of mass exhilaration. Its offspring is the Roller Coaster, patented and built the very next season, 1884: its track parodies the curves, hills and valleys of a regular railway trajectory. Whole train-loads of people tear up and down its slope with such violence that they undergo the magic sensation of liftoff at the peaks; it easily supplants the Loop-the-Loop. The wriggly tracks multiply on their shaky supports, within a few seasons turning the entire middle zone into a vibrating mountain range of steel.

In 1895 Captain Boyton, a professional diver and pioneer of under-water living, introduces a crypto-Freudian complication into the battle against gravity with his Shoot-the-Chutes, a toboggan hoisted mech-anically to the top of a tower from which a diagonal slide descends toward a body of water. Anxiety as to whether the board will stay on top of the water or slip under the surface provides the suspense as the rider slides downward.

A steady flow of visitors climbs the tower for the descent toward the muddy water, which is otherwise inhabited by 40 sea lions. By 1890 "the thing that is furthest from reason, that laughs loudest at the laws of gravitation, is the thing that takes with the Coney Island crowd...."[4] Even before the opening of the Brooklyn Bridge, one venture has in-dicated the future direction of the island's pursuit of irrational ends by entirely rational means: the first "natural" element to be conquered and appropriated in the quest for the New Pleasure is an elephant "as big as a church" that is also a hotel.

"Its legs were 60 feet in circumference. In one front leg was a cigar store, in the other a diorama; patrons walked up circular steps in one hind leg and down the other."[5] Rooms can be had in thigh, shoulder, hip or trunk. Searchlights flash erratically from its eyes, illuminating anyone within range who has decided to spend the night on the beach.

A second annexation of nature is achieved with the creation of the Inexhaustible Cow, a machine constructed to satisfy the insatiable thirst of the visitors, then disguised as a cow.

Its milk is superior to the natural product in the regularity and predictability of its flow, its hygienic quality and its controllable temperature.

ELECTRICITY

Similar adaptations follow at a constantly accelerating rate.

The inordinate number of people assembling on the inadequate acreage, ostensibly seeking confrontation with the reality of the elements (sun, wind, sand, water) *demands* the systematic conversion of nature into a technical service.

Since the total surface area of the beach and the total length of surf line are finite, it follows with mathematical certainty that the hundreds of thousands of visitors will not each find a place to spread out on the sand, let alone reach the water, within a single day.

Toward 1890, the introduction of electricity makes it possible to create a second daytime. Bright lights are placed at regular intervals along the surf line, so that now the sea can be enjoyed on a truly metropolitan shift-system, giving those unable to reach the water in the daytime a man-made, 12-hour extension.

What is unique in Coney Island — and this syndrome of the Irresistible Synthetic prefigures later events in Manhattan — is that this false daytime is not regarded as second-rate.

Its very artificiality becomes an attraction: "Electric Bathing."

CYLINDERS

Even the most intimate aspects of human nature are subjected to experiment. If life in the metropolis creates loneliness and alienation, Coney Island counterattacks with the Barrels of Love. Two horizontal cylinders — mounted in line — revolve slowly in opposite directions. At either end a small staircase leads up to an entrance.

One feeds men into the machine, the other women.

It is impossible to remain standing.

Men and women fall on top of each other.

The unrelenting rotation of the machine fabricates synthetic intimacy between people who would never otherwise have met.

This intimacy can be further processed in the Tunnels of Love, an artificial mountain constructed next to the Barrels of Love. Outside the mountain the newly formed couples board a small boat that disappears

Metropolitan shift-systems (1): Electric Bathing —
the Synthetic becomes Irresistible.

Barrels of Love — anti-alienation apparatus.

Metropolitan shift-systems (2): Steeplechase
horsemen riding through the night.

inside a dark tunnel leading to an interior lake. Inside the tunnel complete obscurity ensures at least visual privacy; from the muffled noises it is impossible to guess how many couples are crossing the lake at any one time. The rocking of the small boats on the shallow water reinforces the sensuality of the experience.

HORSES

The favorite activity of the cosmopolites who enjoyed the island in its virgin state was horseback riding. But the ability to ride a horse is a form of sophistication not available to the people who have replaced the original visitors. And real horses can never coexist in adequate numbers on the same island with the new visitors.

In the mid-nineties George Tilyou — son of Peter Tilyou, the Surf House pioneer — lays out a mechanized track that extends over a large part of the island, a course that leads through a number of natural landscapes, along the oceanfront, and crosses a series of man-made obstacles. Over this track moves a herd of mechanical horses that can be ridden with instant confidence by anyone. The Steeplechase is an "automatic racetrack with gravitation as its motive power"; its "horses resemble in size and model the track racer. Staunchly built, they are to a certain extent under the control of the rider, who can accelerate the speed by the manner in which he utilizes his weight and the position on the descending and ascending grades, making each contest an actual race."[6] The horses operate 24 hours a day and are an unprecedented success. Financial investment in the track is recouped after three weeks of operation. Inspired by the Midway Plaisance, which connected the two halves of the Chicago World's Fair in 1893, Tilyou collects additional facilities — including a Ferris wheel from the same fair — along and around the mechanical course, gradually staking out a discrete amusement area that is formalized when in 1897 he erects a wall around it and channels his visitors through entrances marked by triumphal arches of plaster accumulations of the iconography of laughter — clowns, pierrots, masks. With the act of enclosure, Tilyou has established an aggressive opposition between what he names Steeplechase *Park* and the rest of the island.

FORMULA

Coney Island's reputation has plummeted even as its popularity has risen. The formula of innocent pleasures inside versus corruption outside — implied by Tilyou's enclave — is a first step toward possible rehabilitation. Such a compact oasis can be the planning module for a gradual reclamation of the island's otherwise lost territory. It would clearly be counterproductive for the various intramural facilities to compete by offering identical or incompatible pleasures. A process originates within the walls that generates a spectrum of coordinated facilities. The concept of the park is the architectural equivalent of an empty canvas. Tilyou's wall defines a territory that can — theoretically — be shaped and controlled by a single individual and is thereby invested with a thematic potential; but he fails to exploit fully his breakthrough. He limits his activities to extending the tracks, perfecting the realism of his horses and adding such obstacles as the "water jump," inventing only one more device to alienate further his park from the reality of the island: his entrances now lead directly to the Earthquake floor, where the natural skin of the earth is replaced by a hidden mechanical graft that shakes. The randomness and violence of the tremors demand surrender. To earn the right to enter Steeplechase, the visitor must participate in an involuntary ballet.

Exhausted by his inventions, Tilyou writes poetry and captures in a moment of lucid euphoria the significance of what he has helped create: *"If Paris is France, Coney Island, between June and September, is the World."*[7]

ASTRONAUTS

In 1903, the year the new Williamsburg Bridge injects even more visitors into Coney Island's already overtaxed system, Frederic Thompson and Elmer Dundy open a second park — Luna.

Dundy is a financial genius and an entertainment professional; he has experience with fairs, attractions and concessions. Thompson is Coney's first important outsider: he has no previous experience with any form of amusement. At 26, he has dropped out of architectural school, frustrated by the irrelevance of the Beaux-Arts system to the new age. He is the first professional designer active on the island.

Borrowing Tilyou's park-enclave model, Thompson invests it with systematic intellectual rigor and a degree of deliberation that puts its planning once and for all on a conscious and architectural basis. Steeplechase isolated itself from its surrounding mess on the most literal level: with a wall.

Thompson doubles the isolation of Luna Park by imposing a theme that embraces the entire site in a system of metaphorical meaning: its surface is to be "not of this earth" but part of the Moon. On entering, Luna Park's masses are turned into astronauts in a conceptual airlock through which they all have to pass:

"The Trip to the Moon on the airship Luna IV... Once on board of
the great airship, her huge wings rise and fall, the trip is really begun
and the ship is soon 100 feet in the air. A wonderful, widespread
panorama of the surrounding sea, Manhattan and Long Island seems
to be receding as the ship mounts upward.

"Houses recede from view until the earth fades from sight, while the
Moon grows larger and larger. Passing over the Lunar satellite the barren
and desolate nature of its surface is seen.

"The airship gently settles, the landing made, and the passengers enter
the cool caverns of the Moon...."[8]

In one gesture, the whole structure of mutually reinforcing realities on
earth — its laws, expectations, inhibitions — is suspended to create
a moral weightlessness that complements the literal weightlessness that
has been generated on the trip to the Moon.

THEORY

The center of Luna Park is a large lake, an echo of the lagoon at the
Chicago Fair. At one end of it stands the Shoot-the-Chutes; in this formal
position it more strongly invites descent into the regions of collective
unconscious.

The lake is lined by a forest of needlelike structures, specimens of Moon
architecture. Thompson's own comments indicate the acuteness of his
private rebellion against Beaux-Arts repression.

Traced by a reporter "in the midst of this planetary upheaval ... the
arch-plotter of this embryonic paradise ... [was] seated over an extinct
volcano of his own making and conjuring airy shapes out of the formless
void around him."

For Thompson, Luna Park is a manifesto:

"You see, I have built Luna Park on a definite architectural plan. As it is a
place of amusement, I have eliminated all classical conventional forms
from its structure and taken a sort of free renaissance and Oriental type
for my model, using spires and minarets wherever I could, in order to
get the restive, joyous effect to be derived always from the graceful lines
given in this style of architecture.

"It is marvelous what you can do in the way of arousing human emotions
by the use you can make architecturally, of simple lines. Luna Park is
built on that theory — and the result has proven that theory's worth."
This is 1903.

Thompson's pride is Luna's skyline, "an ensemble of snow-white

Luna Park skyline by day ...

... and by night.

pinnacles and towers limned against the blue firmament [that] is wonderfully pleasing to thousands of eyes heartily tired of the brick, mortar and stone of the Great City."

Before Thompson, single towers have often acted at fairs as lone climaxes of elaborate Beaux-Arts complexes, exclamation marks within carefully coordinated overall designs, deriving their dignity and impact from their singleness.

Thompson's genius is to let these needles proliferate at random, to create an architectural spectacle out of the drama of their frenzied scramble for individuality and to identify this battle of the spires as the definitive sign of otherworldliness, the mark of another condition.

This forest of towers, instead of Coney's virgin nature, now provides an antidote to the grimness of the city.

Season after season Thompson adds towers to his park. After three years he boasts: "Then, for our skyline we have just 1,221 towers, minarets and domes — a great increase over what we had last year." The growth of this architectural plantation becomes the compulsive measure of Luna's vitality: "You see, this being the Moon, it is always changing.

"A stationary Luna Park would be an anomaly."[9]

Even if on the Moon, Thompson has created the first City of Towers: functionless, except to overstimulate the imagination and keep any recognizable earthly realities at a distance. Now he uses electricity — the essential ingredient of the new paraphernalia of illusion — as an architectural duplicator.

In broad daylight Luna's small towers have a pathetic dimension, an aura of cheapness, but by superimposing over its skyline a network of wires and light bulbs, Thompson describes a second, illusory skyline, even more impressive than the first, a separate *city of night.*

"In the wilderness of the sky and ocean rises the magic picture of a flaming city," and "with the advent of night a fantastic city all of fire suddenly rises from the ocean into the sky.... Fabulous beyond conceiving, ineffably beautiful, is this fiery scintillation."

For the price of one, Thompson has created two distinct cities, each with its own character, its own life, its own inhabitants. Now the city *itself* is to be lived in shifts; the electric city, phantom offspring of the "real" city, is an even more powerful instrument for the fulfillment of fantasy.

INFRASTRUCTURE

To perform this miracle in three years, Thompson has compacted on the 38 acres of his park an infrastructure that makes it square inch for

square inch the most *modern* fragment of the world. Luna's infrastructure and communications network are more complex, elaborate,
sophisticated and energy-consuming than those of most contemporary
American cities.

"A few brief facts and figures will give an idea of the immensity of Luna.
1,700 persons are employed during the summer season. It has its own
telegraph office, cable office, wireless office and local and long distance
telephone service. 1,300,000 electric lights are used for illumination.
Throughout its acreage ... are suitable accommodations for 500 head of
animals.... The Towers, spires and minarets number 1,326 [1907]....
The admissions at the front gates since the opening of Old Luna Park
have totalled over 60,000,000...."[10]

If this infrastructure supports a largely cardboard reality, that is exactly
the point. Luna Park is the first manifestation of a curse that is to
haunt the architectural profession for the rest of its life, the formula:
technology + cardboard (or any other flimsy material) = reality.

APPEARANCE

Thompson has designed and built the *appearance,* the exterior, of a magic
city. But most of his needles are too narrow to have an interior, not
hollow enough to accommodate function. Like Tilyou he is finally unable
or unwilling to use his private realm, with all its metaphorical potential,
for the design of culture. He is still an architectural Frankenstein whose
talent for creating the new far exceeds his ability to control its contents.
Luna's astronauts may be stranded on another planet, in a magic city,
but they discover in the skyscraper forest the over-familiar instruments of
pleasure — the Bunny Hug, the Burros, the Circus, the German Village,
the Fall of Port Arthur, the Gates of Hell, the Great Train Robbery, the
Whirl-the-Whirl.

Luna Park suffers from the self-defeating laws that govern entertainment:
it can only skirt the surface of myth, only hint at the anxieties accumulated in the collective unconscious.

If there is a development beyond Steeplechase, it is in the explicit
ambition of the new devices to turn the provincialism of the masses into
cosmopolitanism.

In the Tango, for instance: "The principle of the famous dances that
have monopolized society has been utilized in the more modern rides.
One need not be adept in the terpsichorean arts to be up-to-date.
Convenient cars in which one comfortably reclines *go through the
motions of the dance.*

"They also wind through the wilds of South America, where the Tango originated.... This ride is a feast and a cure for all digestive ills...."[11]
From the mere imitation of a single experience such as horseback riding, the Irresistible Synthetic has progressed to the fusion of previously separate categories. The Tango combines technical emancipation — a machine performing cultivated rituals; an educational experience — a journey through the tropical jungle; and a medical benefit.
In the Fishing Pond, "live and mechanical" fish cohabit in a new round of Darwinian evolution.
For the 1906 season, Thompson injects the myth of Babylon's Hanging Gardens almost casually into Manhattan's bloodstream, growing 160,000 plants on the roofs of his enclave. This green carpet introduces a strategy of "layering" Luna, of improving its performance by superimposing an artificial plane on its original surface: "By the erection of an extremely ingenious and picturesque roof garden that will be known as the Babylonian Hanging Gardens, the capacity of Luna Park has been increased seventy thousand, while at the same time these gardens will afford protection for an even greater number of people in case of rain."[12]

ROOF

Tilyou, upstaged by Luna Park, retaliates with a gesture that anticipates the dilemmas of Modernism; if he encloses all his facilities in a single glass shed not unlike the Crystal Palace and advertises it as "the largest fireproof Amusement Building in the World," the utilitarian iconography of the glass box clashes with the entertainment inside.
The single roof drastically reduces the opportunities for individual facilities to display their own characters; now that they do not have to develop their own skins, they blur together like many molluscs in one gigantic shell in which the public is lost.
Outside, the naked facades repress all signs of pleasure; only one of the mechanical horses jumps through the frigid membrane of this early curtain wall to escape the fun factory.

LEAP

After two years of staggering success, Thompson finally zeroes in on his real target: Manhattan.
The isolation of Luna Park within Coney makes it an ideal architectural testing ground, but also insulates the results of any tests from direct confrontation with reality.

Sen. William H. Reynolds — real-estate
promoter and president of Dreamland.

Metaphoric entrance to Dreamland —
entire park is "underwater."

In 1904 Thompson buys part of a Manhattan block on Sixth Avenue between 43rd and 44th streets so that he can apply his multiple talents to a more critical test of his theories.

DESK

As Thompson plans the conquest of Manhattan from the confinement of his lunar Reich on Coney, Sen. William H. Reynolds plots *the park to end all parks* from behind his desk on the top floor of Manhattan's brand-new Flatiron Building. It is to be the conclusion of a sequence that has begun with Steeplechase and Luna.

Reynolds is a former Republican state senator and real-estate promoter, "always promoting himself into trouble";[13] after rejecting "Wonderland" as too inexact, he chooses the name "Dreamland" for his venture.

The triad of personalities and professions that Tilyou, Thompson and Reynolds represent — amusement expert/professional architect/developer-politician — is reflected in the character of the three parks:

Steeplechase, where the park format is invented almost by accident under the pressure of a hysterical demand for entertainment;

Luna, where this format is invested with thematic and architectural coherence; and finally

Dreamland, where the preceding breakthroughs are elevated to an ideological plane by a professional politician.

Reynolds realizes that to succeed, Dreamland must transcend its compromised origins and become a post-proletarian park, "the first time in the History of Coney Island Amusement that an effort has been made to provide a place of Amusement that appeals to all classes."[14]

Reynolds lifts many of Dreamland's components from the typology of pleasure established by its predecessors but arranges them in a single programmatic composition in which the presence of each attraction is indispensable to the impact of the others.

Dreamland is located on the sea. Instead of the shapeless pond or would-be lagoon that is the center of Luna, Dreamland is planned around an actual inlet of the Atlantic, a genuine reservoir of the Oceanic with its well-tested catalytic potential to trigger fantasies. Where Luna insists on its otherworldliness by claiming an outrageous alien location, Dreamland relies on a more subliminal and plausible dissociation: its entrance porches are underneath gigantic plaster-of-paris ships under full sail, so that metaphorically the surface of the entire park is "underwater," an Atlantis found before it has ever been lost.

This is only one of the strategies Senator Reynolds employs to exclude reality from his state. In a flash-forward to the formal policies of Modernism, he chooses to identify his terrain by the *absence of color*. In contrast to the garishness of the two other parks, the whole of Dreamland is painted snow white, thus laundering whatever concepts it has borrowed through a graphic process of purification.

CARTOGRAPHY

According to an intuitive cartography of the subconscious, Reynolds arranges 15 facilities around his lagoon in a Beaux-Arts horseshoe and connects them with a completely even supersurface that flows from one facility to the next without a single step, threshold or other articulation — an architectural approximation of the stream of consciousness.

"All the walks are level, or inclined. The park being so laid out that there is no possibility of congestion of the crowds, 250,000 people can see everything and move around without fear of congestion."

Scattered across this Wonderpavement are small boys selling popcorn and peanuts, dressed as Mephistopheles to stress the Faustian nature of Dreamland's bargain. They constitute a proto-Dadaist army: every morning their supervisor, Marie Dressler, the famous Broadway actress, instructs them in "nonsense" — meaningless, enigmatic jokes and slo-gans that will sow uncertainty in the crowds throughout the day.

There is no plan left of Dreamland; what follows is a reconstruction based on the best available evidence.

1. Dreamland's steel pier, projecting half a mile into the ocean, is two stories high, with broad walks for 60,000 people. An excursion steamer leaves Manhattan's Battery every hour, so that Dreamland can be visited without setting foot on Coney.

2. The final manifestation of the Shoot-the-Chutes: "The largest ever built ... Two boats will descend side by side, and a moving staircase will take ... 7,000 people an hour to the top...."[15]

Located for the first time on the main axis of a park, the Chutes reinforce Dreamland's underwater metaphor; its toboggans are the perfect vehicles for descent into a world below the world.

3. Straddling the arrival pier is "the largest ballroom in the World" (25,000 square feet), a space so enormous that the intimate patterns of traditional ballroom dancing become meaningless.

Plan of Dreamland.
1. Steel Pier
2. Shoot-the-Chutes leading into Lagoon
3. Ballroom
4. Lilliputia
5. Fall of Pompeii
6. Ride in a Submarine
7. Incubator Building
8. End of the World
9. Circus
10. Creation
11. Flight Over Manhattan
12. Canals of Venice
13. Coasting Through Switzerland
14. Fighting the Flames
15. Japanese Teahouse with Santos Dumont Airship No. 9
16. Leap Frog Railway
17. Beacon Tower

View of Lilliputia — parliament in background.

"Aristocratic" midgets in deceptive pose:
the institutionalization of misbehavior.

In the technological frenzy of the time, the natural movement of the human body appears slow and clumsy. Roller skates are introduced into the delicate formal textures of the ballroom. Their speed and curvilinear trajectories strain the original conventions beyond the breaking point, atomize the dancers and create fresh and random rhythms of coupling and uncoupling between the sexes.

Tracing its own abstract course through this pandemonium, oblivious to the movements of the dancers, is an independent architectural satellite, "a novel contrivance consisting of a motor propelled platform [that] is run out on the floor with the [orchestra and] singers on it so that the entertainment can be enjoyed by everyone."[16] This platform is the harbinger of a truly mobile architecture, a generation of self-propelled tectonic satellites that can be summoned to any location on the globe to perform their particular functions.

4. Lilliputia, the Midget City: if Dreamland is a laboratory for Manhattan, Midget City is a laboratory for Dreamland. Three hundred midgets who had been scattered across the continent as attractions at World's Fairs are offered a permanent experimental community here, "a bit of old Nuremberg in the fifteenth century."

Since the scale of Midget City is half the scale of the real world, the cost of building this cardboard utopia is, at least theoretically, quartered, so that extravagant architectural effects can be tested cheaply. The midgets of Dreamland have their own parliament, their own beach complete with midget lifeguard and "a miniature Midget City Fire Department responding [every hour] to a false alarm" — effective reminder of man's existential futility.

But the true spectacle of Midget City is social experimentation. Within the walls of the midget capital, the laws of conventional morality are systematically ignored, a fact advertised to attract visitors. Promiscuity, homosexuality, nymphomania and so on are encouraged and flaunted; marriages collapse almost as soon as they are celebrated; 80 percent of newborn babies are illegitimate. To increase the *frisson* induced by this organized anarchy, the midgets are showered with aristocratic titles, highlighting the gap between implied and actual behavior.

Midget City represents Reynolds' institutionalization of misbehavior, a continuing vicarious experience for a society preparing to shed the remnants of Victorianism.

Fall of Pompeii — "new inventions which have just been put into *practical* effect."

"Preemies" in incubator — the creation of a private race.

5. The Fall of Pompeii is the perfectionist culmination of a series of simulated disasters that have apparently become a psychological addiction for the metropolitan public. In a single day on Coney Island it is possible to "experience" the San Francisco earthquake, the burnings of Rome and Moscow, various naval battles, episodes from the Boer War, the Galveston Flood and (inside a Classical Greek temple decorated with a fresco of a dormant volcano) the eruption of Vesuvius, realized "with scenic and mechanical equipment coupled with a most extraordinary electric display ... new inventions which have just been put into *practical* effect."[17]

Each nightmare exorcised in Dreamland is a disaster averted in Manhattan.

6. Simulated ride in a submarine — and confrontation with "the inhabitants of the deep."

7. The Incubator Building: here most of the premature babies of the Greater New York area are collected and nursed to health in incubator facilities superior to those of any hospital at the time, in a benevolent variation of the Frankenstein theme. To soften the radicalism of an enterprise that deals openly with the issue of life and death, the exterior of the building is disguised as "an old German Farmhouse," on its roof "a stork overlooking a nest of cherubs" — old mythology sanctioning new technology.

Inside is an ultra-modern hospital divided into two parts, "a large clean room where almost motionless prematures doze in incubators"[18] and a nursery for the "incubator graduates" who have survived the first critical weeks of existence.

"As a scientific demonstration for the nurture of feeble infantile life, it is ... a practical, educational life-saving station...."[19]

Martin Arthur Couney, the first pediatrician in Paris, tries to establish his incubator institute there in the 1890s, but that project is aborted by medical conservatism. Convinced that his invention is an essential contribution to Progress, he exhibits his *Kinderbrut-Anstalt* ("Baby-Hatching Apparatus") at the International Exhibition in Berlin in 1896. Follows the familiar odyssey of a progressive idea/exhibit across the globe — to Rio de Janeiro, then Moscow — with Manhattan as its inevitable destination.

Only in the New Metropolis can Couney find and exploit the confluence of proper conditions: a limitless supply of "preemies", a passion for

Creation.

technology and, especially in Coney Island's middle zone — premature Manhattan — ideological sympathy.

Couney's installation gives the Irresistible Synthetic a new dimension, in which it directly affects the fate of human beings.

In the preemies Dreamland nurtures a private race whose graduates celebrate their survival in a yearly Dreamland reunion sponsored by Reynolds.

8, 9, 10. By the turn of the century it is evident that *creation* and *destruction* are the poles defining the field of Manhattan's abrasive culture; three separate spectacles show this awareness.

10. The Blue Dome of Creation, "Largest Dome in the World," represents the universe. "The visitor to this illusion glides backwards through sixty centuries in a grotesque craft along a water canal encircling the dome for a distance of one thousand feet. A moving panorama of the centuries is passed until the grand spectacular and dramatic climax, the portrayal of the actual Creation, is reached.... The waters part, the earth arises, inanimate and human life appear."[20]

8. Creation's mirror-image is the "End of the World — according to the Dream of Dante." In Dreamland, only 150 feet separate Beginning and End.

9. The Circus, featuring the "greatest aggregation of educated animals on earth," acts as a buffer in between.

The three spectacles unfold simultaneously in apparent independence, but their stages are connected by underground passages so that the casts, human and animal, can shuttle freely between them. An exit from one performance allows reappearance seconds later in another, and so on.

The three theaters — architecturally separate on the surface — form, through invisible connections, one histrionic cluster, prototype of a multiple play with a single cast. The subterranean traffic introduces a new model of theatrical economy where an infinite number of simultaneous performances can be given by a single rotating cast, each play both isolated from and intertwined with all the others.

Reynolds' triple arena is thus a precise metaphor of life in the Metropolis, whose inhabitants are a single cast performing an infinite number of plays.

11. A simulated flight over Manhattan, before the first airplane has ever flown.

Canals of Venice.

Canals of Venice.

12. The Canals of Venice is a gigantic model of Venice inside a reduced version of the Ducal Palace, the largest building in Dreamland. Inside it is night, "with the soft moonlight typical of the city of 'Water Streets' ... accomplished by a newly invented electrical device."

"Real gondolas carry the visitors through a Grand Canal reproduced with faithful regard for detail." The miniature palace is an architectural compression chamber: "all the most famous buildings are here reproduced ... on 54,000 square feet of canvas" mounted in receding planes on both sides of the Grand Canal.

Life in Venice is simulated too. "All along the line of progress [of the gondolas] are the natives of the city engaged in their various occupations, coming and going just as the traveler would find them in a real city...."[21] The Shoot-the-Chutes, the Tunnels of Love, the Submarine, the Creation have all relied on water-based locomotion. The persistence of this mode of travel apparently reflects a deep-seated need of metropolitan inhabitants; the Canals of Venice is its apotheosis, but only provisionally. Dreamland is a laboratory and Reynolds an urbanist: this interior Venice, wrapped in its cocoon of many layers of canvas, is an urban model that will reappear in later incarnations.

13. Coasting Through Switzerland is a machine designed by Reynolds to correct flaws in Manhattan's topography and climate. It is the first entirely mechanical resort, a compressed replica of Switzerland.

"Swelterers in Manhattan's summer sun direct their steps to Dreamland's ... confines, and find relief in a visit to the cooling ice-tipped mountains of 'Switzerland.'" On the facade of the otherwise hermetic box is "a picture of snowy peaks [that] indicates the pleasure to come" as the visitor mounts "a little Red Sleigh."

Like Manhattan, this Switzerland is a compound of anxiety and exhilaration. "The first feature to meet the eye is a scene familiar to all who have visited the Alps.... Roped climbers in their dangerous ascent to the mountain have met ... with the snapping of a guide-rope and the climbers seem to be falling through space." But as the little Red Sleigh passes through a valley "teeming with Swiss life," the impact of the opening drama is "lost in the opening vista of the famous Mt. Blanc."

Now the sleigh penetrates a tunnel 500 feet long to enter Reynolds' Alps. "A notable feature is the cooling apparatus which diffuses iced air throughout the whole structure.

"Deftly concealed pipes with openings in the various snowbanks emit the air from the cooling apparatus, while suction ventilators in the roof make a draught that keeps this artificial 'Switzerland' as cold and as full of sweet pure air as can be found among the picturesque Swiss mountains...."[22]

Through his manipulations in Switzerland Reynolds fully realizes the potential of technology for the support and production of fantasy, of technology as an instrument and extension of the human imagination. Coney is the laboratory of this Technology of the Fantastic.

14. Where Switzerland shows Reynolds taming technology, Fighting the Flames constitutes his most convincing exposition of, and commentary on, the metropolitan condition itself.

It is a building without a roof, 250 feet long, 100 feet deep. Each column on the facade is surmounted by a figure of a fireman; the roofline is an intricate motif of fire hoses, helmets and axes.

The classical exterior gives no indication of the drama inside, where "in the vast expanse of ground a square of a city has been built, showing houses and streets with a hotel in the foreground." Four thousand firemen inhabit, permanently, this metropolitan "set"; they are "recruits from the fire departments of this and nearby cities [who] know their business thoroughly." Waiting in the wings of the synthetic block is a flotilla of disaster prevention: "The fire apparatus will include four engines and hose wagons, an extension ladder truck, a water tower, an ambulance and a battalion chief's wagon."

But the main protagonist on the urban stage is the city block itself: Fighting the Flames introduces the block as actor. "An alarm rings; the men will leap from their beds and slide down the brass poles.... The hotel in the foreground is on fire and there are people inside it. The flames, discovered on the first floor of the hotel, cut off their escape. People throng the square, shouting and gesticulating; the engines arrive, then the water tower, hose wagons, extension ladder truck, the battalion chief and" — once more establishing the connection between rescue and loss — "an ambulance, which runs over a man in its race of relief.

"The flames creep up to the next story.... The inmates at the windows are driven from story to story by fire and smoke.

"When they reach the top floor an explosion is heard, and the roof of the building falls in...."[23]

Yet the hysterical guests are saved, the fire put out and the city block prepared for its next performance.

The entire spectacle defines the dark side of Metropolis as an astro-nomical increase in the potential for disaster only just exceeded by an

Bird's-eye view of Coney Island at night, with regulated Apocalypse of Fighting the Flames: "the dark side of Metropolis — an astronomical increase in the potential for disaster only just exceeded by an equally astronomical increase in the ability to avert it."

Santos Dumont Airship No. 9.

Leap Frog Railway — exhilarating
accident witnessed from parallel track.

equally astronomical increase in the ability to avert it.

Manhattan is the outcome of that perpetual neck-and-neck race.

15. The Japanese Teahouse is converted, after one year and minimal modification, into the Airship Building. Inside a two-story Japanese temple is displayed, from 1905, the Santos Dumont Airship No. 9.

"A cigar-shaped balloon ... 60 feet long of oilskin from which is suspended a framework 35 feet long. A three-horse-power gasoline motor operates a two-blade propeller...."[24]

Earlier in 1905 Santos Dumont has performed maneuvers with this vehicle for the French president and war department; only months later Reynolds is in a position to schedule "a daily flight over Coney Island." To substantiate Dreamland's claims as an autonomous state — with its own intelligentsia — he introduces the aeronaut-inventor Santos Dumont — now his employee — as the "noted Brazilian Scientist"; the small aircraft does, in fact, perform scientific experiments from its base in the backyard of the Japanese temple.

Simultaneously with this daily flight over Coney, Dreamland still accommodates, in apparent conflict, the hourly *simulated* flight over Manhattan. Reality now supersedes dream, reinforcing the suggestion implicit in Dreamland that the Future is gaining on fantasy, and that Dreamland will be the territory where the actual overtaking occurs.

16. The Leap Frog Railway is a special pier with a track leading nowhere, on which Reynolds stages the impossible: two bulletlike trains move toward each other at full speed on the same track, to meet an absurdist challenge once posed by Mark Twain as "the only thing that Yankee Ingenuity had not yet accomplished ... the successful passing of two carloads on a single line of tracks."

The Leap Frog cars rely on a technical invention that mimics animal copulation. They carry a pair of bent rails on their backs that allow them to glide over and under each other. (On the return trip the cars change position.) "The passengers in breathless excitement momentarily anticipating disaster, realizing that their lives are in jeopardy, clinging to one another for safety, closing their eyes to the impending danger....

The cars crash into one another, 32 people are hurled over the heads of 32 others.... They are suddenly awakened to a realization of the fact that they have actually collided with another car and yet they find themselves safe and sound ... proceeding in the same direction in which they started...."[25]

Beacon Tower at night.
(Senator Reynolds would later
promote the Chrysler Building.)

Ostensibly the Leap Frog Railway is a prototype "to reduce the mortality rate due to collisions on railways," but in this apotheosis of the tradition of barely averted disaster Reynolds has blended the mechanics of sex with the imminence of death in a single respectable experience.

17. The Beacon Tower, smallest in plan, is perhaps Dreamland's most important structure.
It "rises 375 feet above a spacious park and is the dominating note around which the general scheme is centered.... The most striking and conspicuous structure for miles around ... When illuminated by over 100,000 electric lights it can be seen for a distance of over 30 miles. The Tower contains two elevators and from the top is obtained a magnificent sea view ... and a bird's-eye view of the Island."[26]
For a year it leads a relatively bland existence as "the finest Tower ever built." Then Reynolds makes it the definitive instrument in the systematic short-circuiting of the external world that is Dreamland's true mission. He equips it with the most powerful searchlight on the eastern seaboard. The US Department of Lighthouses is forced to "crack down on the park in 1906.... Didn't the park realize that the alternating red and white beam was identical with that of the Norton's Point light"[27] — which marks the official entrance to New York's harbor? This surreal competition with reality is Reynolds' masterstroke: the searchlight is to lure ships off course, add real wrecks to the inventory of Dreamland's disasters, confuse and discredit the world outside Dreamland's borders. (Twenty-five years later Reynolds, as the developer of the Chrysler Building, will insist on its silver crown over the objections of his architect.)

SHORTAGE

Dreamland opens only seven years after Steeplechase. Ostensibly seeking to provide unlimited entertainment and pleasure, Tilyou, Thompson and Reynolds have in fact alienated a part of the earth's surface further from nature than architecture has ever succeeded in doing before, and turned it into a magic carpet that can: *reproduce* experience and fabricate almost any sensation; *sustain* any number of ritualistic performances that exorcise the apocalyptic penalties of the metropolitan condition (announced in the Bible and deeply ingrained since in the antiurban American sensibility); and *survive* the onslaught of over a million visitors a day.
In less than a decade they have invented and established an urbanism

based on the new Technology of the Fantastic: a permanent conspiracy against the realities of the external world. It defines completely new relationships between *site, program, form* and *technology*. The *site* has now become a miniature state; the *program* its ideology; and *architecture* the arrangement of the technological apparatus that compensates for the loss of real physicality.

The frenzied pace with which this psycho-mechanical urbanism has extended its tentacles across Coney Island testifies to the existence of a vacuum that had to be filled at all costs.

Just as a given meadow can only support a certain number of cows without being grazed bald, the reality of nature is progressively consumed under the simultaneous escalation of culture and density in the same spot.

The Metropolis leads to Reality Shortage; Coney's multiple synthetic realities offer a replacement.

OUTPOSTS

Coney's new urbanism of Fantastic Technology generates spin-offs all across the United States, even on sites that do not nearly approach an urban density. Outposts of Manhattanism, they serve as advertisements for the metropolitan condition itself.

Steeplechase, Luna and Dreamland are reproduced faithfully: Roller Coaster, Collapsing Alphabet and Fighting the Flames are transplanted to the middle of nowhere. Smoke and flames can be seen for miles on otherwise innocent horizons.

Their effect is stunning: rural Americans who have never been to cities visit the parks. The first high-rise building they ever see is a burning block, their first sculpture is an alphabet about to collapse.

REVOLUTION

Now that the masses have solved the problem of Pleasure, they present the elite elsewhere on the island with the problem of the Masses. Between the comparatively salubrious islands of Steeplechase and Luna Park is an ever-deteriorating community. "There is scarcely any variety of human flotsam and jetsam that is not represented in its permanent population.... Every defaulting cashier, every eloping couple, every man or woman harboring suicidal intent ... comes flocking to it from every part of the land" to be exposed to "a concentrated sublimation of all the mean, petty, degrading swindles which depraved ingenuity has ever devised to prey upon humanity...."[28]

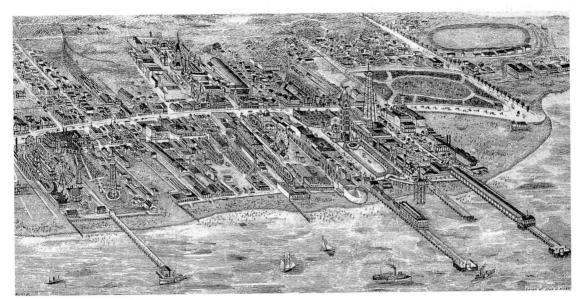

Bird's-eye view of Coney Island's middle zone,
c. 1906 — a Metropolis of the Irrational:
Steeplechase (far left), Luna Park (rear center,
north of Surf Avenue), Dreamland (front right).
The incipient Urbanism of the Fantastic was
extremely unstable — facilities were modified
and replaced continuously to respond to new
demands and latest technological developments; all curves are competing roller coasters.

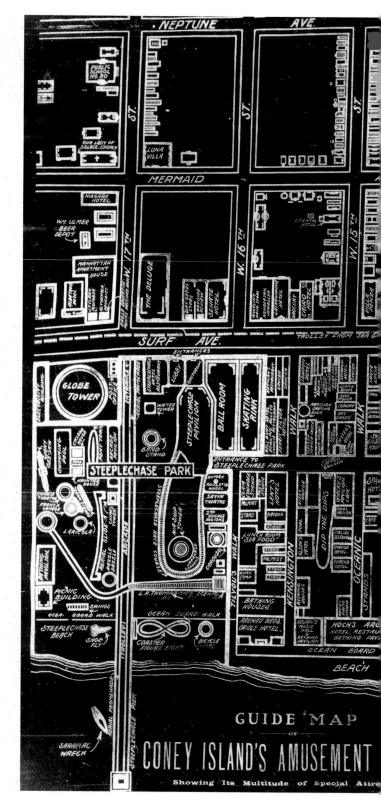

Plan of Coney Island's middle zone, 1907: Steeplechase (lower left), Luna Park (upper right) and Dreamland (lower right). Each rectangle represents a different pleasure-generating unit; entire system of mass irrationality is structured by island's grid.

Metropolitan outposts in the provinces:
Park with Burning Block on Lake Ontario.

The beach itself has become a last resort for the most hopeless victims of metropolitan life, who buy tickets to Coney with their last few cents and huddle together with the wreckage of their families to wait for the end ... staring out over the impassive ocean to the sound of waves crashing on the sand.

"What a sight the poor make in the moonlight,"[29] whispers with an aesthetic shiver the chronicler of the mutant lifestyle of the Metropolis, faced with this terminal front line; each morning Coney's police collect the corpses.

But however outrageous, the situation of the wretched poor is not the real threat to the peace of mind of the reformers now isolated on the east end of the island, forced to retreat inside the still-civilized bastions of the resort hotels by the proliferation of the middle zone.

The gay battlefield of the Reality Shortage, the entertainment generated in Steeplechase, Luna and Dreamland, inspires loathing. Machines going through the motions of the Tango, a lighthouse that lures innocent ships, the masses racing on steel tracks in the moonlight, electric phantom cities more beautiful than anything seen before on earth, all seem to announce the imminent usurpation of a civilization that has taken thousands of years to mature.

They are the symptoms of revolution.

The east panics and becomes the headquarters of a belated campaign to rescue the rest of the island, a last-ditch effort at preservation that intensifies in direct proportion to the success of the Parks.

The issues, tactics and proposed solutions anticipate — in naked form — the tortured misunderstandings between official and popular culture, between elitist taste and popular imagination, that are to agonize the coming century. The debate is a dress rehearsal of the arguments respectable culture will mobilize to denigrate its probable replacement: the potentially sublime is criticized for being cheap and unreal.

FIASCO

In 1906, two years after the opening of Luna, Maxim Gorky visits the USA as a Socialist reporter.

His visit is a fiasco, especially after Manhattan's newspapers organize a mass protest in front of the Times Square Hotel where Gorky, "the Bitter One," is staying. To cheer him up, friends take the Russian to Coney Island. In the essay "Boredom," he articulates his horrified reactions to Coney and its freak culture.

"The City, magic and fantastic from afar, now appears an absurd jungle of straight lines of wood, a cheap, hastily constructed toyhouse for the amusement of children.

"Dozens of white buildings, monstrously diverse, not one with even the suggestion of beauty. They are built of wood, and smeared over with peeling white paint which gives them the appearance of suffering from the same skin disease....

"Everything is stripped naked by the dispassionate glare. The glare is everywhere, and nowhere a shadow.... The visitor is stunned; his consciousness is withered by the intense gleam; his thoughts are routed from his mind; he becomes a particle in the crowd...."

Gorky's disgust represents the modern intellectual's dilemma: confronted with the masses, whom he admires theoretically, in the flesh, he suffers from an acute distaste. He cannot admit to this disgust; he sublimates it by identifying external exploitation and corruption as the reason for the masses' aberrations.

"The people huddled together in this City actually number hundreds of thousands. They swarm into the cages like black flies. Children walk about, silent, with gaping mouths and dazzled eyes. They look around with such intensity, such seriousness that the sight of them feeding their little souls upon this hideousness, which they mistake for beauty, inspires a pained sense of pity....

"They are filled with contented *ennui,* their nerves are racked by an intricate maze of motion and dazzling fire. Bright eyes grow still brighter, as if the brain pales and lost blood in the strange turmoil of the white, glittering wood. The *ennui,* which issues from under the pressure of self-disgust, seems to turn into a slow circle of agony. It drags tens of thousands of people into its somber dance, and sweeps them into a will-less heap, as the wind sweeps the rubbish of the streets....."[30]

INDICTMENT

Gorky's indictment of Fantastic Technology and of the middle zone's arsenal against the Reality Shortage as essentially mediocre and fraudulent is only the most sophisticated display of the compound of prejudice and contempt that feeds the hotel zone's phobias. This fundamental misjudgment and a subsequent series of similar mis-readings guarantees the taste-making establishment's early disquali-fication for further participation in the experiment Manhattan.

Their sensibilities offended by the "peeling white paint," pitying the manipulated masses, disparaging the events in the middle zone as compared to their own unreal well-preserved Arcadia, they look

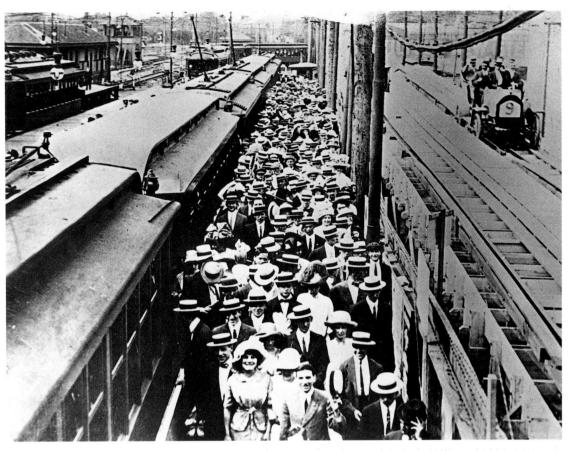

Metropolitan densities arrive at Coney Island.

behind Coney's facade and therefore see nothing.

Based on a false analysis, their solution is doomed to be irrelevant: in the public interest, the island is to be turned into a park.

In what will become a standard remedy against the spontaneous urbanism of the masses — exorcism of the demon of mass irrationality — they propose to raze the City of Towers, to root out every trace of the infamous infrastructure as if it were a poisonous weed and to restore the surface of the earth to its "natural" state, a thin layer of grass.

BARRACKS

But as early as 1899 the patronizing puritanism of the Urbanism of Good Intentions is exposed by more acute observers, who perceive the genius of Coney's phantasmagoric transformation.

"The places of Amusement [on Coney] ... are liberally patronized by those who constitute what we call 'the masses,' meaning thereby persons whom the humanitarians and reformers would like to house in whitewashed barracks, and who possess a sense of the picturesque that I commend to the careful consideration of their would-be benefactors....

"Just now a good many of these reformists and humanitarians and representatives of what they themselves usually term the 'better element' are crying aloud to have the most picturesque and popular summer resort on the continent turned into a public park....

"The enthusiasm with which this proposition has been seconded and approved by everybody who does not know anything about the subject whatever, leads me to fear that our municipal authorities, who are notoriously prone to lend an ear to the clamor of ignorance, may succeed in establishing this park on a site where nothing higher than a currant bush will grow....

"The masses love Coney Island as it is, and although they will probably bear with dumb resignation any attempt to transform it into a region of asphalt walks and patches of scorched 'keep off the grass' sward, they will certainly turn their backs upon it in its new form and seek their summer recreation elsewhere...."[31]

The debate about the park is a confrontation between the reformist urbanism of healthy activities and the hedonistic urbanism of pleasure. It is also a rehearsal of the later showdowns between Modern Architecture and the architecture of Manhattanism.

For the coming century, the battle lines are drawn.

BLOB

Oblivious to the contest for the middle, literally rising above the conflict between mechanical and natural surfaces, is the circular silhouette of a phantom structure that proves — if nothing else — Coney's continuing fertility as a breeding ground for revolutionary architectural prototypes. Early in 1906 advertisements appear in New York papers announcing "a ground floor chance to share profits" in "the largest steel structure ever erected ... the greatest amusement enterprise in the whole world ... the best real estate venture,"[32] the Globe Tower. It will cost $1,500,000 to erect. The public is urged to invest. The stock will pay 100 percent interest annually.

The most voluminous building ever proposed in the history of mankind, it combines in a single gestalt the opposites — needle and sphere — that have been the extremes of Manhattan's formal vocabulary ever since the Latting Observatory and the balloon of the Crystal Palace were juxtaposed in 1853.

It is impossible for a globe to be a tower.

A sketch illustrating the ad — of a skyline dominated by a blob — reveals the Globe Tower's concept: the sphere is to be so colossal that simply by resting on the earth it can claim — through the height of its enormous diameter — also to be a tower, for it is at least "three times as high as the Flatiron building, the present marvel of New York."

SPHERE

The sphere appears throughout Western architectural history, generally coinciding with revolutionary moments. To the European Enlightenment it was a simulacrum of the world, a secular counterpart to the cathedral: typically, it was a monument and, in its entirety, hollow.

It is the American genius of Samuel Friede, inventor of the Globe Tower, to exploit the Platonic solid in a series of strictly pragmatic steps.

For him the globe, ruthlessly subdivided into floors, is simply a source of unlimited square footage. The larger it is, the more immense these interior planes; since the Globe itself will need only a single, negligible point of contact with the earth, the smallest possible site will support the largest reclaimable territory. As revealed to investors, the tower's blueprints show a gigantic steel planet that has crashed onto a replica of the Eiffel Tower, the whole "designed to be 700 feet high, the largest building in the world with enormous elevators carrying visitors to the different floors."[33]

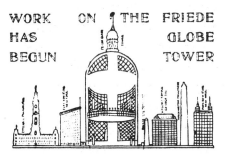

Appearance of the Globe Tower, advertisement in the *New York Herald*, May 6, 1906.

Globe Tower, second version, with exploded exterior. From the top: Roof Gardens; layer of theaters; revolving restaurant; ballroom; *chambres séparées;* Africa, one of the continent/circuses; lobbies; entrances; etc. Special gravity elevator connects interior with underground metropolitan arteries.

SOCLES

A total of eight socles will support the Globe Tower. Otherwise the hovering monument will not directly interfere with life on earth, except where its specially designed gravity elevators penetrate the earth's crust to connect the interior of the sphere with the interior of the earth. Underground will be a multilevel interchange of various modes of transport: a combination of parking garage, subway and railway station with a branch going out to the sea as a pier for boats. As a program, the Globe Tower is an agglomeration of Steeplechase, Luna Park and Dreamland, all swallowed up in a single interior volume, stacked on consecutive floors, the whole parked on a small corner of Steeplechase that Friede has leased from Tilyou.

STATIONS

The capacity of the Globe Tower is 50,000 people at one time. Every 50 feet of its height is a station consisting of a main attraction embedded in subsidiary amusement facilities.

150 feet above the ground: "a Pedestal Roof Garden with popular price restaurant, continuous vaudeville theater, roller skating rink, bowling alley, slot machines, etc."

250 feet above the ground: "the Aerial Hippodrome, seating 5,000 people ... largest Hippodrome in the world, with four large circus rings and four immense animal cages" — incarcerating a vast number of species of wild animals — "giving continuous performances." Each ring represents a continent: a world inside the world. The circus is ringed by "automatic telescopes, automatic opera glasses, slot machines, a miniature railroad...."

300 feet above the ground: in the globe's equatorial zone are concentrated "the Main Hall, the Largest Ballroom in the world, and a moving restaurant enclosed in glass...." A revolving strip 25 feet wide carries "tables, kitchens and patrons around the outer edge of the Tower to give the effect of eating in an airborne dining car" with "a continuous panoramic view of Coney Island, the Ocean, the Countryside and Greater New York."

To stimulate continuous (24-hour) use of the Globe Tower by its 50,000 temporary inhabitants, the middle zone also contains a hotel floor, with small, luxuriously equipped, padded suites, rooms and cubicles.

Connecting the facilities of the main station are a "circular exhibition hall, candy devices, slot machines, toy devices, shows of various kinds, goods manufactured where spectators can see the operation and purchase the goods as souvenirs."

350 feet above the ground: Aerial Palm Garden.

Implicit in Friede's horizontal arrangement is a social stratification; ascent in the Globe coincides with increased refinement and elegance of the facilities.

"Higher up there will be a more expensive restaurant with tables scattered in a palm garden with cascades of running water screened from each other by shrubbery artistically arranged on the Italian Garden plan." Friede hints at his ambition to collect a specimen of every plant known to man: the restaurant as Eden.

500 feet above the ground: Observatory Platform, "containing automatic telescopes, souvenir stand and various small concessions, highest platform in Greater New York."

600 feet above the ground: United States Weather Observation Bureau and Wireless Telegraph Station, "highest observation platform in the United States, equipped with modern weather recording devices, wireless telegraph, etc., surmounted with the largest revolving searchlight in the world.

"Thousands of electric lights make the building a gigantic tower of fire at night."

DISCREPANCY

Because it simply is not of this world, the Globe Tower can do without its predecessors' metaphorical stratagems of discontinuity. The first single *building* to claim the status of resort — "the most popular resort in the whole world" — it has severed all connections with nature; the immensity of its interior precludes any reference to external reality.

The full theoretical ramifications of Friede's quantum leap can best be illustrated mathematically:

1. assuming that the Globe Tower's diameter is 500 feet,
2. assuming further that its floors are spaced 15 feet apart,

then the formula of its total square footage,

$$\pi h^2 \sum_{k=0}^{n} k(n-k)$$

(h = 15' height, n = number of floors + 1),

gives a total of 5,000,000 square feet.

Assuming a total of 1,000 square feet as the surface consumed by the eight socles, then the proportion,

$$\frac{\text{artificial surface}}{\text{area of site}} = \frac{5,000,000}{1,000}$$

The Globe Tower can reproduce that part of the world it occupies
5,000 times.

In light of this colossal discrepancy, the Globe Tower must be seen as the
essence of the idea of Skyscraper, the most extreme and explicit manifestation of the Skyscraper's potential to reproduce the earth and to create other worlds.

FOUNDATION

The first advertisements mention that "work on the foundations of the
Friede Globe Tower has been started by the Raymond Concrete Pile Co.
of Chicago, and will be completed in 90 days according to contract, when
the steel structural work will be rushed to completion."

As the future landing points of the as yet free-floating planet, the socles
are invested with a special mystique.

On May 26, 1906, "the cornerstone laying will be the event of the day at
the Island, and will be celebrated with band concerts, fireworks and
oratory.... In years to come it will be stated with pride that 'I was there
when the cornerstone was laid.'"

There is a rush of investors at the Globe Tower Co. office built next to the
first socle.

At the end of the 1906 season the foundations are still incomplete.
Investors become anxious. Another cornerstone ceremony marks the
beginning of the 1907 season; another socle is completed "and a few
steel girders ... raised on [the socles] as preliminary work on the Tower."

By 1908 it is clear that the most impressive architectural project ever
conceived is a fraud.

Tilyou is stuck with the abortive supports that now obstruct the expansion
of Steeplechase. "On account of the sandy formation at Coney ... long
concrete spiles were sunk to a depth of 35 feet. Eight of these spiles were
grouped together and a solid concrete piece about 3 feet thick was placed
on top to hold them together.... About 30 of these bases were sunk on
the property.... These concrete foundations are massive and it is believed
that they can be removed only by liberal use of dynamite."[34]

FIRE

At the end of his proto-socialist-realist diatribe, Gorky unveils an
alternative solution to Coney that is more imaginative than the artificial

resurrection of nature advocated by the "better element." "The soul is seized with a desire for a living, beautiful fire, a sublime fire, which should free the people from the slavery of a varied boredom."[35]

In May 1911 the lighting system in the devils that decorate the facade of Dreamland's End of the World short-circuits. Sparks start a fire that is fanned by a strong sea wind.

Only weeks before a superior fire-fighting apparatus has been installed; the ground has been dug up once more, to add new water mains and hydrants. But somehow the new ducts have not been connected with the Atlantic, inexhaustible fire extinguisher. In shock, the fire fighters of Fighting the Flames are first to desert their dormitories and the confines of Dreamland.

As real fire fighters arrive on the scene, they find no more pressure in the system than "in a garden hose."

Fireboats are kept at a distance by the heat. Only Lilliputia's midget fire fighters — confronted with the real thing after ± 2,500 false alarms — put up a real fight against the holocaust; they save a small piece of their Nuremberg — the fire station — but otherwise their actions are hopeless. The most pathetic victims of the disaster are the "educated" animals that now become victims of their unlearning of instinct; waiting for their teachers' permission, they escape too late, if at all. Elephants, hippos, horses, gorillas run amok, "enveloped in flames." Lions roam the streets in murderous panic, finally free to kill each other on their way to safety: "Sultan ... roared along Surf Avenue, eyes bloodshot, flanks torn and bleeding, mane afire...."[36] For many years after the holocaust, surviving animals are sighted on Coney, deep in Brooklyn even, still performing their former tricks....

In three hours Dreamland burns to the ground.

END

In the end, Dreamland has succeeded so well in cutting itself loose from the world that Manhattan's newspapers refuse to believe in the authenticity of the final disaster even as their editors see its flames and smoke from their office windows.

They suspect it is one more catastrophe staged by Reynolds to attract attention: the news is printed only after a 24-hour delay.

In an objective postmortem Reynolds admits that the burning of Dreamland is only the formalization of its earlier decline. "The promoters of Dreamland sought to appeal to a highly developed sense of the artistic ... but it did not take long for them to discover that Coney Island

Dreamland burns.

was scarcely the place for that sort of thing.... Architectural beauty was virtually lost upon the great majority of visitors.... From year to year Dreamland was popularized, its original design abandoned."
The disaster concludes Reynolds' preoccupation with Manhattan's prototype. He surrenders the gay battlefield of the Reality Shortage to the Urbanism of Good Intentions — "the City should take the land and turn it into a Public Park"[37] — and shifts his energies to Manhattan itself.

JOY
Follows a period of unsettlement.
In 1914 Luna Park too goes up in flames.
Dreamland becomes a parking lot.
Steeplechase survives, its attractions more debased with every new season.
Manhattan itself has become the theater of architectural invention. Only with the Palace of Joy (1919) does Coney generate another breakthrough, resolving the apparent irreconcilability of *density* and *dignity* that has so upset its enemies. The palace shifts the emphasis in solving the Problem of Pleasure away from the compulsive production of passive entertainment to constructive arrangements of human activity.
The Palace of Joy is a pier, modified to become a condenser of social intercourse: two parallel walls contain an endless number of rooms and other private accommodations that define a linear public realm.
"The Palace of Joy ... will contain the largest enclosed swimming pool in the world; will contain salt water from the Atlantic Ocean and will be open year round.
"A mammoth Dance Hall and Skating Rink ... operated in connection with the Swimming Pool" are planned for the end of the pier.
"The equipment will include Russian, Turkish and Salt Water Baths; there will be 2,000 Private Bath Houses and 500 Private Rooms with 2,000 lockers to accommodate those who wish to stay overnight."[38]
Ballroom *inside* the locker room: an American Versailles for the People.
The Public at the core of the Private — a theoretical inversion that will make Manhattan's inhabitants a population of houseguests.
But the Palace of Joy fails to materialize.
The beach reverts to its earliest condition: overcrowded arena of the dictatorship of the proletariat, "monstrous safety valve of the world's most highly charged metropolis."[39]

CONQUEST

The final conquest and definitive eradication of Coney's original urbanism are assured in 1938 when Commissioner Robert Moses brings beach and boardwalk under the jurisdiction of the Parks Department, ultimate vehicle of the Urbanism of Good Intentions. For Moses, the anti-Reynolds, Coney becomes — again — a testing ground for strategies intended ultimately for Manhattan.

"Engrossed in dreams of lawn-flanked parkways and trim tennis courts,"[40] he considers the thin strip of oceanfront under his control as merely the base for an offensive that will gradually replace Coney's street grid with innocuous vegetation. The first block to fall is the site of Dreamland, where he establishes the new New York Aquarium in 1957.

It is a modern structure, an incarnation of the "whitewashed barracks," painfully cheerful in the upward sweep of its concrete roofline, implanted in a vast lawn.

"Its lines are trim and clean."[41]

The aquarium is a Modernist revenge of the conscious upon the unconscious: its fish — "inhabitants of the deep" — are forced to spend the rest of their lives in a sanatorium.

When he is finished, Moses has turned 50 percent of Coney's surface into parks.

Mother island to the bitter end, Coney Island has become the model for a modern Manhattan of Grass.

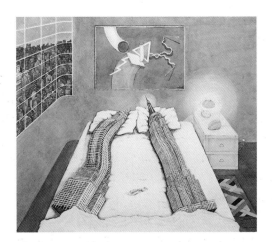

Madelon Vriesendorp, *Après l'amour.*

The Double Life of Utopia: The Skyscraper

There is no easy way from the earth to the stars....
— Text on Medalists' Society Medal, 1933

And finally, in the very last episode, the Tower of Babel suddenly appears and some strongmen actually finish it under a song of new hope, and as they complete the top, the Ruler (of the Olympus, probably) runs off making a fool of himself while Mankind, suddenly understanding everything, finally takes its rightful place and right away begins its new life with new insights into everything....
— Fyodor Dostoyevski, *The Demons*

We take from you what we need and we hurl back in your face what we do not need.
Stone by stone we shall remove the Alhambra, the Kremlin and the Louvre and build them anew on the banks of the Hudson.
— Benjamin de Casseres, *Mirrors of New York*

The Frontier in the Sky

The Manhattan Skyscraper is born in installments between 1900 and 1910. It represents the fortuitous meeting of three distinct urbanistic break-throughs that, after relatively independent lives, converge to form a single mechanism:

1. the reproduction of the World;
2. the annexation of the Tower;
3. the block alone.

To understand the promise and potential of the New York Skyscraper (as distinct from the reality of its now common performance), it is necessary to define these three architectural mutations separately, before they were integrated into a "glorious whole" by the builders of Manhattan.

1. THE REPRODUCTION OF THE WORLD

In the era of the staircase all floors above the second were considered unfit for commercial purposes, and all those above the fifth, uninhabitable.

Since the 1870s in Manhattan, the elevator has been the great eman-cipator of all horizontal surfaces above the ground floor.

Otis' apparatus recovers the uncounted planes that have been floating in the thin air of speculation and reveals their superiority in a metro-politan paradox: the greater the distance from the earth, the closer the communication with what remains of nature (i.e., light and air).

The elevator is the ultimate self-fulfilling prophecy: the further it goes up, the more undesirable the circumstances it leaves behind.

It also establishes a direct relationship between repetition and architec-tural quality: the greater the number of floors stacked around the shaft, the more spontaneously they congeal into a single form. The elevator generates the first aesthetic based on the *absence* of articulation.

In the early 1880s the elevator meets the steel frame, able to support the newly discovered territories without itself taking up space.

Through the mutual reinforcement of these two breakthroughs, any given site can now be multiplied ad infinitum to produce the proliferation of floor space called Skyscraper.

THEOREM

By 1909 the promised rebirth of the world, as announced by the Globe Tower, reaches Manhattan in the form of a cartoon that is actually a *theorem* that describes the ideal performance of the Skyscraper: a slender steel structure supports 84 horizontal planes, all the size

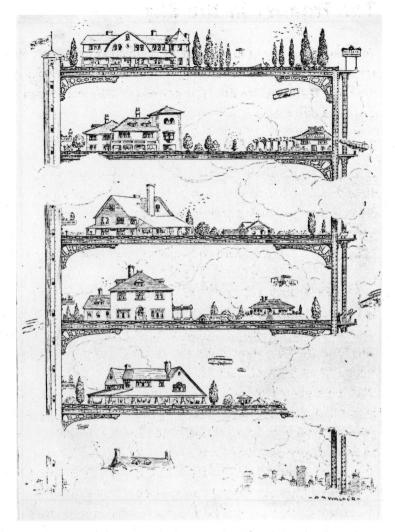

1909 theorem: the Skyscraper as utopian device
for the production of unlimited numbers of
virgin sites on a single metropolitan location.

"THE COSMOPOLIS OF THE FUTURE. A weird
thought of the frenzied heart of the world in
later times, incessantly crowding the possibilities of aerial and inter-terrestrial construction,
when the wonders of 1908 ... will be far out-
done, and the 1,000 foot structure realized;
now nearly a million people do business here
each day; by 1930 it is estimated the number
will be doubled, necessitating tiers of sidewalks, with elevated lines and new creations
to supplement subway and surface cars, with
bridges between the structural heights.
Airships, too, may connect us with all the
world. What will posterity develop?" (Published
by Moses King, rendered by Harry M. Petit.)

of the original plot.

Each of these artificial levels is treated as a virgin site, *as if the others did not exist*, to establish a strictly private realm around a single country house and its attendant facilities, stable, servants' cottages, etc. Villas on the 84 platforms display a range of social aspiration from the rustic to the palatial; emphatic permutations of their architectural styles, variations in gardens, gazebos, and so on, create at each elevator stop a different lifestyle and thus an implied ideology, all supported with complete neutrality by the rack.

The "life" inside the building is correspondingly fractured: on level 82 a donkey shrinks back from the void, on 81 a cosmopolitan couple hails an airplane. Incidents on the floors are so brutally disjointed that they cannot conceivably be part of a single scenario. The disconnectedness of the aerial plots seemingly conflicts with the *fact* that, together, they add up to a single building. The diagram strongly suggests even that the structure is a whole exactly to the extent that the individuality of the platforms is preserved and exploited, that its success should be measured by the degree to which the structure frames their coexistence without interfering with their destinies. The building becomes a stack of individual privacies. Only five of the 84 platforms are visible; lower in the clouds other activities occupy remaining plots; the use of each platform can never be known in advance of its construction. Villas may go up and collapse, other facilities may replace them, but that will not affect the framework.

In terms of urbanism, this indeterminacy means that a particular site can no longer be matched with any single predetermined purpose. From now on each metropolitan lot accommodates — in theory at least — an unforeseeable and unstable combination of simultaneous activities, which makes architecture less an act of foresight than before and planning an act of only limited prediction.

It has become impossible to "plot" culture.

The fact that the 1909 "project" is published in the old *Life*,[1] a popular magazine, and drawn by a cartoonist — while the architectural magazines of the time are still devoted to Beaux-Arts — suggests that early in the century "the people" intuit the promise of the Skyscraper more profoundly than Manhattan's architects, that there exists a subterranean collective dialogue about the new form from which the official architect is excluded.

Flatiron (Fuller) Building, 1902, 22 stories (Daniel Burnham, architect).

World Tower Building, 1915, 30 stories (Edward West, "builder and owner").

Benenson (City Investing) Building, 1908 (Francis H. Kimball, architect). Irregular plot extruded to a height of 480 feet, "13 acres of floor space, and room for 6,000 tenants...."

Equitable Building, 1915, 39 stories "straight up.... The most valuable Office Building in the World — up until 1931...." (E. R. Graham, architect.)

ALIBIS

The skeleton of the 1909 theorem postulates the Manhattan Skyscraper as a utopian formula for the unlimited creation of virgin sites on a single urban location.

Since each of these sites is to meet its own particular programmatic destiny — beyond the architect's control — the Skyscraper is the instrument of a new form of *unknowable* urbanism. In spite of its physical solidity, the Skyscraper is the great metropolitan destabilizer: it promises perpetual programmatic instability.

The subversiveness of the Skyscraper's true nature — the ultimate unpredictability of its performance — is inadmissible to its own makers; their campaign to implant the new giants within the Grid therefore proceeds in a climate of dissimulation, if not self-imposed unconsciousness. From the supposedly insatiable demands of "business" and from the fact that Manhattan is an island, the builders construct the twin alibis that lend the Skyscraper the legitimacy of being *inevitable.*

"The situation of [Manhattan's] financial district with rivers on either side forbidding lateral expansion has encouraged architectural and engineering skill to find room aloft for the vast interests that demand office space in the heart of the New World."[2] In other words: Manhattan has no choice but the skyward extrusion of the Grid itself; only the Skyscraper offers business the wide-open spaces of a man-made Wild West, a *frontier in the sky.*

CAMOUFLAGE

To support the alibi of "business," the incipient tradition of Fantastic Technology is disguised as pragmatic technology. The paraphernalia of illusion that have just subverted Coney Island's nature into an artificial paradise — electricity, air-conditioning, tubes, telegraphs, tracks and elevators — reappear in Manhattan as paraphernalia of efficiency to convert raw space into office suites. Suppressing their irrational potential, they now become merely the agents of banal changes such as improving illumination levels, temperature, humidity, communications, etc., all to facilitate the processes of business. But as a spectral alternative, the diversity of the 84 platforms of the 1909 Skyscraper holds out the promise that all this business is only a phase, a provisional occupation that anticipates the Skyscraper's conquest by other forms of culture, floor by floor if necessary. Then the man-made territories of the frontier in the sky could be settled by the Irresistible Synthetic to establish alternative realities on any level.

"I am business.

"I am Profit and Loss.

"I am Beauty come into the Hell of the Practical."[3]

Such is the lament of the Skyscraper in its pragmatic camouflage.

TRIUMPH

In this branch of utopian real estate, architecture is no longer the art of designing buildings so much as the brutal skyward extrusion of whatever site the developer has managed to assemble.

• In 1902 the Flatiron Building is a model of such sheer multiplication — 300 feet of upward extrusion — nothing more than 22 times its triangular site, made accessible by six elevators. Only its photogenic razor-blade elevation reveals it as the mutation it is: the earth reproducing itself. For seven years "the most famous building in the world," it is the first icon of the *double life of utopia*.

• At 40 West 40th Street the World Tower Building repeats its site 30 times, "one of the highest buildings on so small a plot."[4] As an image, it is evidence of the revolutionary quality of the architecture of sheer territorial multiplication: it looks impossible, but it exists.

• The builders of the Benenson (City Investing) Building multiply their lot 34 times. The site they extrude is irregular in plan; the building they generate therefore even more arbitrary. This flawed shape is compensated for by the perfection of the interior: "The lobby ... is finished in solid marble, 30 to 50 feet wide and 40 feet high [and] extends [the] entire length of the Building, a full block...."[5]

Through volume alone, life inside the Skyscraper is involved in a hostile relationship with life outside: the lobby competes with the street, presenting a linear display of the building's pretensions and seductions, marked by those frequent points of ascent — the elevators — that will transport the visitor even further into the building's subjectivity.

• In 1915 the Equitable Building repeats its block 39 times, "straight up," as it boasts. Its lobby is a sybaritic arcade lined with social facilities such as shops, bars, etc. The surrounding streets are deserted.

The higher the Skyscraper goes, the harder it becomes to suppress its latent revolutionary ambition; when the Equitable is completed its true nature stuns even its builders. "For a while our 1,200,000 square feet of rentable area seemed almost like a new continent, so vast and vacant were its many floors...."[6]

More than the sum of its floors, the Equitable is promoted as a "City in Itself, housing 16,000 souls."[7]

That is a prophetic claim that unleashes one of Manhattanism's most insistent themes: from now on each new *building of the mutant kind* strives to be "a City within a City." This truculent ambition makes the Metropolis a collection of architectural city-states, all potentially at war with each other.

MODEL

By 1910 the process of territorial multiplication has become inexorable. The entire Wall Street area is on its way to a grotesque saturation point of total extrusion where "eventually, the only space not occupied by enormous buildings in Lower Manhattan would be the streets...." There is no manifesto, no architectural debate, no doctrine, no law, no planning, no ideology, no theory; there is only — Skyscraper.

By 1911 the Skyscraper reaches the conceptual barrier of the 100th floor; "when Real Estate brokers shall have found a suitable City Block ... the men and the millions will be ready...."[8]

A coalition of draftsmen, led by Theodore Starrett — member of the construction dynasty already responsible for half Manhattan's Skyscrapers (and which intends to remain in the advance guard of territorial reproduction) — "is working out the plans for the 100-story building...." *Work out* is the right verb; there is no "design," only the extrapolation of Manhattan's irrepressible tendencies and themes; it is no accident that the team lacks architects.

Starrett too believes in metropolitan Manifest Destiny: "Our civilization is progressing wonderfully. In New York — by that I mean Manhattan Island — we must keep building and we must build upward. Step by step we have advanced from the wooden hut to the thirty story Skyscraper.... Now we must develop something different, something larger...."

As the conceptual stratosphere of the 100th floor is approached, the programmatic settlement of the platforms according to the 1909 theorem imposes itself: filling the interior with business alone is inconceivable. If the 39 floors of the Equitable constitute a "City in Itself," the 100-story building is a Metropolis on its own, "a mammoth structure, towering into the clouds and containing within its walls the cultural, commercial and industrial activities of a great city...." Its size alone will explode the texture of normal life. "In New York we travel heavenward as well as on the surface," explains Starrett the futurist. "In the 100 story Building we shall be shot upward with the rapidity that letters are sent across the Brooklyn Bridge."

This ascent is interrupted every 20th floor by public plazas that

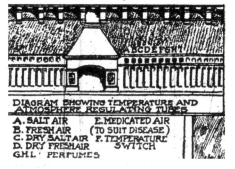

"In New York we must keep building and we must build upward"; Theodore Starrett's proposal for 100-story building, 1906. "Our civilization is progressing wonderfully...."

The 100-story building, detail of nine revolutionary "temperature and atmosphere regulating tubes" emerging in otherwise conventional office suite with fireplace. "A. salt air, B. fresh air, C. dry salt air, D. dry fresh air, E. medicated air (to suit disease), F. temperature switch, G.H.I. perfumes."

articulate the demarcations between the different functional sectors: industry at the bottom, business in the second quarter, living in the third and a hotel in the fourth.

The 20th floor is a general market, the 40th a cluster of theaters, the 60th a "shopping district," the entire 80th floor a hotel and the 100th an "amusement park, roof garden and swimming pool."

To make these programmatic enrichments possible, the implements of efficiency reassume their original identity as paraphernalia of illusion: "Another interesting feature is the made to order climate we shall have. When we shall have at last reached the ideal construction, we shall have perfect control of the atmosphere, so that there will be no need of going to Florida in the winter or to Canada in the summer. We shall have all varieties to order in our big buildings of Manhattan...."

"Total Architecture!" That is Starrett's antihumanistic proposal as he reveals the essence of his Manhattan project: a diagram of "temperature and atmosphere regulating tubes" that are supposed to emerge from the oak-paneled partitions — complete with fireplaces — of his structure.

The outlets of this psychosomatic battery are keys to a scale of experiences that range from the hedonistic to the medical.

The Irresistible Synthetic pervades every corner; each compartment is equipped to pursue its private existential journey: the building has become a laboratory, the ultimate vehicle of emotional and intellectual adventure.

Its occupants are at once the researchers and the researched.

Such structures as Starrett's 100-story building would be definitive; they would mark the point where the index of Manhattan's vitality — "the sound of New York tossing its traditions in the air and devouring its own landmarks"[9] — would be silenced. In the absence of that roar, the 100-story building needs a new index to measure its achievement.

"What would become of the present skyscrapers?" asks the reporter apprehensively. "Some of them would doubtless have to be torn down, but no doubt many of them, on the corners of blocks, could be used in the new structures," reassures Starrett.

This is not generosity; the 100-story building needs an archaeology of dwarfs to tie it down to earth, to remain convinced of its own scale.

2. THE ANNEXATION OF THE TOWER

• In 1853 the Latting Observatory offers Manhattanites the first comprehensive inspection of their domain; it confronts them with the

Singer Building, constructed in two stages: lower 14 floors in 1899, Tower superimposed on block in 1908 (Ernest Flagg, architect).

Metropolitan Life Building, conceived in two separate operations: main ten-story block in 1893, Metropolitan Tower in 1909 (Napoleon LeBrun & Sons, architect).

limitation of Manhattan's islandness, the excuse for all subsequent developments.

• In 1876 the Centennial Tower in Philadelphia is the second needlelike celebrant of Progress, hauled to Coney Island in 1878 to trigger its stampede toward the controlled irrationality of Fantastic Technology.

• From 1904 Luna Park is a breeding ground for Towers, discovering in the clash of Towers the source of architectural drama.

• In 1905 Dreamland's Beacon Tower tries to lure innocent ships aground to flaunt Reynolds' contempt for so-called Reality.

• In 1906 the Globe Tower reveals the potential of the Tower to be — literally — a world on its own.

In 50 years the Tower has accumulated the meanings of: catalyst of consciousness, symbol of technological progress, marker of pleasure zones, subversive short-circuiter of convention and finally *self-contained universe*. Towers now indicate acute breaks in the homogeneous pattern of everyday life, marking the scattered outposts of a new culture.

BUILDINGS

Manhattan's early tall buildings are often taller than many of these Towers, but there is nothing in their cubic outlines to remind anyone of a Tower. They are consistently called *buildings*, not Skyscrapers. But in 1908 Ernest Flagg designs a Tower and places it on top of his existing Singer Building, a 14-story block built in 1899. This architectural afterthought alone makes it "from 1908 to 1913 America's most famous building."

"Thousands of travelers come to New York especially to see this Modern Tower of Babel, gladly paying fifty cents to ride to the 'observation balcony.'" In acknowledgment of the darker side of Metropolis it is also the first "Suicide Pinnacle" — "it seems to have a strong appeal to those who were soured on life...."[10]

The Metropolitan Life Building (1893) is an early "tall block" — ten times its site — on Madison Square. After 1902 it is outflanked by the 22-story wedge of the Flatiron. The management decides to expand, upward; in 1909 they multiply a small adjoining plot 39 times. Because of the small site, their structure copies Venice's campanile on San Marco, its shaft activated for business, holes punctured all over to admit daylight. At the top they perform a more modern annexation by installing a searchlight and other apparatus lifted directly from the lighthouse archetype. A ruby red nipple that caps the structure is supposed, through prearranged signals, to communicate time and weather conditions to imaginary mariners on the Atlantic.

In these steps, the process of sheer multiplication steals the meanings the Tower has accumulated over the previous 50 years.

Building becomes Tower, landlocked lighthouse, ostensibly flashing its beams out to sea, but in fact luring the metropolitan audience to itself.

3. THE BLOCK ALONE

The Horse Show Association — "whose roster was the nucleus for the first social register" — owns Madison Square Garden, on a block east of Madison Avenue between 26th and 27th streets.

In 1890 it commissions a new building — a rectangular box 70 feet high that occupies the entire block. The interior of the box is hollow; its auditorium, the largest in existence, seats 8,000 and is sandwiched between a 1,200-seat theater and a 1,500-seat concert hall, so that the entire surface of the block is a single, articulated field of performance. The arena is designed for the Association's hippodrome events, but is also rented out for circuses, sports and other spectacles; an open-air theater and restaurant are planned for the roof.

Firmly in the tradition of World's Fairs, Stanford White, its architect, marks the box as a site of special interest by constructing a copy of a Spanish Tower on the roof of the hall.

As one of the Garden's promoters he is also responsible for programming the entertainment inside, even after the building is finished, in a form of never-ending architectural design.

But it is difficult to ensure the financial viability of the colossal arena with tasteful performances alone; its size is incompatible with the social strata whose domain it is intended to be. "The Building was a financial lemon from the day it opened."

To avert disaster White is *forced* to experiment, to invent and establish "situations" with a wide popular appeal within the interior acreage.

"In 1893 he sets up a gigantic panorama of the Chicago Exposition, to save New Yorkers the long trip West...." Later he turns the arena into replicas of "the Globe Theatre, old Nuremberg, Dickens' London and the city of Venice, the visitors floating ... from exhibit to exhibit in gondolas."[11] White is caught in the crossfire of the battle between high and low culture that has already flared up at Coney: his spectacles are so "taste-less" that they keep the Social Register away, but they are still not intense enough to attract the masses.

In the difference between a real gondola and Dreamland's mechanical gondola propelled along its mechanical track lies White's dilemma: he is a man of taste who ought to have less. He has no time to resolve it: in 1906 a madman shoots him on the roof of his own project.

TONGUE

In 1905 Thompson, bored with Luna, buys a block east of Sixth Avenue between 43rd and 44th streets. For the first time Coney's Technology of the Fantastic will be grafted onto the Grid.

In one year, Thompson builds his Hippodrome, another box, seating 5,200, topped by "the largest dome in the world after the Pantheon." Two electric Towers, transplants from Luna's forest, identify the Sixth Avenue entrance and mark this block as another miniature state where an alternative reality is established.

The stage itself is the core of Thompson's realm: it breaks out of the traditional proscenium to reach 60 feet into the audience like a gigantic mechanical tongue. This "apron" is capable of instantaneous metamorphosis: among other transformations, "it is possible to turn this portion of the stage into a creek, a lake or a running mountain stream...."

Where Luna's ploy of displacement was the trip to the Moon, Thompson's first Manhattan performance is called "a Yankee Circus on Mars," in an ambitious attempt to turn the surface of his entire block into a spacecraft. "A stranded circus was to be sold at auction by the sheriff, but was saved by a messenger from Mars who bought it for his king...." Once on Mars, "the Martians ask [the performers] to remain permanently and to become inhabitants of that far-away planet...." Such is Thompson's plot, which leaves the visitors to his theater similarly marooned on another planet. The climax of the circus' Martian performance is an eloquent abstract choreography: 64 "diving girls" descend a staircase in squads of eight, "as if they are one." The tongue becomes a lake, 17 feet deep. The girls "walk down into the water until their heads are out of sight," never to return to the surface. (An inverted underwater receptacle that contains air is connected by corridors to the backstage area.)

It is a spectacle of such ineffable emotion that "men sit in the front row, night after night, weeping silently...."[12]

CONTROL

In the tradition of economic free enterprise, control is exercised only at the scale of the individual plot. With Madison Square Garden and Thompson's Hippodrome, the area of such control coincides more and more with the area of an entire block.

The block itself is equipped with technological paraphernalia that

From Coney Island to Manhattan: Frederic
Thompson's Hippodrome on Sixth Avenue (1905).

Scene from "A Yankee Circus on Mars" — entire
city block displaced to another planet.

manipulate and distort existing conditions beyond recognition, establishing private laws and even ideology in competition with all the other blocks. The block becomes a "park" in the tradition of Coney Island: it offers an aggressive alternative reality, intent on discrediting and replacing all "natural" reality.

The area of these interior parks can never exceed the size of a block: that is the maximum increment of conquest by a single "planner" or a single "vision."

Since all Manhattan's blocks are identical and emphatically equivalent in the unstated philosophy of the Grid, a mutation in a single one affects all others as a latent possibility: theoretically, each block can now turn into a self-contained enclave of the Irresistible Synthetic.

That potential also implies an essential isolation: no longer does the city consist of a more or less homogeneous texture — a mosaic of complementary urban fragments — but each block is now *alone* like an island, fundamentally on its own.

Manhattan turns into a dry archipelago of blocks.

FREEZE-FRAME

A 1909 postcard presents a freeze-frame of architectural evolution — three major breakthroughs coexisting on Madison Square: the *multiplication* of the Flatiron, the *lighthouse* of the Metropolitan and the *island* of Madison Square Garden.

At the time the postcard is produced — with its multiple vanishing points it is no simple photograph — the Square "was the center of Metropolitan Life such as New York has never seen reproduced.... Fashion, Clubdom, Finance, Sport, Politics and Retail Trade all met here at high tide.... It was said that someone standing long enough on Fifth Avenue and 23 Street might meet everybody in the world.... Viewing Madison Square from the 'old' Flatiron junction, the scene was Parisian in its kaleidoscopic aspect...."[13]

As Manhattan's social center, this tangle of intersections is the theater where business is being repulsed and replaced by richer forms of activity. That the Square is a front line accounts for its urbanistic fertility in provoking new tendencies. But apart from documenting a multiple breakthrough, the postcard is also a picture of a triple impasse: on its own, each of the three tendencies has no future.

The Flatiron's mere multiplication lacks meaning; the Metropolitan Life Building has meaning, but it is compromised by the contradiction between its pretense of isolation and the reality of its location on just one of many plots on the same block, each poised to steal its thunder; and Madison

Multiple breakthrough but also triple impasse:
Madison Square in 1909, doctored photograph.
From right: Flatiron Building, Metropolitan
Life Building, Madison Square Garden — three
distinct architectural mutations before their
fusion to form the true Skyscraper.

"The Cathedral of Commerce": Woolworth
Building, 1913, 60 floors (Cass Gilbert,
architect) — first *built* amalgamation of the
three mutations.

Square Garden cannot make enough money to justify the extravagance of its metaphors.

But when the three are put together, their weaknesses become strengths: the Tower lends meaning to the multiplication, the multiplication pays for the metaphors on the ground floor, and the conquest of the block assures the Tower isolation as sole occupant of its island.

The true Skyscraper is the product of this triple fusion.

CATHEDRAL

The first *built* amalgamation is the Woolworth Building — completed in 1913, four years after the freeze-frame. Its lower 27 floors are a straightforward extrusion supporting a 30-story tower; the graft occupies an entire block. But this "Glorious Whole, quite beyond the control of human imagination," is only a partial realization of the potential of the Skyscraper. It is a master-piece merely of materialism: none of the programmatic promises of the new type are exploited. The Woolworth is filled, from top to bottom, by business. The Tower is subdivided into office suites with discrete decorative themes — an Empire-style room next to a boardroom that mixes Flemish and Italian Renaissance — while the lower floors accommodate modern administrative operations — files, telexes, tickers, pneumatic tubes, typing pools.

If its interior is business only, its exterior is pure spirituality.

"When seen at nightfall bathed in electric light as with a garment, or in the lucid air of a summer morning piercing space like a battlement of the paradise which St. John beheld, it inspires feelings too deep even for tears.... The writer looked upon it and at once cried out 'The Cathedral of Commerce.'"

The Woolworth does not actually contribute any radical modifications or breaks to the life of the city, but it is supposed to work miracles through the emanation of its physical presence; a larger *mass* than ever constructed before, it is at the same time seen as disembodied, anti-gravitational: "Brute material has been robbed of its density and flung into the sky to challenge its loveliness...."

The building is activated electronically in April 1913, "when President Wilson pressed a tiny button in the White House and 80,000 brilliant lights instantly flashed throughout the Woolworth...."

Through its sheer feat of existing, the Woolworth has a double occupancy, one concrete — "14,000 people — the Population of a City" — the second intangible — "that spirit of man which, through means of change and barter, binds alien people into unity and space, and reduces the hazards of war and bloodshed...."[14]

AUTOMONUMENT

Beyond a certain critical mass each structure becomes a monument, or at least raises that expectation through its size alone, even if the sum or the nature of the individual activities it accommodates does not deserve a monumental expression.

This category of monument presents a radical, morally traumatic break with the conventions of symbolism: its physical manifestation does not represent an abstract ideal, an institution of exceptional importance, a three-dimensional, readable articulation of a social hierarchy, a memorial; it merely *is* itself and through sheer volume cannot avoid being a symbol — an empty one, available for meaning as a billboard is for advertisement. It is a solipsism, celebrating only the fact of its disproportionate existence, the shamelessness of its own process of creation.

This monument of the 20th century is the *Automonument*, and its purest manifestation is the Skyscraper.

To make the Automonument Skyscraper inhabitable, a series of subsidiary tactics is developed to satisfy the two conflicting demands to which it is constantly exposed: that of being a monument — a condition that suggests permanence, solidity and serenity — and at the same time, that of accommodating, with maximum efficiency, the "change which is life," which is, by definition, antimonumental.

LOBOTOMY

Buildings have both an interior and an exterior.

In Western architecture there has been the humanistic assumption that it is desirable to establish a moral relationship between the two, whereby the exterior makes certain revelations about the interior that the interior corroborates. The "honest" facade speaks about the activities it conceals. But mathematically, the interior volume of three-dimensional objects increases in cubed leaps and the containing envelope only by squared increments: less and less surface has to represent more and more interior activity.

Beyond a certain critical mass the relationship is stressed beyond the breaking point; this "break" is the symptom of Automonumentality.

In the deliberate discrepancy between container and contained New York's makers discover an area of unprecedented freedom. They exploit and formalize it in the architectural equivalent of a lobotomy — the surgical severance of the connection between the frontal lobes and the rest of the brain to relieve some mental disorders by disconnecting thought processes from emotions.

The architectural equivalent separates exterior and interior architecture. In this way the Monolith spares the outside world the agonies of the continuous changes raging inside it.

It hides everyday life.

EXPERIMENT

In 1908 one of the earliest and most clinical explorations of this new artistic territory occurs at 228–32 West 42nd Street, which by now is called "Dreamstreet."

The site of the experiment is the interior of an existing building. Officially, its architect, Henri Erkins, describes his project, "Murray's Roman Gardens," as "the realistic *reproduction,* largely from the originals in the form of direct copies, casts, etc.... of the homes of one of the most lavishly luxurious of the world's ancient peoples — the Romans of the Caesarean period — the *reconstruction* of a Roman residence...."[15]

Inside, exact perception of space and objects is made impossible by Erkins' consistent use of mirrors — "so large and artfully disposed that no joint is apparent and it is indeed impossible to discover where the substantial form ceases and the reflection begins...." The center of Erkins' "villa" is "an open court with a colonnade on each side" — an artificial open-air garden, realized through the most advanced technical means: "The ceiling is decorated to represent a blue sky in which electric lights twinkle, while by an ingenious arrangement of optical apparatus, the effect of clouds sweeping over the Sky is produced...." An artificial moon puts in an accelerated appearance, crossing the firmament several times each evening. The mirrors not only disorient and dematerialize, they also "duplicate, triplicate and quadruple the interior exotics" to make the resort a model of decorative economy: the electrified "Roman Fountain" in the Atrium is only one-quarter real, the "barge" one-half. Where there are no mirrors, projecting screens, complex illumination effects and the sounds of a concealed orchestra suggest an infinity of forbidden space beyond the accessible parts of the villa.

Murray's is to be "the storehouse for *all* that was beautiful in the World that the Romans knew, conquered and plundered."

The collector collected is Erkins' formula for harvesting the past, for the borrowing and manipulation of memory.

Overlooking the garden is a mezzanine that gives access to two separate apartments where elaborate three-dimensional murals and a hyper-density of converted objects and decorative motifs represent Egypt/Libya *and* Greece: an obelisk has become a lamp, a sarcophagus an "electric

"Forbidden" space at Murray's: Terrace Room, whose dimensions have been made unknowable through arrangements of screens, walls, lights, mirrors, sounds, decoration. Smoke of Vesuvius hovers ominously over the Greco-Roman idyll as a metaphor for the explosive quality of life in the Metropolis.

Murray's Roman Gardens, first autonomous metropolitan interior generated through architectural lobotomy: view of the "Atrium" with reflected barge, fountain, artificial sky. Further escalation of the Irresistible Synthetic: fabricated history for Manhattan's population. "Take away the scions of the four hundred in their gloomy evening attire, looking like so many scarecrows or undertakers, and the sober-faced attendants, equally sombre as to apparel, and replace them with figures tricked out in the many-hued raiment of ancient days.... Substitute for the begoggled chauffeur, the Roman charioteer, and for the blue-coated guardian of the peace ... the mail clad Roman legionary, and but for such improvements as we owe to our mechanical progress, the visitor to Murray's might readily imagine himself 'turned back' two thousand years to the city of the Caesars at the Zenith of its wealth and splendor...."

car" to transport dishes from one end of a table to the other.

This combination blurs the sense of time and space: periods that were once sequential have become simultaneous. In this three-dimensional Piranesi, iconographies that have remained pure invade each other. Figures from an Egyptian bas-relief play music in a Roman perspective, Greeks emerge from Roman baths at the base of the Acropolis and a "semi-nude female figure in a recumbent position [blows] iridescent bubbles from a pipe, castles in the Air": antiquity is invested with modern sexuality.

The accumulated loot is customized to carry contemporary messages to the metropolitan audience: Nero, for instance, is reinterpreted. "Although he is reported to have been an indifferent spectator of the burning of a considerable part of the Town [Rome], it is shrewdly suggested that he was interested rather in the opportunity the conflagration offered for improvement rather than in the loss it entailed...."

For Erkins, this cross-fertilization represents a true modernity — the creation of "situations" that have never existed before but are made to look as if they have. It is as if history has been given an extension in which each episode can be rewritten or redesigned in retrospect, all past mistakes erased, imperfections corrected: "The latest evolution of the art of past ages, applied to the creation of a veritable modern place of recreation [is] modern, or *modernized* art...." Murray's Roman Gardens is a second chance for the past, a *retroactive utopia.*

HOUSE

Perhaps most original about the tumult of frozen lust of Murray's decoration is its consistent quasi-three-dimensionality: a whole population (the original inhabitants of the villa) is arranged along the walls to enliven the social transactions in the rooms and apartments.

They make the "upper ten ... dressed in somewhat sombre colors" intruders in the sanctity of their empire of the senses. The public are only guests. Reinforcing the house metaphor, relationships generated in the over-saturated downstairs can be consummated upstairs: "In the upper part of the building are twenty-four luxurious bachelor apartments of parlor and bedroom provided with every comfort and convenience, including separate bath room accommodations...."

With the Gardens, Erkins and Murray have stretched the private format of the house to absorb the public. Such is the collective realm in Manhattan: its scattered episodes can never be more than a series of bloated private enclaves that admit "houseguests."

PRIDE

After performing his architectural lobotomy Erkins' pride is that of a successful surgeon.

"The fact that all ingenuity of plan, the wealth of artistic elaboration and the profusion of gorgeous ornamentation, revealed in this unique establishment, have really been 'grafted' as it were onto a building of essentially plain and formal character, planned and erected originally for a purpose *absolutely foreign* to that for which it is today utilized, lends additional interest to the results achieved and reflects the greater credit of the author and originator of this superb exemplification of Modern taste and skill.

"Henry Erkins ... was constrained to adopt, as the basis for this beautiful production, a building originally planned for use as a schoolhouse, but which the magic wand of Mr. Erkins' genius has transformed so happily that in its present arrangement, equipment, adornment and ornamentation, it *nowhere betrays the slightest trace of its original purpose in any way....*"

Lobotomy satisfies the two incompatible demands imposed on the Automonument by generating two separate architectures.

One is the architecture of metropolitan exteriors whose responsibility is to the city as sculptural experience.

The other is a mutant branch of interior design that, using the most modern technologies, recycles, converts and fabricates memories and supportive iconographies that register and manipulate shifts in metropolitan culture.

A *system of Murray's* is planned throughout Manhattan. An Italian Garden on 34th Street and Murray's New Broadway — "3 acres of floor space devoted to Dining Room" — are planned to open in 1909.

From the beginning of the 20th century architectural Lobotomy permits an urbanistic revolution in installments. Through the establishment of enclaves such as the Roman Gardens — emotional shelters for the metropolitan masses that represent ideal worlds removed in time and space, insulated against the corrosion of reality — the fantastic supplants the utilitarian in Manhattan.

These subutopian fragments are all the more seductive for having no territorial ambitions beyond filling their interior allotments with a hyper-density of private meanings. By leaving intact the illusion of a traditional urban landscape outside, this revolution ensures its acceptance through its inconspicuousness.

The Grid is the neutralizing agent that structures these episodes. Within the network of its rectilinearity, movement becomes ideological navigation between the conflicting claims and promises of each block.

CAVE

In 1908 a delegation of American businessmen visits Antonio Gaudí in
Barcelona and asks him to design a Grand Hotel in Manhattan. No site is
known for the project; the businessmen may merely want an initial sketch,
to raise money on and match later with a location. It is unlikely that
Gaudí is aware of the quantum leaps and breakthroughs Manhattanism
has produced; the businessmen themselves must have recognized the
affinity between Gaudí's hysteria and Manhattan's frenzy.

[handwritten annotations: "unable controlled" above "hysteria", "crazy" above "frenzy"]

But in his European isolation, Gaudí is like the man in Plato's cave;
from the shadows of the businessmen's descriptions and requirements
he is forced to reconstruct a reality outside the cave, that of an *ideal
Manhattan*. He synthesizes a premonition of the true Skyscraper that
applies both the lobotomy and the mutant branch of interior design not
only on the ground floor but in layers throughout the interior.

His hotel is a sheaf of stalagmites, combined to form a single conoid that
is, unmistakably, a Tower. It inhabits a podium or island, connected by
bridges to the other islands. It stands aggressively alone.[16]

Gaudí's design is a paradigm of floor-by-floor conquest of the Skyscraper
by social activities. On the outer surface of the structure, low floors
provide individual accommodation, the hotel rooms; the public life of
the hotel is located at the core, on enormous interior planes that admit
no daylight.

This inner core of the Grand Hotel is a sequence of six superimposed
restaurants. The first is decorated with a concentrate of European
mythologies that will be reinforced by the choice of menu and European
music, played by a large symphony orchestra. Each of the other
restaurants, with its own hermetic iconography, represents another
continent; the stack together represents the World.

A theater and exhibition hall are superimposed over the world of the
restaurants. The whole is topped by a small observation sphere
that awaits the moment when the conquest of gravity will be no longer
metaphor but fact.

SCHISM

There is to be no seepage of symbolism between floors. In fact, the
schizoid arrangement of thematic planes implies an architectural strategy
for planning the interior of the Skyscraper, which has become autonomous through the lobotomy: the Vertical Schism, a systematic exploitation
of the deliberate disconnection between stories.

By denying the dependence of one floor on any other, the Vertical Schism

Relative size of Gaudi's Grand Hotel compared to Empire State Building, Chrysler Building and Eiffel Tower.

Gaudi's Grand Hotel, section. Through the lobotomy, the interior of the hotel is disconnected from the reality outside by a skin of bedrooms. As in the 1909 theorem, the central floors are stacked on top of each other as self-contained thematic planes in an essentially random sequence. Through this vertical disconnection, local changes in iconography, function, use can be effected without any impact on the structure as a whole.

Gaudi's Grand Hotel, European restaurant on the fifth floor.

allows their arbitrary distribution within a single building. It is an essential strategy for the development of the cultural potential of the Skyscraper: it accepts the instability of a Skyscraper's definitive composition beyond a single floor, while at the same time counteracting it by housing each *known* designation with maximum specificity, if not overdetermination.

SHADOW

For a time "real" Skyscrapers like the Woolworth and versions of the older type are erected simultaneously; in the latter the simple operation of extrusion takes more and more grotesque proportions. With the Equitable Building (1915) the process of reproduction loses its credibility through the grim deterioration — both financial and environmental — it inflicts on its surroundings. Its shadow alone reduces rents in a vast area of adjoining properties, while the vacuum of its interior is filled at the expense of its neighbors. Its success is measured by the destruction of its context. The time has come to subject this form of architectural aggression to regulation. "It became increasingly evident that the large project was a concern not only of an individual, but of the community, and that some form of restriction must be adopted...."[17]

LAW

The 1916 Zoning Law describes on each plot or block of Manhattan's surface an imaginary envelope that defines the outlines of the maximum allowable construction.
The law takes the Woolworth as norm: the process of sheer multiplication is allowed to proceed up to a certain height; then the building must step back from the plot line at a certain angle to admit light to the streets. A Tower may then carry 25 percent of the plot area to unlimited heights. The last clause encourages the tendency of single structures to conquer the vastest possible area, i.e., a whole block, in order to make the 25 percent that can be Tower as large (profitable) as possible.
In fact, the 1916 Zoning Law is a back-dated birth certificate that lends retroactive legitimacy to the Skyscraper.

VILLAGE

The Zoning Law is not only a legal document; it is also a design project. In a climate of commercial exhilaration where the maximum legally allowable is immediately translated into reality, the "limiting" three-dimensional parameters of the law suggest a whole new idea of Metropolis.

If Manhattan was in the beginning only a collection of 2,028 blocks, it is now an assembly of as many invisible envelopes. Even if it is still a *ghost town of the future*, the outlines of the ultimate Manhattan have been drawn once and for all:

The 1916 Zoning Law defines Manhattan *for all time* as a collection of 2,028 colossal phantom "houses" that together form a *Mega-Village*. Even as each "house" fills up with accommodation, program, facilities, infrastructures, machineries and technologies of unprecedented originality and complexity, the primordial format of "village" is never endangered.

The city's scale explosion is controlled through the drastic assertion of the most primitive model of human cohabitation.

This radical simplification of concept is the secret formula that allows its infinite growth without corresponding loss of legibility, intimacy or coherence.

(As a simple section reveals, each envelope is a gigantic enlargement of the original Dutch gable house with the tower as an endless chimney.

The City of the Zoning Law — the Mega-Village — is a fantastic enlargement of the original New Amsterdam.)

Theoretical envelope of 1916 Zoning Law appearing between the Municipal Building and the Woolworth (rendering by Hugh Ferriss).

"The New York Law, formulated by a group of technical experts, was based on purely practical considerations.... By limiting the bulk of a building, the number of occupants was limited; fewer people required access and egress; traffic on adjoining streets was lightened. The limitation in mass had also of course the effect of permitting more light and air into the streets as well as into the buildings themselves.... The Zoning Law was not at all inspired by concern for its possible effect on architecture...." (Ferriss, *Metropolis of Tomorrow.*) After 1916, no structure in Manhattan could exceed the limitations of this spectral shape. To exploit maximum financial return on any given block, Manhattan's architects were forced to approximate it as closely as possible.

The Skyscraper Theorists

Our role is not to retreat back to the catacombs, but to become more human in skyscrapers....
— Regional Plan Association of New York, *The Building of the City*

OBFUSCATION

In the early twenties identifiable personalities begin to disengage themselves from the nebulae of Manhattanism's collective fantasy to play
more individual roles. They are the Skyscraper theorists.

But each attempt, written or drawn, to create consciousness about the
Skyscraper, its use and design, is at least as much an exercise in
obfuscation: under Manhattanism — doctrine of indefinitely postponed
consciousness — the greatest theoretician is the greatest obscurantist.

ATHENS

As a boy — "where the bias, they say, is set" — Hugh Ferriss is given a
picture of the Parthenon for his birthday.

It become his first paradigm. "The building seemed to be built of stone.
Its columns seemed to be designed to support a roof. It looked like
some sort of temple.... I learned in due time that all those impressions
were true...."

"It was an honest building," built "in one of those fortunate periods when
engineers and artists worked enthusiastically together and when the
populace warmly appreciated and applauded their alliance...."

The image of the Parthenon inspires Ferriss to become an architect;
when he gets his degree he leaves his hometown, St. Louis, for
Manhattan. For him, New York represents a new Athens, the only
possible birthplace of new Parthenons.

"One wanted to get to the Metropolis. In New York ... an indigenous
American architecture would be in the making, with engineers and artists
working enthusiastically together — and maybe even with the populace
warmly appreciating and applauding their alliance...." But at his first job
at Cass Gilbert's office — then designing the Woolworth Building — Ferriss'
"juvenile enthusiasm is in for a jolt."[18] The contemporary architecture
of Manhattan does not consist of the production of new Parthenons but
of the pilferage of all useful elements of past "Parthenons," which are
then reassembled and wrapped around steel skeletons.

Instead of a new Athens, Ferriss finds ersatz antiquity. Instead of
contributing to the design of dishonest buildings, Ferriss prefers the

The "automatic pilot" at the controls: Hugh Ferriss at work in his studio, applying finishing touch to "A Street Vista of the Future"; his paintings together form a fabled series, *Vision of the Titan City — 1975,* based on the research of Manhattanism's progressive thinkers such as Corbett, Hood and Ferriss. Partly hidden against the wall, unfinished version of "Crude Clay for Architects." On shelf, remnants of the Parthenon witness birth of the New Athens.

Evolution of the setback building: Ferriss' variations on the 1916 Zoning Law, in four parts.

First stage: "A representation of the maximum mass which, under the Zoning Law, it would be permissible to build over an entire city block....
Not an architects' design, it is simply a form that results from legal specifications...."

Second stage: "The first step taken by the architect is to cut into the mass to admit daylight.... [He] is not permitting himself any prevision of its final form.... He is accepting, simply, a mass which has been put into his hands; he proposes to modify it step by step.... He is prepared to view the progress impartially and to abide by whatever result is finally reached...."

Third stage: The great slopes of the second stage "cut into the rectangular forms which will provide more conventional interior spaces..."

Fourth stage: "After removing those parts which were found to be undesirable, the mass which finally remains... This is not intended as a finished and habitable building; it still awaits articulation at the hands of the individual designer...."

The renderer as chief architect: in spite of his verbal modesty, Ferriss indirectly circumscribes the role of the individual architect to the point of nonexistence; clearly, the "delineator" would prefer it if architects left him and the Zoning Law alone.

technical and strictly neutral role of renderer; he is made "delineator" in Gilbert's office.

PILOT

By the early twenties he has established himself as independent artist in his own studio. As a renderer Ferriss is the puritanical instrument of a coalition of permissive eclectics: the more convincing his work, the more he promotes the realization of proposals he dislikes.

But Ferriss discovers an escape from this dilemma: a technique that isolates his own intentions from those of his clients.

He draws in charcoal, an imprecise, impressionistic medium that relies on the suggestiveness of planes and the manipulation of what are, essentially, smudges.

By using the one medium incapable of depicting the eclectic surface trivia that preoccupy Manhattan's architects, Ferriss' drawings strip as much as render. With each representation he liberates an "honest" building from under the surface excess.

Ferriss' delineations, even as they are intended to seduce clients for Manhattan's architects — and through them, the larger population — are critiques of the projects that they pretend to embody, polemical "corrections" of the reactionary blueprints on which they are based. That Manhattan's architects have only their dependence on Ferriss' services in common reinforces the cumulative impact of these corrected projects. They coalesce into a coherent vision of a future Manhattan.

That vision becomes increasingly popular with Manhattan's inhabitants — to the point where Ferriss' drawings alone represent Manhattan's architecture, regardless of the individual architect who designed each project. In their calculated vagueness Ferriss' images create exactly that "warmly appreciative and applauding" audience that he has identified in his youth as the condition for the birth of a new Athens. From being a helper, the great delineator becomes a leader.

"He can pump perspective poetry into the most unpromising composition.... The best way to utilize his talent would be to toss over the plans, go to bed and turn up the next morning to find the design all done. "He is the perfect *automatic pilot*...."[19]

RESEARCH

Simultaneously with his commercial work, Ferriss investigates the true issues of Manhattanism with several progressive architects, such as Raymond Hood and Harvey Wiley Corbett. This research centers on the unexplored potential of the 1916 Zoning Law and the theoretical envelope it describes on each Manhattan block.

Ferriss' drawings are the first revelations of the infinite variations — both formal and psychological — contained within its basic legal shape. After exhausting the individual categories, he produces the first concrete image of their final assembly: the Mega-Village that is Manhattan's final destiny.

For Ferriss, this new city of untouched forms is the real new Athens: "As one contemplates these shapes, images may begin to form in the mind of novel types of building which are no longer a compilation of items of familiar styles but are, simply, the subtleizing of these crude masses...."

That city would establish him, Ferriss the renderer, as its chief architect, since its drastic nakedness is what his charcoal medium has always anticipated.

Signs of its imminence are already in the air, baffling the traditional architects; "conservative architectural standards were thrown into confusion. At point after point designers found themselves faced with restrictions which made the erecting of familiar forms impossible...."

LABORS

In 1929 Ferriss publishes the summation of his labors, *The Metropolis of Tomorrow.*
The book is divided into three parts:
Cities of Today, a collection of his renderings for other architects;
Projected Trends, his variations on the theme of the 1916 law; and
An Imaginary Metropolis, Ferriss' new Athens.
There are 50 drawings in the book, each "explained" by a text that is the verbal equivalent of the drawings' charcoal vagueness.
The structure of the book is modeled on the clearing of a persistent fog bank: from "it is again dawn, with an early mist enveloping the scene," via "as the mist begins to disperse," to "a little later, the general clearing of the air allows us to check upon our first impressions...."
This "plot line" corresponds to the three parts of the book: an imperfect past — the work of the other architects; a promising present — the annunciation and theoretical elaboration of the Mega-Village of the 1916 Zoning Law; and the shining future of Ferriss' imaginary Metropolis, which is one version of that village: "a wide plain, not lacking in vegetation, from which rise, at considerable intervals, towering mountain peaks...."[20]

"Crude Clay for Architects": Manhattan as "Ghost Town of the Future," Ferriss' first image of the Mega-Village. "If the maximum masses which are permitted ... were erected over all the blocks of a city, an impression not unlike the one opposite would be produced...."

Man inside the Ferrissian Void,
the womb of Manhattanism.

WOMB

But actually, the divisions are less important than the continuity of all these quasi-nocturnal images. The genius of Ferriss' production is in the medium of his renderings itself, the creation of an artificial night that leaves all architectural incidents vague and ambiguous in a mist of charcoal particles that thickens or thins whenever necessary.

Ferriss' most important contribution to the theory of Manhattan is exactly the creation of an illuminated night inside a cosmic container, the murky *Ferrissian Void:* a pitch black architectural womb that gives birth to the consecutive stages of the Skyscraper in a sequence of sometimes overlapping pregnancies, and that promises to generate ever-new ones.

Each of Ferriss' drawings records a moment of that never-ending gestation.

The promiscuity of the Ferrissian womb blurs the issue of paternity.

The womb absorbs multiple impregnation by any number of alien and foreign influences — Expressionism, Futurism, Constructivism, Surrealism, even Functionalism — all are effortlessly accommodated in the expanding receptacle of Ferriss' vision.

Manhattanism is conceived in Ferriss' womb.

CRASH

Ferriss' book appears in the year of the crash, 1929.

That is not a totally negative coincidence. "It was soon apparent ... that the depression had at least one good side: if architects, for the time being, could not do any real building, at least they could do a lot of real thinking. The skyscraper spree was over; a time for sober reflection had set in."

From his studio Ferriss now looks down on "a strangely quiet Manhattan. The sound of the riveting machines had died upon the air. The architecture of the metropolis, divested of glamor, was telling a story hitherto unsuspected by minds that had been preoccupied with the picturesque.... Of long range planning there was not a Vestige...."[21]

Ferriss' time has come.

CLARIFICATION

In the late twenties most of Manhattan's thinkers and theoreticians are assembled in the committee that prepares — for the Regional Plan Association of New York — a volume on "The Building of the City." Their formal task is to establish pragmatic guidelines for its further development. But in fact their activity contributes to the cloud of unknowing that shields Manhattanism from the glare of objectivity. Like Ferriss, they pretend an interest in planning that cloaks their

The "planning" of Manhattanism: studies for
the Regional Plan Commission. Models showing
maximum bulk of suggested business buildings
for central area, subcentral area, intermediate
area, suburban area. Appropriateness of the
Skyscraper was never questioned; it only became
taller or shorter to respond to local pressure or
lack of pressure.

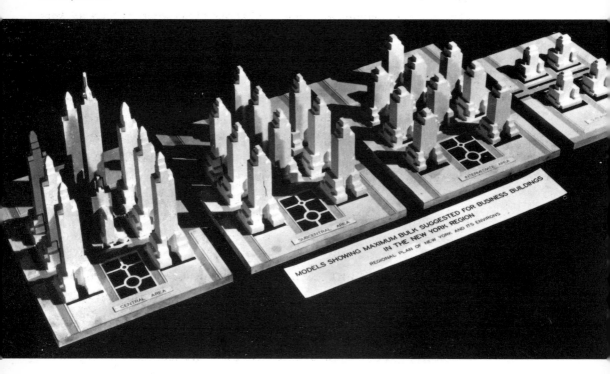

efforts to promote that climate of obscurity in which the Skyscraper will flourish. This complex ambition — to stimulate confusion while paying lip service to clarification — marks the transition between the first, unconscious phase of Manhattanism and the second, quasi-conscious phase. With the first paragraph of their deliberations, the thinkers of the Regional Plan establish the ambiguity of their venture: it is to be an investigation undertaken with the explicit intention of avoiding its logical conclusion.

"All accept the skyscraper as something which serves human needs, but judge it differently as to the value of this service. All know that it has become the dominant feature in the structural composition of large American cities. But is it also to be the dominant feature in the social organization of all urban life in America?... *If we attempt to answer this question we would have had to go deeper than we have dared to go in the Regional Survey and Plan....*"

This early apology sets the tone: everything may be questioned within the framework of the Regional Plan, except the Skyscraper, which remains inviolate. Theory, if there is to be any, will be adapted to the Skyscraper, not the Skyscraper to the theory.

"We will have to accept the skyscraper as inevitable and proceed to consider how it can be made healthy and beautiful...."

QUICKSAND

In the chapter "Magnificence and Limitations of Skyscrapers," the thinkers of the Regional Plan sink still deeper into the quicksand of their own ambivalence. To secure the Skyscraper's continuing license to create congestion, they embark, ostensibly, on a crusade of decongestion.

"There are two aspects in which the bold magnificence of New York skyscrapers cannot be questioned. The great isolated tower that thrusts itself into the clouds and is surrounded by open spaces or very low buildings, so that its shadow does no injury to neighbouring buildings, may in the hands of an artist be an ennobling structure.

"Secondly, the mass effect of a mountain of building, such as is obtained by looking at lower Manhattan from the wide expanse of the Upper Bay, is recognized as one of the great wonders of the world as an artificial creation.

"The pity of it is not that the towers are surging upward beyond 800 feet, but that they are so near to each other; and not that Manhattan has its artificial mountain ranges, but that they are so compact that they keep out light and air from their separate units of building.

"The beauty of both features could have been retained, with more added

beauty as a result of greater display of individual buildings, had more open
areas been preserved in proportion as greater heights were permitted.
"As it is ... more is lost in the closing of the sky between them; in the
consequent dinginess of street and building; in the destruction of many
beautiful low buildings either by dwarfing them or superseding them;
and in want of display of individual skyscrapers and other buildings that
are worthy to be seen, than is gained by magnificence of the great
building masses...."[22]

VENICE

*A hundred profound solitudes together constitute the city of Venice. That is
its charm. A model for the men of the future.*
— Friedrich Nietzsche

*But New York, in addition to being a lot of other things, is a Venice in the
making, and all the ugly paraphernalia by means of which this making is
slowly going forward, all the unlovely processes, physical and chemical,
structural and commercial, must be recognized and expressed and by the
light of poetic vision be made a part of its beauty and romance.*
— J. Monroe Hewlett, President, Architectural League of New York,
New York: The Nation's Metropolis

The most precise and literal proposal to solve the problem of congestion
comes from Harvey Wiley Corbett, prominent thinker about Manhattan and
the Skyscraper, and teacher of the younger generation at Columbia
University.
In his scheme for elevated and arcaded walkways (first proposed in 1923),
the entire ground plane of the city — now a chaos of all modes of
transportation — would gradually be surrendered solely to automotive traffic.
Trenches in this plane would allow fast traffic to rush through the
Metropolis even faster. If cars needed more room again, the edges of existing
buildings could be set back to create still larger areas for circulation.
On the second story pedestrians walk along arcades carved out of the
buildings. The arcades form a continuous network on both sides of streets
and avenues; bridges provide its continuity. Along the arcades, shops
and other public facilities are embedded in the buildings.
Through this separation, the capacity of the original street is increased
at least 200 percent, more if the road consumes still larger sections of
the ground plane.
Ultimately, Corbett calculates, the entire surface of the city could be a

Harvey Wiley Corbett, prominent Manhattan
theoretician, after a lifetime of "visioning."

   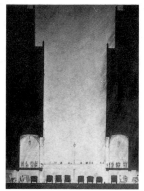

Harvey Wiley Corbett, *Proposals for Relieving Traffic Congestion in New York by Separating Pedestrians and Vehicular Traffic*, sections
1. Present situation.
2. First step: pedestrians are removed from grade level to move along bridges cantilevered from the buildings; cars invade their former domain.

3. Second step, "showing Building cut-ins. Six motor cars moving abreast — parking space for two on each side..."
4. Final stage: "Pedestrians cross streets on overhead bridges and the cities of the future become reincarnations of the City of the lagoons...."

"Towers on a Hudson River Bridge Between New York and New Jersey — 1975, as visioned and designed by Harvey Wiley Corbett."
"Very modernized Venice" in full operation: 20-lane streets, pedestrians walking from "island" to "island" in a "system of 2,028 solitudes."

single traffic plane, an ocean of cars, increasing the traffic potential 700 percent.

"We see a city of sidewalks, arcaded within the building lines, and one story above the present street grade. We see bridges at all corners, the width of the arcades and with solid railings. We see the smaller parks of the city (of which we trust there will be many more than at present) raised to this same side-walk arcade level ... *and the whole aspect becomes that of a very modernized Venice*, a city of arcades, plazas and bridges, with canals for streets, only the canals will not be filled with real water but with freely flowing motor traffic, the sun glistening on the black tops of the cars and the buildings reflecting in this waving flood of rapidly rolling vehicles.

"From an architectural viewpoint, and in regard to form, decoration and proportion, the idea presents all the loveliness, and more, of Venice. There is nothing incongruous about it, nothing strange...."[23]

Corbett's "solution" for New York's traffic problem is the most blatant case of disingenuity in Manhattanism's history. Pragmatism so distorted becomes pure poetry.

Not for a moment does the theorist intend to relieve congestion; his true ambition is to escalate it to such intensity that it generates — as in a quantum leap — a completely new condition, where congestion becomes mysteriously positive.

Far from solving any problems, his proposal is a metaphor that orders and interprets an otherwise incomprehensible Metropolis.

With this metaphor, many of Manhattan's latent themes are substantiated: in Corbett's *"very modernized Venice"* each block has become an island with its own lighthouse, the Ferrissian phantom "house." The population of Manhattan — journeying from block to block — would finally, and literally, inhabit a metropolitan *archipelago* of 2,028 islands of its own making.

CONGESTION

Ferriss, Corbett and the authors of the Regional Plan have invented a method to deal rationally with the fundamentally irrational.

They know instinctively that it would be suicide to solve Manhattan's problems, that they exist by the grace of these problems, that it is their duty to make its problems, if anything, forever insurmountable, that the only solution for Manhattan is the extrapolation of its freakish history, that Manhattan is the city of the perpetual *flight forward.*

The planning of these architects — assembled in the Regional Plan Committee — must be the opposite of objective. It consists of the

Unexpected serenity in the heart of the
Metropolis: two images of Manhattan after
Corbett's metamorphosis — "Looking Down a
Future New York Street in 1975" and "General
view of a city square showing the additional
possibility of a second level of pedestrian
traffic at the height of a ten story setback."

imposition on the explosive substance of Manhattan of a series of meta-phoric models — as primitive as they are efficient — that substitute for literal organization — impossible in any case — a form of poetic control. The "house" and "village" of the 1916 Zoning Law, Ferriss' "buildings like mountains" and finally Corbett's Manhattan as a "very modernized Venice" together form a deadly serious *matrix of frivolity*, a vocabulary of poetic formulas that replaces traditional objective planning in favor of a new discipline of *metaphoric planning* to deal with a metropolitan situation fundamentally beyond the quantifiable.

Congestion itself is the essential condition for realizing each of these metaphors in the reality of the Grid. Only congestion can generate the super-house, the Mega-Village, the Mountain and finally the modernized automotive Venice.

Together, these metaphors are the foundation of a *Culture of Congestion*, which is the real enterprise of Manhattan's architects.

CULTURE

The Culture of Congestion proposes the conquest of each block by a single structure.

Each Building will become a "house" — a private realm inflated to admit houseguests but not to the point of pretending universality in the spec-trum of its offerings. Each "house" will represent a different lifestyle and different ideology.

On each floor, the Culture of Congestion will arrange new and exhilarating human activities in unprecedented combinations. Through Fantastic Tech-nology it will be possible to reproduce all "situations" — from the most natural to the most artificial — wherever and whenever desired.

Each *City within a City* will be so unique that it will naturally attract its own inhabitants.

Each Skyscraper, reflected in the roofs of an endless flow of black limousines, is an island of the "very modernized Venice" — *a system of 2,028 solitudes*.

The Culture of Congestion is *the* culture of the 20th century.

1931

In the chill of the crash, Ferriss and Manhattan's theoreticians have successfully negotiated the transition between Manhattanism's pre-conscious phase to a stage of quasi-consciousness. Amid all the *signs* of demystification, they have preserved the essential mysteries intact. Now, Manhattan's other architects have an equally delicate rite of "modernization" to perform, without succumbing to self-consciousness. After 11 Beaux-Arts costume balls devoted to nostalgic historical tableaux ("A Pageant of Ancient France," "The Gardens of Versailles," "Napoleon," "Northern Africa") that serve as opportunities for the Beaux-Arts graduates of New York to reconsummate their love affair with French culture, the backward-looking flow is reversed in 1931, when the organizers admit that the future cannot be delayed forever.

They decide to use the format of the ball this time to probe the Future. It is an appropriate beginning for 1931.

The Crash — an enforced break in the previous frenzy of production — demands new directions. The reservoir of historical styles is finally depleted. Various versions of Modernism announce themselves with increasing urgency.

"Fête Moderne: A Fantasie in Flame and Silver" is the theme for the 12th ball, to be held on January 23, 1931: an invitation to the Beaux-Arts architects and artists to participate in a collective search for the "Spirit of the Age."

It is *research,* disguised as costume ball.

"What is the modern spirit in art? No one knows. It is something toward which a lot of people are groping and in the course of this groping interesting and amusing things should be developed...."

To preclude superficial interpretations of their theme, the organizers warn that "the modern spirit in art is not a new recipe for designing buildings, sculpture and painted decoration but is a quest for something more characteristic and more vital as an expression of modern activity and thought....

"In the decoration, as in the costumes, the effect sought is a rhythmic, vibrant quality expressive of the feverish activity which characterizes our work and our play, our shop windows and our advertisements, the froth and the jazz of modern life...."[24]

Weeks in advance, the public is informed of this manifesto by a press release. "The Fête Moderne is to be modernistic, futuristic, cubistic, altruistic, mystic, architistic and feministic.... Fantasy is the note, originality will be rewarded...."[25]

VOID

On the night of the ball, 3,000 guests come to the Hotel Astor on Broadway for "a program of eventful events and delightful delights." The familiar interior of the hotel has disappeared and is replaced by a pitch black void that suggests the infinity of the universe, or that of Ferriss' womb.

"From the darkness above prismatic lanterns stab the gloom like great projectiles from the sky...."

Guests, in their two-tone silver- and flame-colored costumes, trace rocket-like trajectories. Weightless pieces of decor float in midair. A "cubistic main-street" seems a fragment of a future USA distorted by Modernism. "Futuristic refreshments" — a drink that looks like liquid metal — and "miniature meteorites" — roasted marshmallows — are served by silent servants dressed in black and thus almost invisible. Familiar melodies collide with the sounds of a frantic Metropolis; "the orchestra will be assisted by nine riveting machines, a three-inch pipe for live-steam, four ocean-liner whistles, three sledge hammers and a few rock drillers. The music however will penetrate through all this on account of the modernistic quality of the dissonances."

Certain subliminal but serious messages float around and can be isolated from the overdose of suggestive information. They remind New York's architects that this ball is in reality a congress — that this ceremony is Manhattan's counterpart of the CIAM Congress on the other side of the Atlantic: a delirious grope after the Spirit of the Age and its implications for their increasingly megalomaniac profession.

"Painted upon a great draped frieze, level with the third balcony, a vague procession of colossal figures rushes as through space with silver arrows poised for flight. These are the guards of the void, the inhabitants of the upper air, charged with the duty of placing some limit upon the vaulting ambition of our builders whose works are soaring ever nearer to the stars."[26]

BALLET

Now Manhattan's builders gather in the wings of the small stage to prepare for the climax of the evening: becoming their own Skyscrapers, they will perform a "Skyline of New York" ballet.

Like their towers, the men are dressed in costumes whose essential characteristics are similar; only their most gratuitous features are involved in fierce competition. Their identical "Skyscraper dresses" taper upward in attempted conformity to the 1916 Zoning Law. Differences occur only at the top.

This agreement is unfair to some of the participants. Joseph H. Freedlander, who has only designed the four-story Museum of the City of New York, never a Skyscraper, nevertheless prefers the embarrassment of the shared Skyscraper dress to the alternative of being alone but honest in his evening costume. His headdress represents the whole building.

Leonard Schultze, designer of the soon-to-be-opened Waldorf-Astoria, has

Manhattan's architects perform "The Skyline
of New York." From left: A. Stewart Walker as
the Fuller Building, Leonard Schultze as the
new Waldorf-Astoria, Ely Jacques Kahn as the
Squibb Building, William Van Alen as the
Chrysler Building, Ralph Walker as One Wall
Street, D. E. Ward as the Metropolitan Tower
and Joseph H. Freedlander as the Museum of
the City of New York — *research*, disguised
as costume ball.

had to represent that twin tower structure in a single headdress. He has settled for one.

The elegant top of A. Stewart Walker's Fuller Building has so few openings that faithfulness to its design now condemns its designer to temporary blindness.

The close fit of head- and Skyscraper-dress on Ely Jacques Kahn reflects the nature of his buildings: never straining for dramatic pinnacles, they are squat mountains.

Ralph Walker appears as One Wall Street, Harvey Wiley Corbett as his Bush Terminal; James O'Connor and John Kilpatrick are inseparable as the twin Beaux-Arts Apartments. Thomas Gillespie has managed the impossible: he is dressed as a void to represent an unnamed subway station.

Raymond Hood has come as his Daily News Building. (He works day and night on the design of Rockefeller Center, a project so complex and "modern" that it would resist translation into a single costume.)

PAROXYSM

Outshining all of these, as it has since 1929 on the stage of mid-Manhattan, is the Chrysler Building.

Its architect, William Van Alen, has spurned the Skyscraper dress: his costume — like his tower — is a paroxysm of detail. "The entire costume, including the hat, was of silver metal cloth trimmed with black patent leather; the sash and lining were of flame-colored silk. The cape, puttees and cuffs are of flexible wood, the wood having been selected from trees from all over the world (India, Australia, Philippine Islands, South America, Africa, Honduras and North America). These woods were teakwood, Philippine mahogany, American walnut, African prima vera, South American prima vera, Huya and Aspen, maple and ebony, lace wood and Australian silky oak. The costume was made possible by the use of 'Flexwood,' a wall material of a thin veneer of wood with a fabric backing. The costume was designed to represent the Chrysler Building, the characteristic features in the composition being carried out by using the exact facsimile of the top of the building as a headpiece; the vertical and horizontal lines of the tower were carried out by the patent leather bands running up the front and around the sleeves. The cape embodied the design of the first floor elevator doors, using the same woods as were used in the elevator doors themselves, and the front was a replica of the elevator doors on the upper floors of the building. The shoulder ornaments were the eagles' heads appearing at the 61st-floor setback of the building...."[27]

This evening is Van Alen's swan song, a brittle triumph. Inconspicuous on this stage, but undeniable on the Grid at 34th Street, the Empire State Building already dominates Manhattan's skyline, outranking the Chrysler by (1,250 − 1,046 =) 204 feet. It is almost complete now, except for the shameless airship mooring mast that grows taller every day.

WOMAN

Architecture, especially its Manhattan mutation, has been a pursuit strictly for men. For those aiming at the sky, away from the earth's surface and the natural, there has been no female company.

Yet among the 44 men on the stage, there is a single woman, Miss Edna Cowan, the "Basin Girl."

She carries a basin as an extension of her belly; two taps seem even further entwined with her insides. An apparition straight from the men's subconscious, she stands there on the stage to symbolize the entrails of architecture, or, more precisely: she stands for the continuing embarrassment caused by the biological functions of the human body that have proved resistant to lofty aspirations and technological sublimation. Man's rush to the nth floor is a neck-and-neck race between plumbing and abstraction. Like an unwanted shadow, plumbing will always finish a close second.

CONTEST

In retrospect it is clear that the laws of the costume ball have governed Manhattan's architecture.

Only in New York has architecture become the design of costumes that do not reveal the true nature of repetitive interiors but slip smoothly into the subconscious to perform their roles as symbols. The costume ball is the one formal convention in which the desire for individuality and extreme originality does not endanger collective performance but is actually a condition for it.

Like the beauty contest, it is a rare format in which collective success is directly proportionate to the ferocity of individual competition.

New York's architects, by making their Skyscrapers compulsively competitive, have turned the entire population into a jury. That is the secret of its continuing architectural suspense.

"The new age is … feministic": Miss Edna Cowan as the Basin Girl — apparition straight from the men's subconscious.

The Lives of a Block:
The Waldorf-Astoria Hotel and
the Empire State Building

A well-planned life should have an effective climax.
— Paul Starrett, *Changing the Skyline*

SITE

One of the 2,028 blocks defined by the 1811 Commissioners' Plan lies
west of Middle (Fifth) Avenue between 33rd and 34th streets.
The transformations of this one block in a period of less than 150 years —
from virgin nature to launching pad of two of Manhattan's most definitive
Skyscrapers, the Empire State Building and the Waldorf-Astoria Hotel —
represent a summary of the phases of Manhattan's urbanism, featuring
all the strategies, theorems, paradigms and ambitions that sustain
the inexorable progress of Manhattanism. The layers of its past occupancies still exist on the block as an invisible archaeology, no less
real for being disembodied.
In 1799 John Thompson acquires (for $2,500) 20 acres of wilderness —
"fertile, partly wooded and eminently suitable for the raising of various
produce" — to cultivate as farmland. He builds "a new and convenient
house, barn and several out-houses."[28]
In 1827 the site ends up, via two other owners, in the possession of
William B. Astor for $20,000.
The Astors' myth is young and fresh. "From the humblest beginnings,
John Jacob Astor (William B.'s father) lifted himself upward and placed
his family at the topmost peak of wealth, of influence, of power, of social
importance...."
Myth meets Block when William B. builds the first Astor Mansion on the
new property. Only five stories tall, it represents a monument of social
climbing that "fixes the seal of perpetual prestige on the famous site." Its
emanations make the corner one of New York's major attractions.
"Many an arriving immigrant looked on the Astor Mansions as a promise
of what America might yield to him, too, through work and energy and
through determination...."[29]

SPLIT

William B. Astor dies.
The block is divided between branches of his family that quarrel,

First Waldorf-Astoria Hotel: Waldorf built in
1893, Astoria (taller part) three years later—
"a distinctive change in the Urban Civilization
of America."

grow apart and finally stop communicating altogether. But they still share the block.

In the 1880s the 33rd Street corner carries the original Astor Mansion, now inhabited by grandson William Waldorf Astor; the other Fifth Avenue corner accommodates the almost identical residence of his cousin Jacob Astor. Separated by a walled garden, the cousins are not on speaking terms. The spirit of the block is split.

Toward the nineties, William Waldorf Astor decides to go to England.
A new destiny awaits his half of the block.

AURA

Throughout the century, the aura of the Astor Mansions has attracted an assembly of similar residences; the block has become the heart of Manhattan's more desirable area, its famous Astor ballroom the epicenter of New York's high society.

But now Astor and his advisers sense "that an extraordinary growth would take place in the ranks of society — the rich were springing up, in the East and West alike, like mushrooms after a rain — that a quicker tempo would infect the life in the city ... that the nineties were ushering in a whole new era."[30]

In a single gesture, he exploits both the old *cachet* and the imminence of new times: the house will be replaced by a hotel, but a hotel that will remain, in Astor's instructions, "a house ... with as little of the typically hotel features in evidence as humanly possible," so that it can preserve the Astor aura.

For Astor, the destruction of a structure does not preclude the preservation of its spirit; with his Waldorf he injects the concept of reincarnation into architecture.

After finding a manager to run the new type of "house" — George Boldt, "a man who could stand on the blueprint plan of a hotel and see the folks come piling in the front doors" — Astor finally leaves for England. Further suggestions for the hotel arrive by cable — architecture in Morse code. The 20th century is approaching.

TWIN

As soon as the 13-story Waldorf is finished, Boldt diverts his attention to the other half of the block. He knows that he can only realize the full potential of location and site by reuniting the two halves.

After years of negotiations he convinces Jacob Astor to sell. Now the *Astoria*, postponed twin of the Waldorf, can be built. (In secret anticipation

Boldt has already counteracted the slope of Fifth Avenue and "caused the main floor of the Waldorf to be set high enough to come just even with the pavement of Thirty-fourth Street.... It meant that the ground floor of the combined hotels could be at an absolute single level.")

In 1896, three years after the opening of the Waldorf, the 16-story Astoria is completed. On the ground floor its dominant feature is Peacock Alley, an interior arcade that runs parallel to 34th Street for more than 300 feet, from an interior carriage driveway to the Rose Room on Fifth Avenue.

On the ground floor the two hotels are joined by shared facilities that puncture the dividing wall: the two-story Palm Room, a branch of Peacock Alley, kitchens. On the second and third floors are the Ballroom — democratic enlargement of the famous Astor ballroom — and the Astor Gallery, "an almost exact replica of the historic Soubise ballroom in Paris."

The transplantations from the Astor mansions — literal or merely by nomenclature — suggest that the Waldorf-Astoria is conceived by its promoters as a haunted house, rife with the ghosts of its predecessors. To construct a House haunted by its own past and those of other buildings: such is the Manhattanist strategy for the production of vicarious history, "age" and respectability. In Manhattan the new and revolutionary is presented, always, in the false light of familiarity.

CAMPAIGN

As William Waldorf Astor intended, the "very coming [of the united hotels] seemed to mark a distinctive change in the Urban Civilization of America." In spite of the reassurance of its iconographies, the program of the new hotel involves it in a campaign to change and manipulate the social patterns of the new Metropolis by offering services that implicitly attack the domain of the individual household to the point where they challenge its reason for being.

To those without the space at their apartments, the Waldorf-Astoria offers modern accommodation for entertainment and social functions; and to those encumbered with mansions, the sophisticated services that liberate their energies from the logistics of running a small private palace.

Day after day the Waldorf pulls society from its hiding places to what becomes in effect a colossal collective salon for exhibiting and introducing new urban manners (such as women alone — yet clearly respectable — smoking in public).

As it becomes, in a few years, "the accepted scene of a great variety of concerts, dances, suppers and theatrical entertainments," the Waldorf-Astoria can claim to be Manhattan's social center of gravity, "a semi-

New Waldorf-Astoria as reincarnation of the
old, "pictured by Lloyd Morgan."

"AND NOW — the EMPIRE STATE, an office
building, taking its logical position on
this site"; final Skyscraper rendered as
summation of all previous occupancies of
the block (advertisement).

public institution designed for furnishing the prosperous residents of the New York metropolitan district with all of the luxuries of urban life." Block makes good: in the twenties the Waldorf-Astoria has become "the Unofficial Palace of New York."

DEATH

But two parallel tendencies announce the death of the hotel, or at least the end of its material being.

The Waldorf has instigated a paradoxical *tradition of the last word* (in creature comfort, supportive technologies, decor, entertainments, metropolitan lifestyles, etc.) which, to preserve itself, is forced continuously to self-destruct, eternally to shed its latest incarnation. Any architectural container that fixes it to a site degenerates sooner or later into a battery of outdated technical and atmospheric apparatus that prevents the hasty surrender to change that is the tradition's *raison d'être*.

After barely 20 years of confident existence the twin hotel is abruptly diagnosed — by a consensus of commercial intuition and public opinion — as "old," unfit to accommodate true modernity.

In 1924 Boldt and his partner, Lucius Boomer, propose gradually to "reconstruct the Waldorf-Astoria and make it vastly more modern." Over the Astor Court — a crevice that separates the hotel from the other occupants of the block — their architects design "a vaulted roof of glass and steel ... creating one of the most magnificent arcades in all New York."[31] The Ballroom is enlarged to twice its original size.

The final remedy is to perform cosmetic surgery on the older part of the twin, so that the Waldorf reaches the same height as the Astoria. But each proposal is an additional argument for the hotel's death warrant.

LIBERATION

The real problem of the Waldorf-Astoria is that it is not a Skyscraper. The more the hotel's success enhances the value of the block, the more urgent it becomes to realize a definitive structure that is at once: a new incarnation of the *idea* of the Waldorf as defined by William Waldorf Astor — a colossal "house" with the preserved atmosphere of a private mansion — and a *Skyscraper* that reaps the financial harvest allowed by the Zoning Law.

In drawings, the block is now contested by two equally phantasmagorical occupants: the first, the final Skyscraper that strives, almost beyond the control of man, toward the full exploitation of the 1916 model; and the second, the re-reincarnation of the Waldorf idea.

The first image is drawn as culmination of a sequence of occupancies —
from virgin nature to Thompson's farm, to the Astor Mansions, to
the Waldorf-Astoria Hotel, to finally, the Empire State. It suggests that
the model for Manhattan's urbanism is now a form of architectural
cannibalism: by swallowing its predecessors, the final building accumu-
lates all the strengths and spirits of the previous occupants of
the site and, in its own way, preserves their memory.

The second drawing suggests that the spirit of the Waldorf will, once
more, survive physical destruction to reappear triumphantly on another
location in the Grid.

The *Empire State Building* is the last manifestation of Manhattanism as
pure and thoughtless process, the climax of the subconscious Manhattan.
The *Waldorf* is the first full realization of the conscious Manhattan. In any
other culture the demolition of the old Waldorf would have been a philis-
tine act of destruction, but in the ideology of Manhattanism it constitutes
a double liberation: while the site is freed to meet its evolutionary destiny, the idea of the Waldorf is released to be redesigned as the example
of an explicit Culture of Congestion.

PROGRAM

The Empire State Building is to be "a skyscraper surpassing in height
anything ever constructed by man; surpassing in its simple beauty any
Skyscraper ever designed, meeting in the interior arrangements the most
exacting requirements of the most critical tenant...."[32]

The program, as described by William F. Lamb, its architect, is so rudimen-
tary as to become epigrammatic. "[It] was short enough — a fixed bud-
get, no space more than 28 feet from window to corridor, as many stories
and as much space as possible, an exterior of limestone, and completion by May 1931, which meant a year and six months from the beginning
of sketches....

"The logic of the plan is very simple. A certain amount of space in the
center, arranged as compactly as possible, contains the vertical circulation,
toilets, shafts and corridors. Surrounding this is a perimeter of office
space 28 feet deep. The sizes of the floors diminish as the elevators
decrease in number. In essence there is a pyramid of non-rentable space
surrounded by a pyramid of rentable space."[33]

TRUCK

While the Empire State is being planned, the European avant-garde is
experimenting with automatic writing, a surrender to the *process* of

writing unhindered by the author's critical apparatus.

The Empire State Building is a form of *automatic architecture,* a sensuous surrender by its collective makers — from the accountant to the plumber — to the *process* of building.

The Empire State is a building with no other program than to make a financial abstraction concrete — that is, *to exist.* All the episodes of its construction are governed by the unquestionable laws of automatism. After the sale of the block there is a dreamlike ceremony of desecration, a performance for Truck and Hotel. "Promptly following the first announcement a motor-truck [was it driverless?] drove through the wide door which had received presidents and princes, rulers of states and uncrowned kings and queens of society. The truck, like a roaring invader, thrust its great bulk into the lobby, where surely such an invader had never been seen before. It churned across the floor, then turned and roared down 'Peacock Alley,' down that proud corridor lined with gold mirrors and velvet draperies.

"The end of the Waldorf had come."[34]

SAW

On October 1, 1929, demolition is formally begun. A second "act" is performed, this one for two gentlemen and a saw. With crowbars they dislodge the topmost stone of the cornice.

The destruction of the Waldorf is planned as part of the construction. Fragments that are useful remain, such as the elevator cores that now reach into the as yet immaterial floors of the Empire State: "We salvaged four passenger elevators from the old building and installed them in temporary positions in the new framework."[35]

Those parts that do not serve any purpose are carted off in trucks and loaded on barges. Five miles beyond Sandy Hook, the Waldorf is dumped in the sea.

The dream's outrageousness activates dormant nightmares: might the building's heaviness make it disappear through the earth? No — "Empire State is not a new load placed on bedrock. Instead, the inert load of earth and stones put there by Nature has been dug away and a *useful* load in the form of a building has been placed there by man."

DREAMPLANNING

According to the logic of automatism, workers on the site are described as passive, almost ornamental presences.

"It was, as Shreve the architect said, like an assembly line placing the

"Messrs. Raskob and Smith begin to demolish the Waldorf...."

"As if by magic, their supplies appeared at their elbows...."

"A dream well-planned..."

same materials in the same relationship over and over....

"So perfect was the planning, so exact the fulfillment of schedule that workmen scarcely had to reach out for what they next required. As if by magic, their supplies appeared at their elbows...."

Since the base of Empire State occupies the entire site, all new supplies vanish inside the building, which now seems to generate itself, feeding on the never-ending stream of materials that arrive with split-second regularity.

At one point the "velocity" of this automatic architecture reaches $14\frac{1}{2}$ stories in ten days.

The cladding joins the frame: "On each floor, as the steel frame climbed higher, a miniature railroad was built, with switches and cars, to carry supplies. A perfect timetable was published each morning. At every minute of the day the builders knew what was going up on each of the elevators, to which height it would rise and which gang of workers would use it. On each floor, the operators of every one of the small trains of cars knew what was coming up and where it would be needed.

"Down below, in the streets, the drivers of the motor trucks worked on similar schedules. They knew, each hour of every day, whether they were to bring steel beams or bricks, window frames or blocks of stone, to Empire State. The moment of departure from a strange place, the length of time allowed for moving through traffic and the precise moment of arrival were calculated, scheduled and fulfilled with absolute precision. Trucks did not wait, derricks and elevators did not swing idle, men did not wait.

"With perfect teamwork, Empire State was built."

Pure product of process, Empire State can have no content. The building is sheer *envelope*.

"The skin is all, or almost all. Empire State will gleam in all its pristine beauty, for our children's children to wonder at. This appearance comes from the use of chrome-nickel steel, a new alloy that never tarnishes, never grows dull.

"The disfiguring shadows which so often come from deeply recessed windows, to mar the simple beauty of line, in Empire State are avoided by setting the windows, in thin metal frames, flush with the outer wall. Thus, not even shadows are allowed to break the upward sweep of the tower...."

After the building is finished, all participants wake up and look at the structure, which, inexplicably, does not go away.

"Empire State seemed almost to float, like an enchanted fairy tower, over New York. An edifice so lofty, so serene, so marvelously simple, so

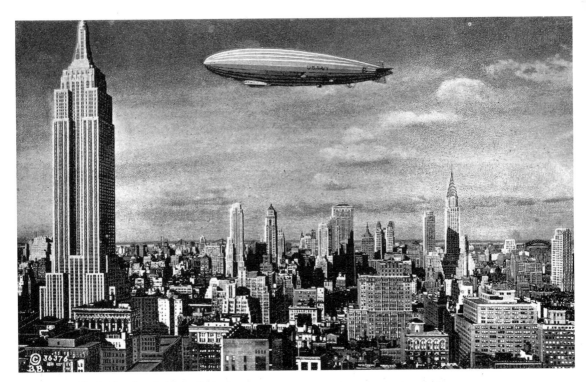

Rendezvous with destiny: the airship meets its
metropolitan lighthouse.

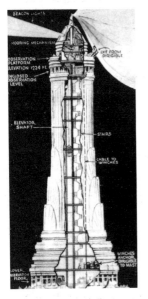

Empire State Building, details
of airship mooring mast.

luminously beautiful, had never before been imagined. One could look back on a dream well-planned."[36]

But exactly its character of dream, of automatic architecture, prevents it from being also an example of the conquest of the Automonument by higher forms of culture.

It was and is, literally, *thoughtless.*

Its ground floor is all elevator; there is no place left between the shafts for metaphor.

The upper floors too are strictly business, for 80,000 people. Maybe a businessman finds himself puzzled by its grandiosity; secretaries gaze at vistas never before seen by man.

AIRSHIP

Only at the top is there symbolism.

"At the eighty-sixth floor level is the observation tower, a sixteen story extension shaped like an inverted test-tube, buttressed by great flanking corner piers...."[37]

It is also an airship mooring mast and thus resolves Manhattan's paradoxical status as a city of landlocked lighthouses.

Only an airship could select its favorite harbor among all Manhattan's needles and actually dock to make the metaphorical literal once more.

DISPLACEMENT

Meanwhile, during its short period of displacement, the concept of the Waldorf continues to exist in the form of rights to its name, owned by Lucius Boomer, its last manager. It is left to him to reformulate the *tradition of the last word,* to plan and design the Waldorf's reappearance as the first Skyscraper fully conquered by social activity.

For over a century, Manhattan's lifestyle avant-garde has wandered from type to type in search of ideal accommodation. "In the beginning, private and detached houses were the only available residences for well-to-do New Yorkers. Then came the famous Brownstones, which were sometimes 'two-family' affairs; then the day of the flats arrived. Flats went up in the social scale and became 'apartments.' Next, because of their economic advantages, real or fancied, cooperative apartments had their day of favor. There then followed the vogue for Duplex apartments, with large rooms for entertaining purposes and many facilities of living that had previously been unknown...."[38]

The stages of this quest correspond to ever greater accumulations of individual units that, however combined, do not surrender their independence.

But as the Culture of Congestion reaches its zenith in the early thirties, a final homecoming is imminent.

The model of the hotel undergoes a conceptual overhaul and is invested with a new experimental ambition that creates Manhattan's definitive *unit of habitation*, the Residential Hotel — place where the inhabitant is his own houseguest, instrument that liberates its occupants for total involvement in the rituals of metropolitan life.

By the early thirties, what used to be *everyday* life has reached a unique level of refinement, complexity and theatricality. Its unfolding requires elaborate mechanical and decorative support systems that are uneconomical in the sense that peak use of decor, space, personnel, gadgetry and artifacts is only sporadic, while their idle presence is detrimental to the optimum experience of privacy.

In addition, this infrastructure is perpetually threatened with obsolescence by the pressure of fashion — of change as index of Progress — which results inevitably in a growing aversion to make household investments. The Residential Hotel transcends this dilemma by separating the private and public functions of the individual household and then bringing each to its own logical conclusion in a different part of the Mega-House.

In such a hotel, "patrons, whether permanent or transient, could avail themselves not only of the usual living facilities in an ultramodern hotel but, in addition, of services that might readily enable them to expand and supplement their own living quarters, and so arrange for the occasional entertainment of their friends on an elaborate scale...."[39]

COMMUNE

Such a unit of habitation is in effect a commune.

Its inhabitants pool their investments to finance a collective infrastructure for the "method of modern living."

Only as a commune can they afford the machinery to sustain the expensive and strenuous *tradition of the last word*.

By the same logic the hotel also becomes the shared headquarters of clubs and organizations that do not have their own accommodations. Freed from overhead, they can reconstitute themselves at regular intervals with maximum splendor at minimal cost.

With the development of the Residential Hotel, the metaphor implied by the 1916 Zoning Law finally coincides with the interior program: the Skyscraper as single unit of the Mega-Village. The phantom envelope of 1916 can become a single metropolitan household.

PROBLEM

"A problem of planning indeed was the new Waldorf-Astoria, combining ...
a transient hotel, an apartment house, a great ballroom and entertainment layout, a garage for private railroad cars (off the New York Central
tracks), various exhibition rooms and everything one can think of, the
whole thing mounting to forty stories....

"The architects' job was to plan the greatest hotel of all time, a structure
designed to take care of dozens of functions at the same moment, leaving
any of the house guests who weren't invited to a certain party quite
ignorant of such an affair going on right under their noses...."[40]

Its site does not really exist: the entire hotel is built on steel columns
wedged between the railroad tracks. It occupies a whole block, 200 by
600 feet, between Park and Lexington avenues and 49th and 50th streets.
Its silhouette closely follows the Ferrissian envelope, even if it has two
pinnacles instead of one, an echo of its origins in the two Astor Mansions
on 34th Street.

The lowest floors contain three layers of entertainment and public facilities, each the size of the original block, subdivided into circles, ovals,
rectangles and squares: Roman baths without water.

The hotel guests are housed in the four lower flanges, which reach
halfway to the top. The permanent residents live in the Waldorf Towers,
accessible through a private midblock tunnel.

SOLITUDES

The three lowest floors of the Waldorf form one of the most elaborate
manifestations yet of Manhattan's concept of a modern Venice.

Even though all their spaces are easily accessible, they are not exactly
public; they form a sequence of theatrical "living rooms" — an interior for
the Waldorf's houseguests that admits visitors but excludes the general
population. These living rooms constitute one of the bloated private
realms that together form Manhattan's Venetian *system of solitudes*.

The first floor, the Piano Nobile level, is a maze of circulation ("for truly,
there should be no end to circulation")[41] that leads to the Sert Room —
"favorite of New York's most interesting people ... decorated with murals
that show episodes of Don Quichotte" — the Norse Grill — "a rustic
Scandinavian space with a mural that marks the location of all sports
activities in the greater New York area"[42] — the Empire Room, the
Jade Room, the Blue Room and the Rose Room.

The third floor is a system of interconnecting larger spaces culminating
in a colossal ballroom that is also a theater.

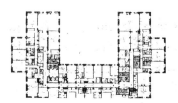

New Waldorf-Astoria, plans of typical
Waldorf Towers floor, typical hotel sector
floor, first floor and ground floor.

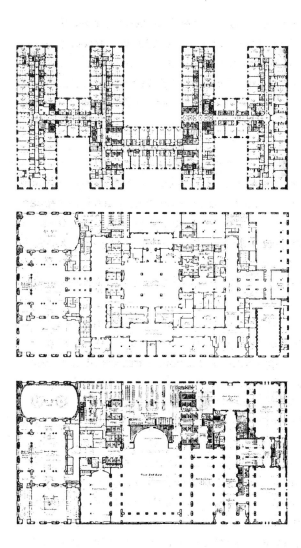

The two are separated by a layer of utilitarian facilities — kitchens, lockers, offices.

All floors are punctured by 16 passenger elevators, in a configuration that reflects the plan of the towers, and an additional 15 elevators for employees and freight. (One of the cars is large enough — 20 by 8 feet — to take a limousine to the center of the ballroom for the yearly automobile exhibit.)

To complement the cavelike lower floors, other facilities are placed near the extremities of the Mountain, such as the Starlight Roof on the 18th floor, which offers a sudden communication with the elements. "The entire ceiling can be rolled back by means of electrical machinery.... A tropical background of decoration, plants, flowers, pink flamingos suggests tropical Florida...."[43]

HISTORY

The Waldorf's theme of reincarnation is reinforced by the transplantation of Peacock Alley from the old Waldorf and by a nomenclature that repeats the old Waldorf's famous names, transferring to the new building their accumulated memories and associations. Thus, parts of the new Waldorf are famous before they have even been built.

Apart from the "historic" names, actual fragments and memorabilia from the old Waldorf, rescued from the demolition on 34th Street, are reassembled in the new Mountain to ensure further atmospheric continuity. More "history" is bought all over the globe by interior decorators who reconstruct their trophies in appropriate locations throughout the new structure: the disintegration of Europe provides ample material for the assembly of Manhattan's interiors.

"In the early planning of the Waldorf-Astoria, Basildon Park, England, was about to be dismantled.... Following a visit by Mr. Boomer negotiations were begun, which ended in the purchase of the beautifully painted and decorated salon." It is reconstituted on the ballroom floor.

Similar transplants — they cause a busy transatlantic traffic of dismantled mantelpieces — are inserted in the towers, where "floors alternate in modified French and English styles of decoration, while some of the terraced suites have been decorated and furnished in contemporary style...."[44]

TENTACLES

Its nonexistent site forces the Waldorf's designer to rethink a number of hotel-planning conventions.

Since the railroad is unwilling to give up parts of its tracks, the hotel is without a basement, the traditional location for services such as kitchens and laundry. These facilities are therefore atomized and scattered throughout the structure in optimal locations for serving the farthest reaches of the building.

Instead of a kitchen, the Waldorf has a *system of kitchens*. The main station is located on the second floor; "from there octopus-like tentacles in the form of service pantries were extended in all directions providing contact with all the Rooms and innumerable private dining rooms on the 3rd and 4th floors." On the 19th floor, in the residential part, is a Home Kitchen where all the cooking is done by women.

"Suppose that you want a dinner in your own language? Instead of the exotic masterpiece of a French chef, you may pine for your country ham and eggs, or Vermont cakes and maple syrup.... It was for that reason that I put a home kitchen in the Waldorf. There are times that we all long for everyday food, so for instance if you wake up feeling hungry for chicken dumplings, or cherry pie, you simply call the American kitchen...."[45]

The concept of Room Service is also elevated. For the benefit of those guests who choose to remain in the tower rather than descend to the living floors, it is transformed into a transcendental service that offers each visitor a choice between remaining a provincial or becoming a cosmopolite without ever leaving his room.

All these services are orchestrated and coordinated by means of the telephone, which becomes an extension of the architecture. "The volume of telephone calls and special services rendered by telephone to the Waldorf's guests requires equipment that is extensive enough to serve a city with a population of more than 50,000...."[46]

Through all these revolutionary arrangements and the facilities that "take care of elaborate private or public functions — balls, banquets, expositions, concerts, theatrical performances — all of them in self-contained spaces that include halls, theater, restaurants, cloakrooms, dance floors, etc.," the Waldorf-Astoria becomes "the social and civic center which it is today...."[47] Manhattan's first Skyscraper House.

MOVIE

In the thirties — when the second Waldorf is being built — the "Hotel" becomes Hollywood's favorite subject.

In a sense, it relieves the scriptwriter of the obligation of inventing a plot. A Hotel *is* a plot — a cybernetic universe with its own laws generating random but fortuitous collisions between human beings who would never have met elsewhere. It offers a fertile cross section through the

Axonometric section through new Waldorf-Astoria Hotel.

TOWER SUITES · TOWER SUITES

STARLIGHT ROOF

JUNIOR LEAGUE

PALM BAR · CANADIAN CLUB · CANADIAN CLUB

TRANSIENT · TRANSIENT

JANSEN SUITE

CENTER COURT

RADIO & TELEVISION · LIGHTING

SERT ROOM

EAST COURT

TERRACE

WEST COURT · WEST GALLERY · BALL ROOM · EAST GALLERY · SILVER GALLERY · ASTOR GALLERY

SERVICE · LOCKERS · SHOP · LOCKERS · BARBER SHOP

FOYER · KITCHENS · KITCHENS · PEACOCK ALLEY

GALLERY · PEACOCK ALLEY · LOBBY · SHOP · SHOP · SHOP · BANK

PARK AVENUE · MENS BAR · DRIVEWAY

BAKERY · KITCHEN · STORAGE · LEXINGTON AVENUE

EMPLOYEES LOCKERS · NEW YORK CENTRAL TRACKS

HEATING · LIGHTING · VENTILATING

HEATING · LIGHTING · VENTILATING · NEW YORK CENTRAL TRACKS · EXPRESS LEVEL · EMPLOYEES LOCKERS · STORAGE · BANK · KITCHEN · BAKERY · SHOPS · DRIVEWAY · MENS BAR · GALLERY · FOYER · KITCHENS · PEACOCK ALLEY

SHOPS · BARBER SHOP · EXECUTIVE OFFICES · ASTOR GALLERY · SILVER GALLERY · EAST COURT · EAST GALLERY · BALL ROOM · WEST GALLERY · WEST COURT · SERVICE · TERRACE · SERT ROOM · RADIO & TELEVISION

TRANSIENT · TRANSIENT · JANSEN SUITE · STARLIGHT ROOF · PALM BAR · CANADIAN CLUB · CANADIAN CLUB · JUNIOR LEAGUE · TOWER SUITES · TOWER SUITES · PARK AVE · 50TH ST · LEXINGTON AVE.

population, a richly textured interface between social castes, a field for the comedy of clashing manners and a neutral background of routine operations to give every incident dramatic relief.

With the Waldorf, the Hotel itself becomes such a movie, featuring the guests as stars and the personnel as a discreet coat-tailed chorus of extras.

By taking a room in the hotel, a guest buys his way into an ever-expanding script, acquiring the right to use all the decors and to exploit the pre-fabricated opportunities to interact with all the other "stars."

The movie begins at the revolving door — symbol of the unlimited sur-prises of coincidence; then subplots are instigated in the darker recesses of the lower floors, to be consummated — via an elevator episode — in the upper regions of the building. Only the territory of the block frames all stories and lends them coherence.

EPIC

Together, the cast performs an abstract epic entitled *Opportunity, Emancipation, Acceleration.*

One (sociological) subplot describes a careerist's shortcut to the top through a stay in the Hotel. "I would invest my savings in living at the Waldorf and doing my utmost to rub shoulders with the financial and business great.... This was the best investment I have ever made in my life," confides Forbes, the future tycoon.[48]

In another part of the intrigue women guests are freed to pursue careers by the Hotel's takeover of all the annoyances and responsibilities of housekeeping, which leads to an accelerated liberation that baffles the males, suddenly surrounded by "hyper-emancipated creatures."

"The bluer their eyes, the more they know about Einstein's theory and you can depend upon a clinging vine to give you the real lowdown on the diesel engine...."[49]

In a more romantic story, the boy next door becomes the man on the floor above, his tap dancing an indispensable medium of Skyscraper communication — a Morse code of the heart performed by the feet.

COW

Until 1800 real cows grazed on the site of the first Waldorf.

A hundred years later, the pressure of popular demand invests the concept of the cow with a technical dimension, producing the Inexhaustible Cow on Coney Island: stiff and lifeless, but effective in its production of an endless flow of milk.

Thirty-five years later still, the Waldorf witnesses the final (re)appearance of the concept Cow, in one of the Hotel's most ambitious subplots. Gossip columnist Elsa Maxwell — a self-described "hotel pilgrim" — has lived in the Waldorf Towers since their opening. To cultivate her connections, she organizes a yearly party somewhere in the building. Because she likes to test the management, the theme of each of these events is chosen to be as incompatible as possible with the existing interiors. In fact, "the vain, mad endeavor to break down Captain Willy" (who is in charge of the Waldorf's Banquet Department) becomes, after a while, "the only reason for the continuing and ever-growing extravagance of my costume balls...."

In 1935, when her favorite Starlight Roof is already reserved and only the Jade Room — a somber modern interior that reminds her of the Temple of Karnak near Luxor — is available, Maxwell sees her chance to ask the impossible.

"'Captain Willy, in this Jade Ballroom I am going to give a farmyard party, a barn dance.

"'I am going to have trees with real apples on them, even if the apples have to be pinned on. I'm going to cover those enormous chandeliers with hayricks. I'm going to have clotheslines stretched across the ceiling on which the family wash will be hung. I'm going to have a beer well. I'm going to have stalls with sheep, real cows, donkeys, geese, chickens and pigs and a hillbilly band....'

"'Yes, Miss Maxwell,' said Captain Willy. 'Certainly.'

"To my surprise, I blurted out, 'Impossible. How are you going to get live animals to the third floor of the Waldorf?'

"'We can have felt shoes made for the animals,' said Captain Willy firmly. A Mephistopheles in coat-tails....."[50]

The centerpiece of Maxwell's party is *Molly the Moët Cow*, a cow that milks champagne on one side and whiskey and soda on the other.

Maxwell's farm completes a cycle: the super-refined infrastructure of the hotel, its architectural ingenuity, all its accumulated technologies together ensure that in Manhattan the last word is the same as the first. But it is only one of many last words.

A haunted house such as the Waldorf is not simply the end product of a long pedigree, but even more its *sum,* the simultaneous existence — on a single location, at a single point in time — of all its "lost" stages. It was necessary to destroy those early manifestations in order to preserve them. In Manhattan's Culture of Congestion, destruction is another word for preservation.

Definitive Instability:
The Downtown Athletic Club

We in New York celebrate the black mass of Materialism.
We are concrete.
We have a body.
We have sex.
We are male to the core.
We divinize matter, energy, motion, change.
— Benjamin de Casseres, *Mirrors of New York*

APOTHEOSIS

The Downtown Athletic Club stands on the bank of the Hudson River
near Battery Park, the southern tip of Manhattan. It occupies a lot "varying
from 77 feet wide on Washington Street to 78 feet 8 inches wide on West
Street with a depth of 179 feet 1¼ inches between streets...."[51]
Built in 1931, its 38 stories reach a height of 534 feet. Large abstract
patterns of glass and brick make its exterior inscrutable and almost indistinguishable from the conventional Skyscrapers around it.
This serenity hides the apotheosis of the Skyscraper as instrument of the
Culture of Congestion.
The Club represents the complete conquest — floor by floor — of the Skyscraper by social activity; with the Downtown Athletic Club the American
way of life, know-how and initiative definitively overtake the theoretical
lifestyle modifications that the various 20th-century European avant-
gardes have been insistently proposing, without ever managing to
impose them.
In the Downtown Athletic Club the Skyscraper is used as a Constructivist
Social Condenser: a machine to generate and intensify desirable forms
of human intercourse.

TERRITORIES

In only 22 years the speculations of the 1909 theorem have become
reality in the Downtown Athletic Club: it is a series of 38 superimposed
platforms that each repeat, more or less, the original area of the site,
connected by a battery of 13 elevators that forms the north wall of the
structure.
To the financial jungle of Wall Street, the Club opposes a complementary
program of hyper-refined civilization, in which a full spectrum of facilities — all ostensibly connected with athletics — restores the human body.

Downtown Athletic Club, 1931 (Starrett & Van Vleck, architect; Duncan Hunter, associate architect). Successful lobotomy made this apotheosis of the Skyscraper as instrument of revolutionary metropolitan culture almost indistinguishable from surrounding Towers.

Downtown Athletic Club, site plan: a small rectangle, repeated 38 times.

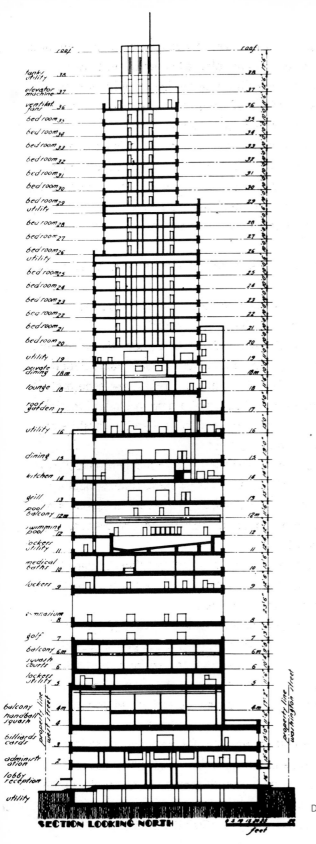

SECTION LOOKING NORTH

feet

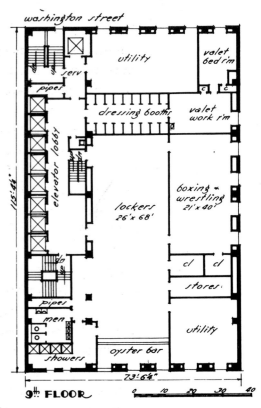

9th FLOOR

Downtown Athletic Club, plan of ninth floor: "eating oysters with boxing gloves, naked, on the *n*th floor ..."

Downtown Athletic Club, section.

154

The lowest floors are equipped for relatively conventional athletic pursuits: squash and handball courts, poolrooms, etc., all sandwiched between locker rooms. But then ascent through the upper layers of the structure — with its implied approximation of a theoretical "peak" condition — leads through territories never before tread upon by man.

Emerging from the elevator on the ninth floor, the visitor finds himself in a dark vestibule that leads directly into a locker room that occupies the center of the platform, where there is no daylight. There he undresses, puts on boxing gloves and enters an adjoining space equipped with a multitude of punching bags (occasionally he may even confront a human opponent).

On the southern side, the same locker room is also serviced by an oyster bar with a view over the Hudson River.

Eating oysters with boxing gloves, naked, on the nth floor — such is the "plot" of the ninth story, or, the *20th century in action.*

In a further escalation, the tenth floor is devoted to preventive medicine. On one side of a lavish dressing lounge an array of body-manipulation facilities is arranged around a Turkish bath: sections for massage and rubbing, an eight-bed station for artificial sunbathing, a ten-bed resting area. On the south face, six barbers are concerned with the mysteries of masculine beauty and how to bring it out.

But the southwest corner of the floor is the most explicitly medical: a special facility that can treat five patients at the same time. A doctor here is in charge of the process of *"Colonic Irrigation":* the insertion into the human intestines of synthetic bacterial cultures that rejuvenate man by improving his metabolism.

This final step brings the sequence of mechanical interference with human nature, initiated by such apparently innocent attractions as Coney Island's Barrels of Love, to a drastic conclusion.

On the 12th floor a swimming pool occupies the full rectangle; the elevators lead almost directly into the water. At night, the pool is illuminated only by its underwater lighting system, so that the entire slab of water, with its frenetic swimmers, appears to float in space, suspended between the electric scintillation of the Wall Street towers and the stars reflected in the Hudson.

Of all the floors, the interior golf course — on the seventh — is the most extreme undertaking: the transplantation of an "English" landscape of hills and valleys, a narrow river that curls across the rectangle, green grass, trees, a bridge, all real, but taxidermized in the literal realization of the "meadows aloft" announced by the 1909 theorem. The interior

Downtown Athletic Club, 12th floor: swimming pool at night.

Downtown Athletic Club, seventh floor: interior golf course.

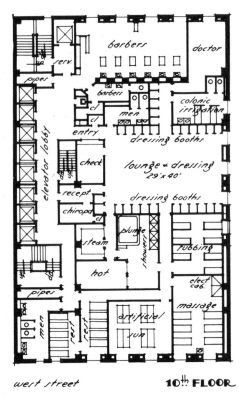

west street   10th FLOOR

Downtown Athletic Club, plan of tenth floor.

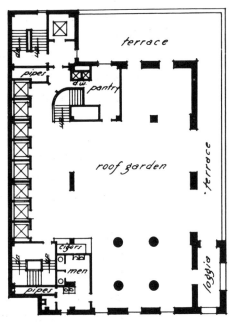

Downtown Athletic Club, plan of 17th floor: interior roof garden with metropolitan verandas.

golf course is at the same time obliteration and preservation: having been extirpated by the Metropolis, nature is now resurrected *inside* the Skyscraper as merely one of its infinite layers, a technical service that sustains and refreshes the Metropolitanites in their exhausting existence. The Skyscraper has transformed Nature into Super-Nature.

From the first to the twelfth floors, ascent inside the Downtown Athletic Club has corresponded to increased subtlety and unconventionality of the "programs" offered on each platform. The next five floors are devoted to eating, resting and socializing: they contain dining rooms — with a variety of privacies — kitchens, lounges, even a library. After their stringent work-outs on the lower floors, the athletes — puritanical hedonists to a man — are finally in condition to confront the opposite sex — women — on a small rectangular dance floor on the 17th-story roof garden.

From the 20th to the 35th floors, the Club contains only bedrooms.

"The plan is of primary importance, because on the floor are performed all the activities of the human occupants";[52] that is how Raymond Hood — the most theoretical of New York's architects — has defined Manhattan's version of functionalism distorted by the demands and opportunities of density and congestion.

In the Downtown Athletic Club each "plan" is an abstract composition of activities that describes, on each of the synthetic platforms, a differ-ent "performance" that is only a fragment of the larger spectacle of the Metropolis.

In an abstract choreography, the building's athletes shuttle up and down between its 38 "plots" — in a sequence as random as only an elevator man can make it — each equipped with techno-psychic apparatus for the men's own redesign.

Such an architecture is an aleatory form of "planning" life itself: in the fantastic juxtaposition of its activities, each of the Club's floors is a separate installment of an infinitely unpredictable intrigue that extols the complete surrender to the definitive instability of life in the Metropolis.

INCUBATOR

With its first 12 floors accessible only to men, the Downtown Athletic Club appears to be *a locker room the size of a Skyscraper,* definitive manifestation of those metaphysics — at once spiritual and carnal — that protect the American male against the corrosion of adulthood. But in fact, the Club has reached the point where the notion of a "peak" condition transcends the physical realm to become cerebral.

It is not a locker room but an *incubator for adults,* an instrument that

permits the members — too impatient to await the outcome of evolution —
to reach new strata of maturity by transforming themselves into new
beings, this time according to their individual designs.

Bastions of the antinatural, Skyscrapers such as the Club announce the
imminent segregation of mankind into two tribes: one of *Metropolitanites* —
literally self-made — who used the full potential of the *apparatus of
Modernity* to reach unique levels of perfection, the second simply the
remainder of the traditional human race.

The only price its locker-room graduates have to pay for their collective
narcissism is that of sterility. Their self-induced mutations are not repro-
ducible in future generations.

The bewitchment of the Metropolis stops at the genes; they remain the
final stronghold of Nature.

When the Club's management advertises the fact that "with its delightful
sea breezes and commanding view, the 20 floors devoted to living
quarters for members make the Downtown Club an ideal home for men
who are free of family cares and in a position to enjoy the last word
in luxurious living,"[53] they suggest openly that for the true Metropolitan,
bachelorhood is the only desirable status.

The Downtown Athletic Club is a machine for metropolitan bachelors
whose ultimate "peak" condition has lifted them beyond the reach of
fertile brides.

In their frenzied self-regeneration, the men are on a collective *"flight
upward"* from the specter of the Basin Girl.

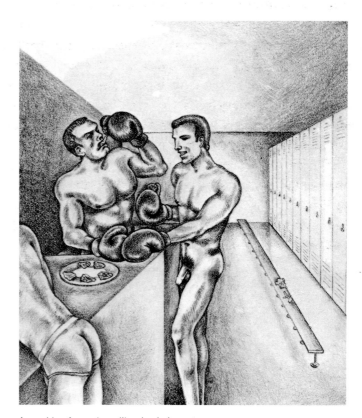

A machine for metropolitan bachelors ...

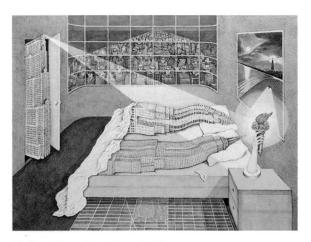

Madelon Vriesendorp, *Flagrant délit*.

How Perfect Perfection Can Be: The Creation of Rockefeller Center

I get so sentimental when I see
How perfect perfection can be....
— Fred Astaire in *Top Hat*

The Talents of Raymond Hood

*Architecture is the business of manufacturing adequate shelter for
human activities.*
My favorite form is the sphere.
*The test of a first-rate intelligence is the ability to hold two opposite ideas in
the mind at the same time, and still retain the ability to function.*
—F. Scott Fitzgerald, *The Crack-Up*

REPRESENTATIVE

Manhattanism is the urbanistic doctrine that suspends irreconcilable
differences between mutually exclusive positions; to establish its
theorems in the reality of the Grid, it needs a human representative.
Only he could conceive of the two positions quoted above *at the same
time* without unbearable strains developing in his psyche.
This representative is Raymond Hood.[1]
Hood is born in 1881 in Pawtucket, Rhode Island, son of an affluent
Baptist family; his father is a box manufacturer. Hood attends Brown
University, then MIT School of Architecture. He works in Boston archi-
tectural offices but wants to go to the École des Beaux-Arts in Paris; in
1904 he is turned down for lack of drawing ability.
In 1905 he is accepted. Before leaving for Paris, he warns his colleagues
in the office that one day he will be "the greatest architect in New York."
Hood is small; his hair grows straight up from his scalp at a remarkable
90-degree angle. The French call him "le petit Raymond."
As a Baptist, he refuses at first to enter Notre Dame; friends convince
him to drink his first wine, then to enter the cathedral.
In 1911 his final project at the École is for a city hall in Pawtucket. It is
his first Skyscraper: a fat Tower, inadequately anchored to the ground
by a timid socle.
He travels in Europe — the Grand Tour — then returns to New York.
Paris represents "years to think," he writes; "in New York one falls too
easily in the habit of working without thinking on account of the amount
of work that there is to do."[2]
Manhattan: no time for consciousness.
Hood opens his office in a brownstone at 7 West 42nd Street. In vain he
listens for "footsteps on the staircase."
He papers his office in gold, but the money runs out and it remains
half-gilded.
A client asks Hood to redecorate her bathroom. She expects the Prince

Raymond Hood.

of Wales; a large crack in the wall might upset him. Hood advises her to hang a painting over the crack.

There are odd jobs: Hood supervises "the removal of 8 bodies from one family vault to another."

He is restless in the absence of work; he "marks up many a tablecloth with his soft pencil" with architect friends Ely Jacques Kahn (the Squibb Building) and Ralph Walker (One Wall Street).

He marries his secretary.

His nervous system gets intertwined with that of the Metropolis.

GLOBE 1

In the Concourse of Grand Central Station he meets his friend John Mead Howells, one of ten American architects invited to enter the Chicago Tribune Competition; the first prize is to be $50,000. Howells, too busy to accept, offers Hood the chance to enter for him.

On December 23, 1922, their entry, no. 69, a Gothic Skyscraper, wins first prize. Mrs. Hood drives around town in a taxi to show all creditors the check.

Hood is 41.

He refers to the moon as "his"[3] and designs a house in the form of the globe.

His involvement with the Skyscraper deepens.

He buys Le Corbusier's first book, *Towards a New Architecture;* the next ones he only borrows.

THEORY

He has a discreet, private theory about the Skyscraper but knows that, in Manhattan, it would be unwise to admit it.

In his vision the future Manhattan is a *City of Towers,*[4] a subtly modified version of what already exists; instead of the ruthless extrusion of arbitrary individual plots, larger sites within a block will be assembled in new building operations. The space around the Towers within the blocks will be left unbuilt, so that each Tower can regain its integrity and a measure of isolation. Such pure skyscrapers can insinuate themselves strictly within the framework of the Grid and gradually take over the city without major disruptions. Hood's City of Towers will be a forest of freestanding, competing needles made accessible by the regular paths of the Grid: a practical Luna Park.

GOLD

Soon after building the Chicago Tribune Tower, Hood is asked to do his first Skyscraper in New York, the American Radiator Building, on a lot facing Bryant Park.

In the standard "solution" — the direct multiplication of the site as often as the zoning envelope permits — the west face of such a Tower would have a blind wall, so that a similar structure could be built directly against it. By shrinking the area of the Tower, Hood is able to perforate the west facade with windows, and so designs the first example of his City of Towers. The operation makes pragmatic and financial sense; the quality of the office space increases, therefore the rents, and so on.

But the exterior of the Tower presents different — i.e., artistic — issues to the architect. He has always been irritated by the boring window openings in the facades of Towers, a potential tedium that increases in direct proportion to their height — acres of meaningless black rectangles that threaten to reduce their soaring quality.

Hood decides to build the building in black brick, so that the holes — embarrassing reminder of the other reality inside — can be absorbed within the stem and thus become unnoticeable.

The top of the black building is gilded. Hood's down-to-earth alibi for the top briskly severs all connections between gold and any possible associations with Ecstasy. "The incorporation of publicity or advertising features in a building is frequently an item for consideration. It stimulates public interest and admiration, is accepted as a genuine contribution to architecture, enhances the value of the property and is profitable to the owner in the same manner as other forms of legitimate advertising."[5]

GLOBE 2

In 1928 Colonel Paterson, owner of the *Daily News,* comes to Hood. He wants to build printing works on 42nd Street combined with a negligible amount of office space for his editors.

Hood calculates that a Skyscraper would ultimately be cheaper. He designs the second fragment of his City of Towers (unbeknownst to his client) by "proving" that through yielding a thin midblock strip this Tower too can have windows in a wall that would otherwise be blind, transforming cheap loft space into expensive office accommodation.

Inside he goes even further: builder so far only of Towers, he consummates here his overwhelming love for the sphere. He designs "a circular space, 150 feet in circumference — to be enclosed by a wall of black glass which rises, unbroken by any windows, to a black glass ceiling; in

 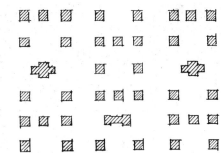

Raymond Hood, "A City of Towers," first published in 1927; diagram of suggested transformations presented as "Proposals for the Solution of New York's Problem of Overcrowding." Against the 1916 Zoning Law, which can never control the ultimate *bulk* of Manhattan's buildings, only their *shape* — and is therefore incapable of defining the upward limit of Manhattan's density — Hood wanted to "establish a constant ratio between the Volume of Building and the street area.... For each foot of street frontage a *definitive* volume is allowed by law. A property owner can [only] exceed this volume allowance provided he sets back," so that "each building as it imposes additional load on street traffic provides the additional street area to carry it...." In this way, Hood enlisted the natural greed of the developer — who invariably wanted to build the largest possible volume, which, under the terms of Hood's proposal, would coincide with the *highest* possible tower on the *smallest* possible site — in the service of an aesthetic vision: a city of sheer, freestanding needles. But that vision was never revealed; officially the proposal would only solve "the problems of light, air and traffic...."

"A City of Towers ... Operation at the end of a block..."

"A City of Towers ... Three operations have completed one block ..."

Manhattan halfway to becoming a City of Towers:
model combining various end-, mid- and complete-
block operations; gradual metamorphosis without
major disruption or conceptual reorganization.

Harvey Wiley Corbett, "Proposed Separation of
Towers," 1926. Analogous proposal to Hood's.
As complement to his "Venetian" proposals
Corbett projects here a *Metropolitan Suburb* that
corresponds to "the smallest maximum bulk
for business buildings" suggested by the Regional
Plan models. The random placement of the
Towers — which are connected by a frivolous geom-
etry of footpaths through a park enlivened
by a multitude of female forms, yet intersected by
the regularity of the Grid — combined with the
intimate, suburban scale of the miniature
Skyscrapers makes Corbett's *Metropolitan Suburb*
the most appealing version of the tower-in-the-
park formula ever proposed.

Study model of the theoretical zoning envelope on the Daily News site, 1929. "It is a shape that the law puts in the architect's hands. He can add nothing to it; but he can vary it in detail as he wishes...." (Ferriss, *Metropolis of Tomorrow*; model and photo by Walter Kilham, Jr.)

Daily News Building, second prototype of the City of Towers, halfway modeled from the crude form of the zoning envelope: "clay emerging into practical form ..."

Daily News Building, definitive model.

the center of a brass-inlaid floor, a cup-shaped well from which light —
the sole illumination of the room — is to stream.

"Bathed in this light, a ten-foot terrestrial globe is to revolve — its
even revolutions reflected darkly in the night-like ceiling above": with
understandable pleasure Ferriss describes the Daily News lobby in his
Metropolis of Tomorrow.[6]

The lobby is, after all, a three-dimensional realization of that murky
Ferrissian void — the pitch-black womb of Manhattanism, cosmos of charcoal smudges — which has given birth already to the Skyscraper and
now, finally, to a Globe.

"Why is so bizarre a design included in so utilitarian a building?"
Ferriss asks with feigned innocence. It is because Raymond Hood is now
the leading agent of the collapse of oppositions that is Manhattan's
true ambition. The lobby is a chapel of Manhattanism. (Hood himself con-
fesses that Napoleon's Tomb in Les Invalides is the model for the sunken
installation.)

ICEBERG

With the McGraw-Hill Skyscraper (1929–31), Hood becomes more openly
fanatic as he prepares a final dose of hedonism for his City of Towers.
The building accommodates three categories of activity that correspond
to the setbacks of its section: printing works in the base, loft spaces for
book production in the middle and offices in the slender shaft.

Once, when it suited him, Hood pretended to have no feeling for color:
"What color? Let's see. How many colors are there — red, yellow and blue?
Let's make it red."[7] Now he considers yellow, orange, green, gray, red,
Chinese red and black with orange trimming for the building.

The tower is to be shaded from a darker tone at the base to a lighter one
toward the top, "where it finally blends off into the azure of the sky...."
To realize this denial of the tower's presence, one of Hood's assistants
checks the location of each single tile — its fit within the overall project
of "disappearance" — with binoculars from a window opposite the
construction site.

The result is stunning: "The exterior of the building is finished entirely in
polychrome.... The horizontal spandrel walls are faced with rectangular
blocks of *blue-green* glazed terra-cotta.... The metal-covered vertical piers
are painted a *dark green-blue,* almost *black.* The metal windows are painted
an *apple-green* color.... A narrow band of *vermillion* is painted on the
face of the top jambs of the windows and across the face of the metal-
covered piers. *Vermillion* is also used on the underside of the horizontal

Raymond Hood, McGraw-Hill Building, 1931:
the fire of Manhattanism raging inside the
iceberg of Modernism.

projections on the penthouse and over the front entrance. The *golden* color of the windowshades effectively complements the cool tone of the building. They have a broad *blue-green* vertical stripe in the corner tying them into the general color scheme. Their color is an unusually important element in the exterior design.

"The entrance vestibule is finished in sheet steel bands, enameled *dark blue* and *green* alternatively, separated by metal tubes finished in *silver* and *gold*.... The walls of the main and elevator corridor are finished in sheet steel enameled a *green* color."[8]

The relentlessness of such a color scheme betrays obsession.

Once again Hood has combined two incompatibles in a single whole: its golden shades pulled down to reflect the sun, the McGraw-Hill Building looks like a fire raging inside an iceberg: the fire of Manhattanism inside the iceberg of Modernism.

SCHISM

In the tradition of the dime novel, one day in the mid-twenties a pastor comes to see Hood in his office. He represents a congregation that wants to build the greatest church in the world.

"The congregation was one of businessmen and the site was an extremely valuable one.... Therefore they wished not only to build the greatest church in the world, but to combine it with revenue producing enterprises including a hotel, a YMCA, an apartment house with a swimming pool, and so on. On the street level would be shops, to bring in high rentals, and in the basement, the largest garage in Columbus, Ohio. The garage was very important, because, in giving his congregation a place to park their cars on coming to work weekdays, the pastor would indeed make the church the center of their lives...."

The pastor had first gone to Ralph Adams Cram, a traditional church architect, who rejected him, especially indignant about the suggested garage. "There would be no room for cars because this noble structure would be constructed on tremendous granite piers ... that would support [it] through all time as a monument to their faith."

New York — Hood — is the pastor's last resort. He cannot go back to the businessmen to tell them that the basement will be completely occupied by piers instead of cars.

Hood reassures him. "The trouble with Mr. Cram is that he has no faith in God. I will design a church for you that will be the greatest church in the world. It will include all the hotels, swimming tanks and candy stores you desire. Furthermore, in the basement will be the largest garage in

Central Methodist Episcopal Church, first
floor plan: Cathedral shares ground floor
with, clockwise, candy stores, Sunday
school, hotel kitchens and dining rooms.

Raymond Hood, Central Methodist
Episcopal Church, Columbus, Ohio, 1927.
Vertical Schism at its most blatant: directly
below the Cathedral, "the largest garage
in Christendom" — actually room for only
2 x 69 cars.

Central Methodist Episcopal Church,
general view showing uneasy coexistence
of heterogeneous elements collected in
Hood's first multifunctional Skyscraper.
The Tower — in spite of its lofty expression — contains strictly secular accommodation: YMCA, pool, apartments, hotel
and offices. The church is articulated as
a quasi-autonomous volume.

Christendom because I will build your church on toothpicks and have faith enough in God to believe it will stand up!"[9]

For the first time Hood works on a multipurpose building. Indifferent to programmatic hierarchy, he simply assigns parts of the Mountain to the necessary functions. With barefaced literalness he projects two floors — the Cathedral and the Parking Garage, separated only by inches of concrete — that realize his boast to the pastor *and* represent the final implementation of the Great Lobotomy's indispensable complement: the Vertical Schism, which creates the freedom to stack such disparate activities directly on top of each other without any concern for their symbolic compatibility.

SCHIZOPHRENIA

The church episode is emblematic of Hood's, and his colleagues', state of mind in the mid-twenties; they have developed a schizophrenia that allows them simultaneously to derive energy and inspiration from Manhattan as irrational fantasy *and* to establish its unprecedented theorems in a series of strictly rational steps.

The secret of Hood's success is a radical command of the language of fantasy-pragmatism that lends Manhattanism's ambition — the creation of congestion on all possible levels — the appearance of objectivity.

Hood's rhetoric leaves the most hard-headed businessman — especially him — hopelessly entrapped. He is a captivating architectural Scheherazade, holding the real-estate men in thrall with his 1,001 fairy tales of philistinism:

"All this beauty stuff is bunk,"[10] or "Consequently, contemporary architecture is disclosed and established as logic...."[11]

Or, almost poetic: "The plan is of primary importance, because on the floor are performed all the activities of the human occupants...."[12]

When Hood concludes his tale with a description of the ideal architect — that theoretical human representative of Manhattanism who alone can exploit the overlap between the businessmen's fantasies of practicality and the architects' dreams of a Culture of Congestion — he is merely describing the enviable topography of his own personality:

"The architect of aesthetically acceptable buildings must possess an analytical and logical type of mind; have a knowledge of all the elements of a building and of its purpose and function; possess a lively imagination and a cultivated inherent sense of form, proportion, appropriateness and color; possess a spirit of creation, adventure, independence, determination and bravery, and also, a large measure of humanistic instincts and ordinary common sense."[13] The businessmen have to agree: Manhattanism is the only program where the efficiency intersects with the sublime.

PREMONITION

After the City of Towers and the rediscovery for his profession of the well-integrated schism of the church/garage, Hood undertakes two more theoretical projects.

They share a premonition of a new age contained in the extrapolation of the trends as they are, grafted onto a continuing devotion to the existing metaphoric infrastructure, a refusal to consider any part of the magic carpet of the Grid as subject to reconsideration. Hood wants to adapt the new age to the real Manhattan, not the reverse. The "City under a Single Roof"[14] (1931), the first of these projects, "has been founded on the principle that concentration in a metropolitan area ... is a desirable condition...." According to the stratagem of self-induced schizophrenia, the scheme is actually presented as the answer to the condition it is determined to exacerbate: "The growth of cities is getting beyond control. Skyscrapers create congestion. Subways are built resulting in more skyscrapers and so on in an ascending spiral. Where will it end? Here is the answer...." Hood knows.

"The tendency is toward related communities in the city — communities whose activities are confined within certain areas whose traffic does not need to travel distant streets to collect supplies and orders. It seems to me that the salvation of New York depends on the wider application of this principle.

"Every businessman in the city must have realized what an advantage it would be to live in the Building where his office is located. It is toward this ideal that real estate firms and architects should work....

"Whole industries should be united into interdependent developments with clubs, hotels, stores, apartments and even theaters. Such an arrangement would make possible great economies in time as well as diminish wear and tear on human nerves. Put the worker in a unified scheme and he need hardly put his feet on the sidewalk during the entire day...."

In Hood's City under one Roof, all the movement that contributes to congestion — horizontally across the surface of the earth — is replaced by vertical movement inside buildings, where it causes *de*congestion.

MOUNTAINS

That same year, Hood develops his thesis of the *City within a City* further. In his project "Manhattan 1950"[15] — even more emphatic about the

Raymond Hood, "A City under a Single Roof,"
model in typical midtown context (smoke added),
"... founded on the principle that concentration in
a metropolitan area ... is a desirable condition ...
The Unit Building, covering three blocks of ground
space, will house a whole industry and its auxiliary
businesses. Only elevator shafts and stairways
reach the street level. The first ten floors house
stores, theaters and clubs. Above them is the
industry to which the Building is devoted. Workers
live on the upper floors...." Hood's second theoretical proposal abandons the formula of the City
of Towers in favor of much larger metropolitan
structures that exceed the limitations of a single
block and that—through their colossal size—
absorb and interiorize all traffic—and thus congestion—that smaller single structures such as
Hood's Towers would generate between them.

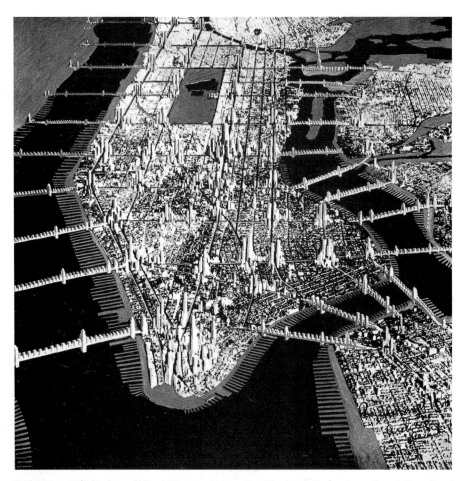

"Manhattan 1950," collage. "Island throws out tentacles.... Bird's-eye view of the Manhattan of 1950 with its ranges of Skyscrapers over transportation lines and the mountain peaks of industry over each entrance. The great bridges empty into business centers...." Hood's third "theory" — for a definitive Manhattan — is a variation on the "City under a Single Roof" theme, a proposal to break through the *Congestion Barrier* by the careful implantation of the new mega-scale of autonomous, man-made universes on the existing city. By this time, Hood's success in blurring the distinction between pragmatism and idealism had his contemporaries utterly confounded. How could an allegedly straightforward accommodation of business interests — the simple extrapolation of implacable tendencies — generate such artistic images? "These visions place their emphasis upon the increasing concentration occurring in Manhattan. To the extent that they apparently follow the characteristic growth of the city they may be considered practical rather than visionary. Only in greatness of scale and boldness in employment of bridges may they be judged skeptically. Their implied acquiescence, however, to the principle of Congestion in city growth detracts considerably from their value as Utopian schemes...." (*Creative Arts.*)

inviolate character of the Grid as *sine qua non* of Manhattan — he proposes a regular, reasonable implantation of the new scale on chosen locations within the Grid. A total of 38 Mountains are positioned on the intersections of alternate avenues and the wider streets of the Grid, roughly every tenth street.

The bulk of each Mountain exceeds the size of a single block, but neither Mountain nor Grid is compromised: the Grid simply cuts through the Mountain to create a solid/void configuration. Four peaks face each other across the intersection and gradually terrace down toward the perimeter where, like the 100-story building, they connect with the remaining traces of the older urban landscape.

Secondary tentacles develop along the island: suspension bridges overloaded with apartments — streets that have become buildings. Hood's bridges are like the drawbridges surrounding a fortress. They mark Manhattan's gates.

The "Manhattan 1950" project proposes a specific, limited number of Mountains. That in itself is proof that a new phase of Manhattanism has begun: a knowable Manhattan.

BARRIER

The paradoxical intention to solve congestion by creating more congestion suggests the theoretical assumption that there exists a "congestion barrier." By aiming for a new order of the colossal, one would break through this barrier and suddenly emerge in a completely serene and silent world, where all the hysterical and nerve-wracking activity that used to occur outside, in the subways, etc., would now be completely absorbed within the buildings themselves. Congestion has been removed from the streets and is now swallowed by the architecture. This City is permanent; there is no reason that the buildings should ever be replaced. The eerie calm of their exteriors is ensured through the Great Lobotomy. But inside, where the Vertical Schism accommodates all possible change, life is in a continuous state of frenzy. Manhattan is now a quiet metropolitan plain marked by the self-contained universes of the Mountains, the concept of the Real definitively left behind, superseded.

The gates define a hermetic Manhattan, a Manhattan with no external escape, a Manhattan with only interior pleasures.

After the Manhattan of Change, a Manhattan of Permanence.

These Mountains are, finally, the realization of the 1916 Zoning Law: the Mega-Village, the definitive Manhattan on the other side of the congestion barrier.

All the Rockefeller Centers

Americans are the Materialists of the abstract.

— Gertrude Stein

PARADOX

At the heart of Rockefeller Center — the first installment of that final, definitive Manhattan — is a double paradox that only Manhattanism could transcend:

"The Center must combine the maximum of congestion with the maximum of light and space," and

"All planning ... should be based upon 'a commercial center as beautiful as possible consistent with a maximum income that should be developed.'"[16]

The program of Rockefeller Center is to reconcile these incompatibles.

An unprecedented coalition of talents works on this enterprise, unusual in both numbers and composition. As Raymond Hood describes it: "It would be impossible to estimate the number of official minds that have engaged in untangling the complexities of the problem; and certainly the number of unofficial minds that have pondered over it is even a more meaningless guess. Architects, builders, engineers, real estate experts, financiers, lawyers — all have contributed something from their experience and even from their imagination."[17]

Rockefeller Center is a masterpiece without a genius.

Since no single creative mind is responsible for its definitive form, the conception, birth and reality of Rockefeller Center have been interpreted — in the traditional measuring system of architectural judgment — as an elaborate *compromise,* an example of "architecture by committee."

But Manhattan's architecture cannot be measured with conventional instruments; they give absurd readings: to see Rockefeller Center as a compromise is to be blind.

The essence and strength of Manhattan is that *all* its architecture is "by committee" and that the committee is Manhattan's inhabitants themselves.

SEED

The seed of Rockefeller Center is a search, begun in 1926, for new accommodation for the Metropolitan Opera.

In an architectural odyssey, the theoretical container of the new Opera wanders across the Grid in a quest for an appropriate location.

Scenes from the campaign of specification:
"Corbett's Move," or "Design by Committee."
Associated Architects and developers
playing with miniature Centers. "Standing:
J. O. Brown, Webster Todd, Henry Hofmeister,
Hugh S. Robertson. Seated: Harvey Wiley
Corbett, Raymond Hood, John R. Todd,
Andrew Reinhard, Dr. J. M. Todd."

Benjamin Wistar Morris, proposal for Metropolitan Square, 1928, on site of present Rockefeller Center. From Fifth Avenue a central axis leads to plaza in front of the Metropolitan Opera. 49th and 50th streets continue through the two frontal Towers. The dilemma of cultural facility vs. fund-raising commercial structures is resolved by shaping the offices into the protective walls of a "forbidden city" and using the four Skyscrapers as monumental totems that define a bastion of high culture. Apart from the central plaza, many other features that recur in later schemes by other architects are already present here: an intimation of roof gardens, and bridges across 49th and 50th streets that connect a network of elevated arcades and walkways on the second-floor level, in the manner of Corbett's so-called anti-congestion proposals.

John D. Rockefeller, Jr., measuring plans of the future RCA Building with his four-foot rule. Office interior, originally bought in Spain, was reconstructed first in Rockefeller's private offices, then dismantled again to be resurrected on the 56th floor of the RCA Building.

Its architect-to-be, Benjamin Wistar Morris, is subjected to a fundamental Manhattan paradox: it has become literally impossible to be conventional in the Manhattan of the late twenties, even if determined to be so: Morris' Opera can only exist on its own, as a dignified object, in the most undesirable areas of the Grid. At better locations, the ground becomes so expensive that additional commercial functions are needed to make the enterprise financially feasible.

The better the site, the more the theoretical Opera is in danger of being overwhelmed — physically and symbolically — by these commercial superimpositions, to a point where the original concept collapses under their weight.

The Opera's trajectory is from a site on 57th Street between Eighth and Ninth avenues, where it can exist on its own in a slum, to a location on Columbus Circle where it is already incorporated into a Skyscraper. Finally, sometime in 1928, Morris discovers a three-block site, owned by Columbia University, between Fifth and Sixth avenues and between 48th and 52nd streets.

There he designs a final scheme, stubborn in his Beaux-Arts determination to make the Opera a freestanding symbolic object at the end of a symmetrical vista. The center of his site is now a plaza where he locates the cube of the Opera. A ceremonial approach flanked by two Skyscrapers leads to it from Fifth Avenue. Opera and plaza are surrounded by a ten-story wall of deep loft space; on Sixth Avenue two more Skyscrapers — a hotel and an apartment building — flank the Opera.

RIVET

When this scheme is officially unveiled at the Metropolitan Club, whose members have sponsored its design, John D. Rockefeller, Jr., begins to take an interest.

The Opera does not have the means to construct its own new headquarters, let alone finance the surrounding mountain range of what is to be the largest building operation ever conceived in Manhattan.

Rockefeller offers to take responsibility for the further planning and actual execution of the entire operation.

Feeling unequipped, as a nonexpert, to lead such a colossal real-estate operation, Rockefeller delegates the logistical responsibilities to a friend, John R. Todd, a businessman, contractor and real-estate developer.

On December 6, 1928, the Metropolitan Square Corporation is founded as the vehicle for the enterprise.

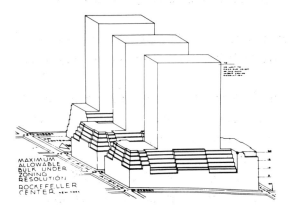

Diagram of maximum allowable bulk on three-block Radio City site according to 1916 Zoning Law. Morris' project sacrifices the volume of the middle block in favor of the Beaux-Arts dignity of his Opera.

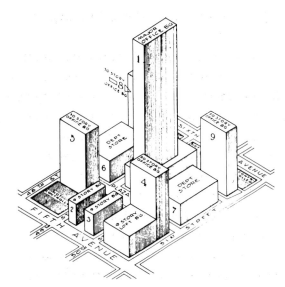

Diagram by architect Reinhard & Hofmeister for developer Todd, correcting Morris' mistake by adding major central tower to exploit fully commercial potential of allowable bulk. Closeness of this diagram to Center as built is remarkable, but that does not make Reinhard & Hofmeister the "designer" of Rockefeller Center. These unspecified outlines correspond rather to Ferriss' "shape that the law puts in the architect's hands." In the *specification* of this envelope — its "conquest" by architectural and programmatic detail — lies the genius of Rockefeller Center.

Rockefeller himself remains responsible for preserving the idealistic dimensions of the project.

He is obsessed with the process of building. "I suspect he always had a suppressed desire to drive a rivet,"[18] is how Nelson Rockefeller diagnoses his father's condition.

Through the late twenties, John D. Rockefeller, Jr., has been chairman of the building committee of Riverside Church — emphatic graft of the spiritual onto the Grid to counter the commercial frenzy everywhere else — and involved himself in all its architectural details.

Simultaneously with Rockefeller Center, he is preparing the restoration of Colonial Williamsburg; one enterprise is the fabrication of a past, the other — in a collapsing economy — the restoration of a future.

During the design of the Center, Rockefeller spends years "living knee deep in blueprints"[19] in his Gothic office (later transplanted in its entirety to the higher regions of the RCA). He always carries a four-foot rule with him, to check the smallest details of the emerging project, occasionally insisting on the addition of spiritual details such as the Gothic decoration at the top of the RCA slab (a suggestion accepted by the architects because they know that altitude alone will make it invisible).

CRATER

Todd has his own architects, Reinhard and Hofmeister, both young and inexperienced.

With them, he scrutinizes Morris' proposal in light of the paradox of maximum congestion combined with maximum beauty. The weakness of Morris' scheme is its avoidance of the maximum zoning envelope — which by now is both financial necessity and irresistible architectural model. Compared to the Ferriss-Hood *Mountain* — the configuration of the definitive Manhattan — Morris' project, with the plaza's emptiness as its center, is like the crater of an extinguished volcano.

In a gesture of commercial and metaphoric repair, Todd and his architects replace the crater with the peak of an office building.

This correction defines and fixes the primordial Rockefeller Center; all later versions are variations of the same architectural motif: a supertower at the center, four smaller towers on the corners of the site. The shrunken remnants of Morris' plaza survive only insofar as they facilitate further planning.

After the formulation of the fundamental diagram, Todd invites Hood, Corbett and Harrison — more experienced than his own architects — to become consultants.

CRASH

In 1929 the Great Crash shatters the assumptions on which the Center is based: from a financially reasonable enterprise it becomes commercially irrational. But this sudden suspension of financial gravity forces the committee to be, if anything, less commercial and more idealistic.

The original impetus — construction of a new Metropolitan Opera — becomes more and more implausible, while the demand for the type of office space the scheme provides also evaporates. Yet Rockefeller has signed a lease that stipulates payment of $3.3 million a year to Columbia University.

What is left after the collapse of all predictions — and of the structures that make prediction of any kind possible — is only the Center's zoning envelope, a colossal volume that now somehow has to be made desirable for new forms of human occupancy through the originality of the architects and builders.

There is a metaphor — Ferriss' Mountain.

There is a series of strategies — the Great Lobotomy, the Vertical Schism, real-estate calculations that have been geared, since the twenties, to prove the impossible — and there is a construction industry specialized in building it.

Finally, there is the doctrine of Manhattanism — the creation of congestion on all possible levels.

FACTS

Todd is committed to a tradition of relentless pragmatism and financial cold-bloodedness. But because of the financial uncertainties of the enterprise, what should have been the ultimate pragmatic operation unfolds in a complete shortage of facts. In the uncertain climate after the Crash, there simply *are* no demands, no empirical necessities to be met — in short, no *facts* that could compromise the purity of the conception. The financial crisis guarantees the Center's theoretical integrity.

The committee — stacked with alleged philistines — has no choice but the Ideal.

Intended as empirical, their specifications merely bring into focus the outlines of the archetype.

TEST

For Hood, Rockefeller Center is a test of the doctrine, the strategies to establish it and the individuals committed to it.

"I have, and I suppose every architect has, done things of which I was not entirely certain. On a single building operation, something may be risked for the sake of experimentation, but on a two hundred fifty million development, and one which may set a precedent for many in the future, mistakes can be so costly that they become catastrophes. It is needless to say that every man associated with Rockefeller Center knows that he is risking his professional reputation, his professional future on the success of Rockefeller City."[20] What all the men on the committee have in common is their involvement in the previous unconscious stages of Manhattan; in different degrees, they are responsible for developing Manhattan's already existing architecture. Now they have to carve the final Manhattan archetype from the invisible rock of its zoning envelope in a campaign of specification: each invisible fragment will have to be made concrete in terms of activity, form, materials, servicing, structure, decoration, symbolism, finance.

The Mountain must become architecture.

COMPETITION

At the beginning each of the Associated Architects is asked to develop a private scheme in competition with the others. This ploy creates an overabundance of architectural images and energy for partial inclusion in the diagram while it drains ego from the individual members.

The two most famous of the Associated Architects, Corbett and Hood, the only theoreticians, propose retroactive versions of earlier, aborted projects.

Corbett sees a chance finally to impose his 1923 traffic/island metaphor to cure congestion by turning Manhattan into a "very modernized Venice." Ferriss' renderings bring only the Venetian elements of Corbett's scheme into sharp focus: a Bridge of Sighs spans 49th Street; San Marco–like colonnades and a stream of shiny black limousines monopolize the atten-tion. The other outlines of the scheme disappear in a mist of charcoal particles.

Corbett's Rockefeller Center, located on a synthetic midtown Adriatic, redeems a subconscious promise made as long ago as Dreamland's Canals of Venice.

INTERSECTION

Hood's proposal too is testimony to the persistence of his obsession; since the three blocks of the site frustrate his intention finally to implant one of his mega-Mountains on a major intersection, he creates within the

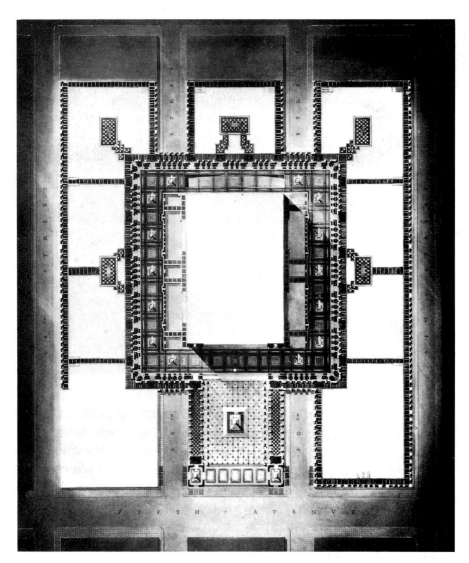

"Proposal for the Development of Metropolitan Square," plan at elevated arcade level, Corbett, Harrison & MacMurray, 1929, or "The Persistence of Memory (1)." Corbett's private project for Rockefeller Center is the apotheosis of his *planning through metaphor*, a last attempt to create "a very modernized Venice" in his lifetime, presented as a logical series of anti-congestion measures. The three blocks of Radio City are treated as "islands"; the center of the middle island is occupied by the Metropolitan Opera, surrounded by seven Skyscrapers. As to be expected, the essence of his scheme is the separation of vehicular traffic — assigned to the ground — and pedestrians, for whom he creates a continuous elevated network on the second floor; its arcades line the full perimeter of the outer blocks and form, at the core of the scheme, a *Square* around the Opera, a metropolitan ambulatory whose circuit is completed by half-arcaded bridges — the width of the plaza itself — across 49th and 50th streets. From the Square, subsidiary bridges lead to side entrances in the Opera. The arcade network also gives access to the recessed lobbies of the seven Skyscrapers — three on the outer blocks and one, the tallest, west of the Opera on Sixth Avenue. The central Square is connected to the city's conventional pedestrian plane — i.e., the ground — by an inclined platform that slopes down toward Fifth Avenue between two colossal pergolas. The whole arrangement resembles the "circumferential plaza" around Grand Central Station, with the station replaced by the Opera, the cars by people and the ramp from Park Avenue by the sloping plaza.

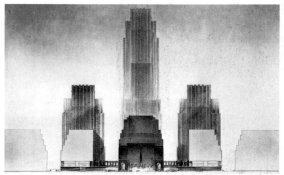

"Development of Metropolitan Square," section/elevation from Fifth Avenue, showing, in center, sloping plaza between pergolas ascending toward Metropolitan Square in front of Opera, and section through the two outer blocks. Here a problematic aspect of Corbett's scheme is revealed: not only are the arcades on the main pedestrian level on the second floor lined with shops — a valuable commercial proposition — but the ground floor, which ought, to be consistent, to have been completely surrendered to cars, shows a second arcade with shopping on both sides, while all other features of the scheme conspire to *remove* pedestrians from grade level.

"Development of Metropolitan Square," west-east section through 49th Street, central Square and sloping plaza on Fifth Avenue. From left to right: silhouette of tallest Skyscraper, outline of Opera, cut through Metropolitan Square and sloping plaza.

"Development of Metropolitan Square," model from northeast showing north elevation of block with three Towers and car access to covered area under pedestrian square on site of present Rockefeller Plaza.

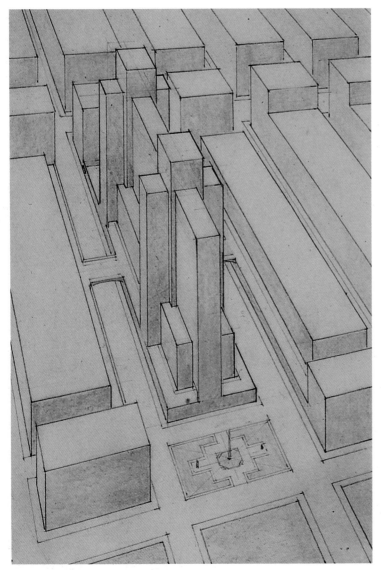

Between December 19 and 23, 1929, Walter Kilham, Jr. — working for Hood — drew up at least eight Rockefeller Centers. Each alternative was developed as a diagrammatic plan and in three-dimensional outline. Scheme O dates from December 19. Like Corbett's "private" project it proposes a continuous elevated level for pedestrians that counteracts the discontinuity of the three separate blocks. In the O scheme the center block is occupied by an extremely tall longitudinal slab that terminates in Skyscrapers at both ends. Thus, the O project marks the first appearance in Manhattan's architecture of a "slab" — itself a regression to the *extrusion* buildings of the early part of the century — the form that would soon spell the end of the Manhattanist Skyscraper. It was dictated — Hood would claim — by logic alone: access to air and light. The two outer blocks are designated as "Department Stores." Facing the central Skyscraper Slab are two metropolitan balconies along the inside of the outer blocks, connected by two bridges to similar terraces around the perimeter of the center block; both balconies and terraces are lined with shops. The two elevator cores at either end of the Skyscraper Slab are connected by an interior arcade. Further schemes were variations on the O scheme, with alternative arrangements of high-rise elements on the center block and relocations of the bridges to create different pedestrian networks.

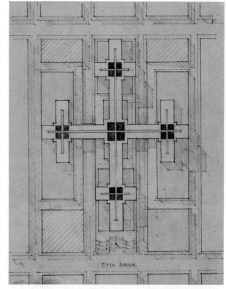

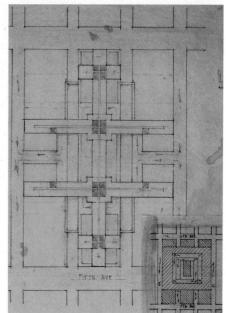

In further proposals, like "Loft & Office scheme on 3 New York Blocks" and the plans for V and X schemes, the proto-project of Rockefeller Center consists — not unlike the "City under a Single Roof" — of a center slab intersected by one, two and even three north-south wings that span 49th and 50th streets, with elevator banks at those points where the transverse slabs rest on the lower outer blocks. These plans make the project a "Grid within the Grid," with premonitions of Mondrian's *Victory Boogie-Woogie*.

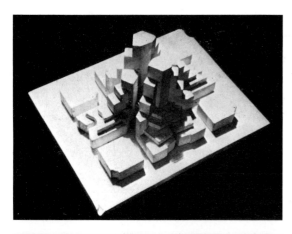

Hood's personal project for Rockefeller Center —
"The Persistence of Memory (2)": "Superblock
scheme for Rockefeller Center," also called "The
Fling," described by Hood as "an attempt to
build a pyramid unit," model. "The Fling" is a
barely disguised version of one of the business
centers of his "Manhattan 1950." Since the site
lacks the major intersection for which those
"peaks" were intended, Hood connects the outer
corners of the site to create an artificial intersection, then fits the business center in by
twisting it 45 degrees. Four Skyscrapers face
each other across a miniature Rockefeller
Square in the center; they are connected by
bridges at intervals along their length. From
the quadruple central peak "The Fling" slopes
down toward the perimeter to connect with the
existing city.

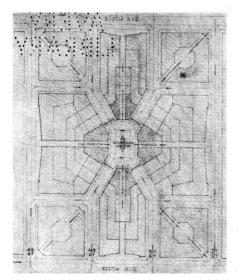

Grid an artificial intersection, two diagonals that connect its four corners, the traffic "shortcut" first applied in his City of Towers. On this artificial crossing, he places a four-part peak that slopes down in terraces toward the perimeter of the site. The peaks of the four buildings concentrate services and elevator shafts. At regular intervals along these towers, bridges connect the four shafts, so that congestion is assured. Hood's scheme is a proposal for a perpetual rush hour in three dimensions.

BRAIN

Before the Center itself, the most impressive creation of Todd and his architects, now assembled as the Associated Architects — Reinhard & Hofmeister; Corbett, Harrison & MacMurray; Hood, Godley & Fouilhoux — is the theater they design to accommodate the campaign of specification.

Its purpose is not the fastest possible determination of all the details of the Center but, on the contrary, the *postponement of its final definition* to the last possible moment so that the concept of the Center remains an open matrix that can absorb any idea that can increase its ultimate quality.

The Associated Architects are organized on two floors in Todd's own Graybar Building. The office is an almost literal diagram of the consecutive stages of the creative process.

On the top floor, all the Associated Architects have their individual cubicles; they meet together once a day in a conference room for collective brainstorming, so that their separate ideas can be inserted in the collective matrix. Renee Chamberlain, an architectural sculptor, and the "delineators" of Drafting Room #1 give the still-fluid concepts of the designers a provisional embodiment, so that they can make quick decisions.

On the floor below, connected only by a small spiral staircase, the professional specificators are arranged in a grid of tables in Drafting Room #2. Here the zoning envelope is dismantled into separate frag-ments numbered one to thirteen, each with its own team of supervisors and technicians. They translate the ideas from above into precise working drawings that will be submitted to those who turn the blueprint into three-dimensional reality.

"In addition to a main telephone switchboard, with direct lines to consulting engineers and the blueprinting companies, is a dictograph system of interoffice communication. All departments are connected by dictograph substations, connected in turn with a master dictograph,

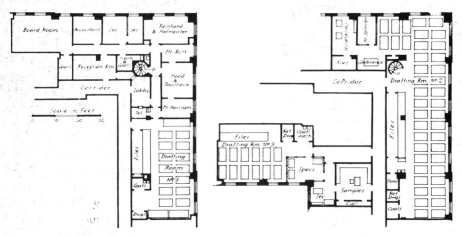

Theater of the campaign of specification: the office as a three-dimensional flow diagram of the creative process. "Executive offices are located on the 26th floor of the Graybar Building and are connected with 3 drafting rooms, 2 of which are on the 25th floor. Drafting Room #1 is used for designing and modeling; the other two for general production work...."

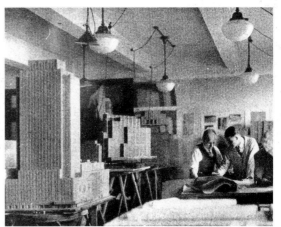

Center's bulk was dismantled in fragments that were studied and developed by separate teams of architect, sculptor/modelmaker, delineators, draftsmen, specification writers.

Raymond Hood, Wallace K. Harrison and
Andrew Reinhard: "the architects of Rockefeller
Center as they inspect a plaster model of
La Maison Française and the British Empire
Building ..." Ashtray-like objects on pedestal are
models for fountain in sunken plaza.

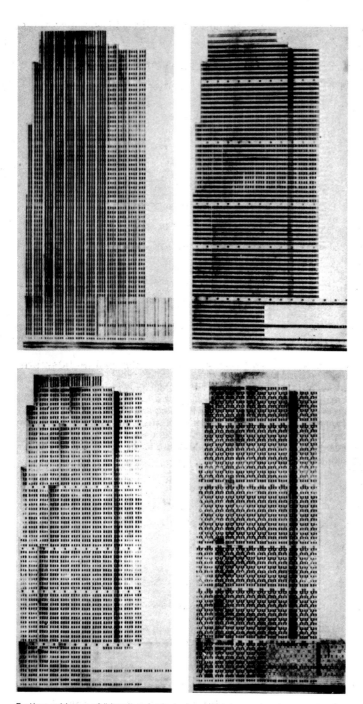

Further evidence of "density of rejected possibilities": facade alternatives for RCA Building; cladding in painted corrugated iron was also considered.

from which a conference report can be carried on with all the substations at the same time.

"Each substation is connected with an executive office. In addition to this system is a corps of runners who transmit interoffice memoranda, mail and conference notes,"[21] writes Wallace Harrison, the futurist "manager" of this quasi-rational circuitry of creation.

MARRIAGE

The rejection of the personal projects in favor of the diagram established in the committee's brainstorming causes no resentment. When Hood describes the committee's mechanics — the collapse of philistinism into creativity — he seems, for once, free from disingenuousness. "Far from being a handicap, this discipline, I am convinced, of being obliged to make a project stand on its own financial feet and to submit its details and materials to a constant critical analysis leads to honesty and integrity of design. Under this stimulation, the cobwebs of whimsy, taste, fashion and vanity are brushed aside, and the architect finds himself face to face with the essentials and elements that make real architecture and real beauty."[22]

If not responsible for the Center's initial diagram, it is obvious that Hood dominates *the campaign to specify the envelope*. Specialist in pragmatic sophistry at the service of pure creation, Hood is the most effective member of the committee. He speaks all the different "languages" represented by its members.

When Todd, for instance, balks at the cost of cladding the entire RCA slab in limestone, Hood retaliates by suggesting they cover it with corrugated iron, "painted, of course."[23]

Todd wants limestone after all.

(Perhaps Hood really does prefer painted iron?)

If the committee is a forced marriage between capital and art, it is a marriage eagerly consummated.

SIEGE

Outside Rockefeller Center's "brain" reigns the Great Depression: the cost of both labor and materials keeps dropping during the design period.

The two floors are under constant siege from outsiders who want to contribute ideas, services and products to the realization of the Mountain. With the economy desperate and the Center one of the few works in progress, the pressure from these outsiders is often irresistible. It is one more reason for the committee to avoid premature definition; the longer

"I would not attempt to guess how many ... solutions were made: I doubt ... if there were any possible schemes that were not studied before the present plan was adopted. And, even *after* arriving at a definite scheme, changes were continually being made to coincide with rental developments...." (Raymond Hood.) Once the individual schemes were out of the way, their metaphors — Venice, the pyramid — digested, the Associated Architects worked on the elaboration of the Reinhard & Hofmeister envelope: tallest Skyscraper at the center, four secondary Skyscrapers on the far corners of the outer blocks. In front of the central Tower, a midblock plaza — as in Morris' scheme — sunken to facilitate communication between underground and grade levels. Lower structure on Fifth Avenue was first an oval bank, soon replaced by two identical seven-story structures — the French and the British buildings — which channel pedestrians toward the sunken plaza. Symmetry of the initial concept was abandoned, with northeast Tower now facing Fifth Avenue. Originally it had a solid department store fronting it on Fifth Avenue; this block soon "split," to form, as an echo of the French and British buildings, an entrance court to the International Building, whose slab repeated the stepping motif of the RCA ("necessitated" by the dropping-out of elevator banks). Southeast tower became the Time-Life Building. As the thirties proceeded and the Center was realized in installments, overall design became less recognizable — to suit demands of specific tenants, and in response to creeping Modernism.

they postpone nonessential decisions, the more the answers appear to them in the form of luxuries that were impossible before.

They appoint a *Director of Research* to exploit this unexpected potential. Thus the Center continuously raises its sights. While the usual process of architectural creation is like a narrowing horizon, the horizon of Rockefeller Center becomes ever wider. In the end, each fragment of the structure has been exposed to unprecedented scrutiny and is chosen from a terrifying number of alternatives.

This density of rejected possibilities still emanates from the Center as built: there is at least one idea for each of its 250 million dollars.

ARCHAEOLOGY

Rockefeller Center is the most mature demonstration of Manhattanism's unspoken theory of the simultaneous existence of different programs on a single site, connected only by the common data of elevators, service cores, columns and external envelope.

Rockefeller Center should be read as five ideologically separate projects that coexist at the same location. Ascent through its five layers exposes an archaeology of architectural philosophies.

PROJECT #1

The most prominent New York architects, like Hood, have been marked by the teachings of the École des Beaux-Arts, with its reliance on axes, vistas and the articulation of civic monuments against a background of neutral urban fabric. But each and every one of these doctrines is invalidated and denied *a priori* by New York's Grid.

The Grid assures every structure it accommodates exactly the same treatment — the same amount of "dignity." The sanctity of private owner-ship and its inbuilt resistance to overall formal control preclude the crea-tion of premeditated perspectives, and in the city of the Automonument, the isolation of symbolic objects from the main fabric is meaningless; the fabric itself is already an accumulation of monuments.

In New York, the Beaux-Arts sensibility can only go where there is no Grid, that is: underground.

Rockefeller Center's –1 level, the basement, is a traditional Beaux-Arts composition finally established on Manhattan: buried vistas that culminate not in the monumental entrance of a new Opera but in the subway. In the Center's basement, Beaux-Arts planning establishes surreptitious connections between blocks that are scrupulously avoided above ground: a grand design that never makes it to the surface.

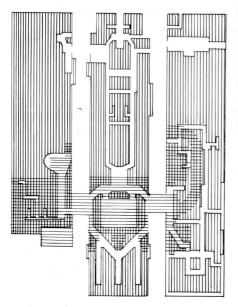

Project #1: Underground Beaux-Arts, plan of concourse (basement) level. Counteracting surface independence of the three Rockefeller Center blocks, a system of underground arcades radiates from Rockefeller Plaza — turned into a skating rink in 1937 after a listless existence as shop window/entrance to the subterranean domain — to form a grandiose, if pathetically two-dimensional, Beaux-Arts composition.

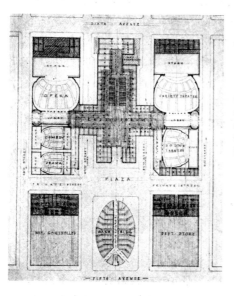

Project #2: Metropolitan resort, three-block theatrical carpet of five to eight theaters — where, theoretically, a single cast could perform up to eight simultaneous spectacles — connected by "Radio Forum," a hybrid bridge at grade level blocking 49th and 50th streets, which dive underneath it. Concentration of elevator banks shows tallest Skyscraper on Sixth Avenue, two smaller ones east of "private street." The five theaters were eventually reduced to single Radio City Music Hall.

At the east end of the composition, the sunken plaza negotiates the transition between the surface of the Grid and the Beaux-Arts intricacies underneath it.

PROJECT #2

The 0 level of the present Rockefeller Center, dominated by the RCA lobby and Radio City Music Hall, is a drastically reduced version of much more daring alternatives that were projected and even almost built.

When plans for the new Metropolitan Opera are discarded, the Associated Architects continue to consider theaters. They design versions of a fantastic ground floor *entirely* occupied by more and more theaters: a three-block ocean of red velvet chairs, acres of stage and backstage, square miles of projection screens — a field for performance where seven or eight spectacles can unfold at the same time, however contradictory their messages may be.

An enormous suspended lobby — three blocks wide — bridging 49th and 50th streets will connect all these theaters, reinforcing the simultaneity of clashing performances. This metropolitan lounge will turn the separate audiences into a single fantasy-consuming body, a temporarily hypnotized community.

The antecedents of this theatrical carpet are Steeplechase, Luna Park and Dreamland. It is exactly within the megalomaniac ambition of the definitive Manhattan to want to provide this kind of escape — a metropolitan *resort* — within its territory.

In the process of realization, the size of the carpet is reduced; Radio City Music Hall is its last bastion, a measure of its ambition.

PROJECT #3

The third project of Rockefeller Center is the ten-story extrusion of the site in the early Skyscraper tradition of sheer multiplication of surface. It is a volume unpenetrated by daylight, artificially lit and ventilated and filled with public and semipublic spaces.

This entire artificial domain is planned for nonexistent clients in anticipation of straightforward applications of the Great Lobotomy; it finds its perfect occupant when the Radio Corporation of America and its subsidiary NBC sign up as tenants of the Center. RCA takes the slab, NBC the block.

"The National Broadcasting Company will occupy ... twenty-six broadcasting studios in this building ... supplemented by six audition rooms. One studio, the largest in the world, will be more than three stories high.... All the studios will be electrically shielded and provided with suitable lighting facilities for Television. Many of them will have observation galleries for visitors.

"Four studios grouped around a central control room will be used for complicated dramatic productions. The actors will be in one studio, the orchestra in a second, crowd scenes will be staged in a third and the fourth will be used for sound effects. This plan for grouping several studios around a central control room is admirably adaptable, also, to the presentation of television programs."[24]

In anticipation of the imminent application of TV technology, NBC conceives of the entire block (insofar as it is not punctured by RCA's columns) as a single electronic arena that can transmit itself via airwaves into the home of every citizen of the world — the nerve center of an electronic community that would congregate at Rockefeller Center without actually being there. *Rockefeller Center is the first architecture that can be broadcast.*

This part of the Center is an anti–Dream Factory; radio and TV, the new instruments of pervasive culture, will simply broadcast *life,* "realism," as it is organized at the NBC studios.

By absorbing radio and TV, Rockefeller Center adds to its levels of congestion electronics — the very medium that denies the need for congestion as condition for desirable human interaction.

PROJECT #4

The fourth project is the resuscitation of the original, virgin state of the site now occupied by the Center, on the roofs of the lower blocks. In 1801 Dr. Davis Hosack, a botanist, established the Elgin Botanic Garden, a scientific horticultural enclave with an experimental greenhouse. He filled the garden "with plants from all parts of the world, including 2,000 duplicate plants from the laboratorium of Linnaeus, renowned Swedish botanist...."

Only 130 years later Hood convinces Todd — with one of his most seductive pragmatic fairy tales, about the higher rent that can be charged for the privileged windows that would look down on one of the Wonders of the World — finally to install the hanging gardens of a contemporary Babylon.

Only the negligible surfaces of the Center's high-rise elements — the RCA slab, RKO tower, International Building, etc. — subtract "from the landscaped roofs which will tower above the area formerly devoted to the Elgin Botanic Garden."[25]

From the early thirties, a series of postcards recorded each step in Radio City's design — almost *before* it occurred. These images reflect an unbearable suspense on the part of the metropolitan public about its final appearance — a collective impatience for these speculative shapes to become tangible. In Manhattan, postcards acted as a populist semaphore about architecture, a medium that nourished Ferriss' "populace warmly appreciating and applauding" the architects of the "New Athens."

"Phantom" scheme, imagined entirely by postcard publisher.

First "official Radio City" presented to the public.

Official perspective from Fifth Avenue with "hanging gardens" joined by Venetian bridges.

Bird's-eye view of definitive scheme, based on John Wenrich rendering.

Collage of spectral Radio City in midtown.

Under any other doctrine of urbanism, Rockefeller Center's past would be suppressed and forgotten; under Manhattanism the past can coexist with the architectural permutations it has given rise to. The park extends over the three blocks. A greenhouse for scientific experimentation is a reminder of Hosack. The roofs are to be connected by Venetian bridges that create a continuous park with a marionette theater, a permanent sculpture exhibition, an open-air flower exhibit, music stands, restaurants, elaborate formal gardens, tea garden, etc.

The garden is only a more advanced variation of the synthetic Arcadian Carpet of Central Park, nature "reinforced" to deal with the demands of the Culture of Congestion.

PROJECT #5

Project #5, the final project, is "a Garden City aloft."[26]
But the garden is a double image: two projects at the same time. It can be read as the *roof* of the lower blocks but also as the *ground floor* of the towers.

During the design and building of Rockefeller Center, the impact of European Modernism on American architectural practice can no longer be ignored. But Hood and the Associated Architects are representatives of Manhattanism first, and Modernism second.

Hood's projects before Rockefeller Center may be seen as a more or less erratic "conversion" from eclecticism toward Modernism; but his production can also be read as a consistent enterprise to salvage Manhattanism, to develop, clarify and refine it. In the face of the Modernist *Blitzkrieg* of the thirties, Hood always defends the hedonistic Urbanism of Congestion against the puritanical Urbanism of Good Intentions.

In this light, the roof gardens of the Center are an attempt of the Manhattan sensibility to ingest the Modernist Radiant City of "happy" light, air and grass, by reducing it to one layer among many. In this way, the Center will be both metropolitan and antiurban.

Implanted in the synthetic vegetal past of their airborne site, standing on the fabricated meadows of a New Babylon, amid the pink flamingos of the Japanese Garden and imported ruins donated by Mussolini, stand five towers, co-opted totems of the European avant-garde coexisting for the first and the last time with all the other "layers" their Modernism intends to destroy.

The roof of Rockefeller Center is both a flashback and a flash-forward: ghost of the Elgin Garden *and* Ville Radieuse, masterstroke of architectural cannibalism.

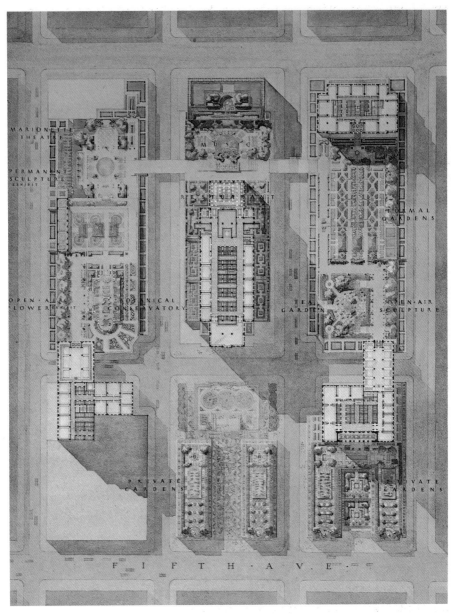

Project #4: "hanging gardens on the roof... land-scaped roofs will tower above the area formerly devoted to the Elgin Botanical Gardens," plan (John Wenrich, rendering). Bridges connect the parks on each of the three blocks; public and entertainment facilities are scattered through the parks. Pale areas are high-rise towers; orange squares within them, elevators. The two Skyscrapers nearest Fifth Avenue were supposed to bridge the private street, forming porches to Rockefeller Plaza. Babylonian "hanging gardens" connected by Manhattan's last "Venetian" bridges: a triumph of mixed metaphor.

The Center is the apotheosis of the Vertical Schism: Rockefeller Center =
Beaux-Arts + Dreamland + the electronic future + the Reconstructed
Past + the European Future, "the maximum of congestion" combined with
"the maximum of light and space," "as beautiful as possible consistent
with the maximum income that should be developed."

FULFILLMENT

Rockefeller Center is the fulfillment of the promise of Manhattan. All
paradoxes have been resolved.
From now on the Metropolis is perfect.
"Beauty, utility, dignity and service are to be combined in the completed
project. Rockefeller Center is not Greek, but it suggests the balance of
Greek architecture. It is not Babylonian, but it retains the flavor of Babylon's
magnificence. It is not Roman, yet it has Rome's enduring qualities of
mass and strength. Nor is it the Taj Mahal, which it resembles in mass-
composition, though in it has been caught the spirit of the Taj — aloof,
generous in space, quieting in its serenity.
"The Taj Mahal lies in solitary grandeur on the shimmering bank of the
Jumna River. Rockefeller Center will stand in the mid-stream rush of New
York. The Taj is like an oasis in the jungle, its whiteness tense against the
gloomy greenness of the forest. Rockefeller Center will be a beautiful
entity in the swirling life of a great metropolis — its cool heights standing
out against the agitated man-made skyline. And yet the two, far apart in
site and surroundings, are akin in spirit.
"The Taj, in tribute to pure beauty, was designed as a temple, a shrine.
Rockefeller Center, conceived in the same spirit of aesthetic devotion, is
designed to satisfy, in pattern and in service, the many-sided spirit of our
civilization. By solving its own varied problems, by bringing beauty and
business into closer companionship, it promises a significant contribution
to the city planning of an unfolding future."[27]

"General airview seen from above 47th Street
looking NE over roof gardens and RCA Building
complete with bridges over City Streets"
(John Wenrich, rendering). The "restored" virgin
territory of the Center as synthetic Arcadia on
the roof. Foreground right: the "Botanical
Conservatory," retroactive homage to Hosack;
waterfall leads to sculpture garden.

Radio City Music Hall:
The Fun Never Sets

In Radio City Music Hall the fun never sets.
— Advertisement

DREAM

"I didn't conceive of the idea, I dreamed it. I believe in creative dreams.
The picture of Radio City Music Hall was complete and practically
perfect in my mind before architects and artists put pen on the drawing
paper...."[28]
In the congestion of hyperbole that is Manhattan, it is relatively
reasonable for Roxy, the animator of Radio City Music Hall, to claim a
crypto-religious revelation as inspiration for his amazing theater.

EXPERT

Roxy — real name Samuel Lionel Rothafel of Stillwater, Minnesota — is the
most brilliant showbiz expert in the hysterical New York of the twenties.
After abandoning the ideal of the new Metropolitan Opera as cultural
epicenter of his complex, John D. Rockefeller, Jr., buys Roxy away from
Paramount and gives him carte blanche to create instead a "Showplace
of the Nation" at the Center.

NEW YORK–MOSCOW

In this venture — "the greatest theatrical adventure the World has ever
known" — Roxy cannot expect much enthusiasm from the Center's
Associated Architects, who want to be sober and modern; they even
convince Roxy to join them on a study tour of Europe, where they want
him to see with his own eyes the advances modern architecture has
made in theater construction.
Summer 1931: the consummate showman Roxy, two businessmen-
architects, Harrison and Reinhard, and a delegation of technical experts
make the transatlantic journey.
The mission opposes Roxy, expert in the production of illusions in
sufficient quantity and density to satisfy the metropolitan masses, to the
European architects, puritanical enemies of the tradition of showbiz
that Roxy embodies.
Roxy is bored in France, Belgium, Germany and Holland; his architects
even force him to take the train to Moscow so that he can inspect and

Revelers at the Metropolitan Resort facing
synthetic sunset: "A visit to Radio City Music
Hall is as good as a month in the Country."

experience firsthand the Constructivist clubs and theaters built there
since the mid-twenties.

ANNUNCIATION

Somewhere in mid-ocean during his return to New York, a revelation
strikes a melancholy Roxy. Staring at a sunset, he receives the
"Annunciation" of his theater: it is to be an incarnation of this sunset.
(*Fortune* magazine dates the moment of this architectural visitation much
later, i.e., a week before the theater's opening. In that case Roxy's is
merely a retroactive revelation — late, but no less valid.)[29] Back in New
York, Roxy's pregnancy only needs to be substantiated by his architects
and decorators.

From the beginning, Roxy insists on the literalness of his metaphor. Within the rectangular section and plan of the Hall's external envelope, the
sunset theme is established through a series of consecutive plaster semi-
circles that diminish toward the stage to create a vaguely uterine hemi-
sphere whose only exit is the stage itself.

This exit is "masked by the beautiful contour curtain"[30] made of a specially
developed synthetic fabric whose reflectivity makes it an acceptable
substitute for the sun. The "rays" from the curtain continue along the
plaster arches, reaching around the entire auditorium. The arches
are covered in gold to better reflect the purple of the setting sun and
the glow of the red velvet which Roxy insists on for the chairs.

The consequence of Roxy's dream is that, while the effect of a sunset is
successfully achieved when the lights of his auditorium are dimmed,
the return of electricity in the intermissions and at the end of each performance corresponds to a sunrise.

In other words, the 24-hour cycle of day and night is repeated several
times during a single performance at Radio City Music Hall. Day and
night are drastically reduced, time accelerated, experience intensified,
life — potentially — doubled, tripled....

CHILL

Roxy's understanding of Fantastic Technology inspires a further
intensification of his metaphor: questioning the conventional use of the
air-conditioning system — ventilation and cooling — he realizes that this
would only add chill to the sunset.

With the same maniacal logic that characterized his earlier visions,
Roxy then considers adding hallucinogenic gases to the atmosphere of
his theater, so that synthetic ecstasy can reinforce the fabricated sunset.

A small dose of laughing gas would put the 6,200 visitors in a euphoric mood, hyper-receptive to the activity on the stage.

His lawyers dissuade him, but for a short period Roxy actually injects ozone — the therapeutic O_3 molecule with its "pungent refreshing odor" and "exhilarating influence" — into the air-conditioning system of his theater.

Combining super-time with super-health, Roxy defines the definitive formula of the metropolitan resort with his slogan, *"A visit to Radio City Music Hall is as good as a month in the Country."*[31]

MUTATIONS

The perfection and metaphorical stringency of Roxy's artificial paradise — the "ultimate countryside" — sets off a chain reaction of further, unforeseen cultural mutations.

"In grandeur of conception, in glory of planning, in perfection of fulfillment nothing like Radio City has ever been dreamed,"[32] claims its creator, with justice; but the container is so perfect that it ridicules its imperfect contents.

On the night of the official opening of Radio City, the exhausted remnants of a stale and spent vaudeville tradition — a tradition that peaked 20 years earlier in Coney Island — fall flat into Roxy's sparkling new apparatus.

The old histrionics do not survive the test. People sitting 200 feet from the footlights cannot follow the grimaces on the comedians' faces as they embark on their tired routines; the size of the theater alone precludes reliance on conventional use of the human voice or even the human body; the gigantic stage — wide as a city block — denies the meaning of *mise en scène,* where suggested vastness can always rely on actual intimacy. On this stage, "atmosphere" is atomized.

Under these crisis conditions, "feelings" are mercilessly exposed as both unreal *and* human, or worse, human, *therefore* unreal.

"Much of it," writes a critic on the first night, "seemed sadly second rate stuff, out of place amid such triumphs of architecture and mechanics."[33] Light years separate the architecture of Roxy's theater from the activity on its stage.

Unintentionally, Radio City represents a more radical break with the past than any consciously revolutionary theater has managed so far.

PARTICLES

In the early thirties only Hollywood is producing the kind of scenarios that equal Roxy's fantastic landscape in anti-authenticity.

Control booth of the Metropolitan Resort:
"The great stage, which he watches constantly
(sometimes with a pair of binoculars), is a
full city block away...."

Hollywood has developed a new dramatic formula — *isolated human parti-cles floating weightlessly through a magnetic field of fabricated pleasure, occasionally colliding* — that can match the artificiality of Radio City Music Hall and fill it with abstracted, formalized emotions of sufficient density. The production of the Dream Factory is nowhere more at home than in Roxy's brainchild.

BACKSTAGE

After the first-night fiasco, humanity — in the form of superannuated vaudeville — is abandoned, and the Music Hall becomes a movie theater. A movie theater needs only a projection booth, an auditorium and a screen; but behind Radio City's screen still exists another realm, "a perfectly organized entity of 700 souls": backstage.

Its elaborate facilities include dormitories, a small hospital, rehearsal rooms, a gymnasium, an art department, costume workshops. There is Radio City Symphony and a permanent troupe of 64 female dancers — the Roxyettes, all between 5'4" and 5'7" — a scriptless chorus line with-out any action to sustain.

Furthermore, there is a menagerie — horses, cows, goats and other animals. They live in ultramodern stables, artificially lit and ventilated; an animal elevator — dimensioned to carry even elephants — not only deposits them on the stage but also on a special grazing ground on Radio City's roof.

Finally, there is Roxy's own apartment fitted in between the roof trusses of his theater. "It is round, all white plaster and the walls describe a parabola to meet in a domed top. The whole thing is really breathless — vague, spaceless, timeless. Makes you feel like an unhatched chicken looking up at the top of his eggshell. To make the whole thing even more fantastic, there are telephone dials in the walls. When you turn a dial, a red light starts to flash on and off — something to do with radio."[34]

But most painfully inactive is the colossal theatrical machine, "the most complete mechanical installation in the world, including a revolving stage; three manipulable sections of stage flooring; a power-driven orchestral dais; a tank; an electrically draped curtain; seventy-five rows of fly lines for its scenery, ten of which are electrically operated; a cyclorama 117 feet by 75; six horns for motion pictures and two motion picture projection sheets; a fountain in the middle of the revolving stage which can be used for water effects while the turntable is in motion; a public-address system for amplifying speech and producing thunder and wind effects (played from records with fifty-four ribbon type); semi-invisible microphones on the stage, in the footlights, in the orchestra pit and in the sub-basement and an amplifier and six loud-speakers concealed above the proscenium; a monitor system in connec-tion with the public address system which reproduces words spoken on the stage in the projection booths and the director's office and even in the foyer and lobbies if desired, and which also carries the directions of the stage manager to the dressing rooms and electrical stations; an elaborate lighting system with six motor-operated light bridges over the stage, each 104 feet long, from which lens units and floods can be used for special lighting; eight portable sixteen-floor lighting towers; four spotting galleries, two on each side of the stage, and a spotting booth in the auditorium ceiling; a cyclorama strip in the floor and a floor battery of self-leveling, disappearing footlights; six projection machines, four effect machines and the usual, or rather more than usual, complica-tion of controls."[35]

The waste of this mechanical potential behind the movie screen is unacceptable.

The frenetic sunsets and daybreaks, and the permanent availability of the Roxyettes and the cosmopolitan livestock, combined with the inactivity of "the most complete mechanical installation in the world," create multiple pressures for a new stage show that can exploit in the shortest possible time the maximum capacities of this top-heavy infrastructure.

Under these critical conditions Roxy, general director of production Leon Leonidoff and the director of the Roxyettes (their name soon stream-lined to Rockettes) invent a stunning ritual: a new routine that is, in a sense, a record of the crisis; a systematization of the concept of "lack of inspiration"; variations on the theme of "no content," founded on a process, a display of inhuman coordination that relies on frenzied synchro-nization, an exhilarating surrender of individuality to the automatism of a synthetic year-round rite of spring.

The essence of this performance is a mass high-kick: a simultaneous display of sexual regions, inviting inspection but on a scale that transcends personal provocation.

The Rockettes are a new race, exhibiting their superior charms to the old one.

PYRAMID

For the sake of the Music Hall audience, this pure abstraction is occasionally intersected with a recognizable reality. Producer Leonidoff

Rockettes and Machines "Members of the Corps Ballet wait by elevators' gleaming pistons to be lifted to stage level during performance...."

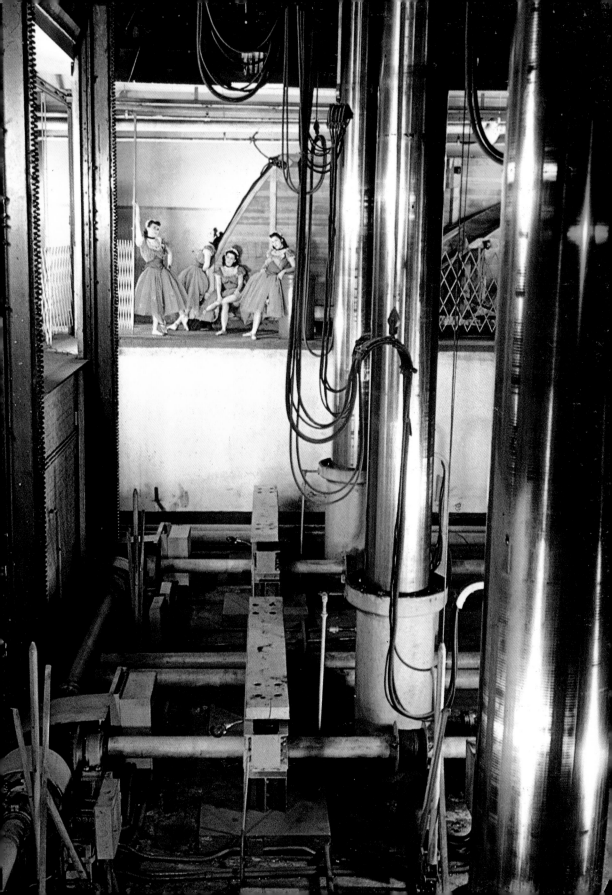

Essence of the Rockettes' performance:
plotless theatrical energy.

invades traditional stories with his man-made race, rejuvenating tired mythologies.

Especially his Easter show becomes a classic of such cross-fertilization. A pyramid of eggs occupies center stage. Cracks develop, marked by neon scars.

After some struggling the Rockettes emerge intact from the shattered shells in a direct reference to the Resurrection.

The stage magically cleared of debris, the reborn Rockettes assume their traditional formation, lift their legs as high as they will go....

CHORUS

Only the Rockettes' abstract movement can generate completely plotless theatrical energy commensurate with the theater Roxy has created.

It is as if the chorus of a Greek tragedy decided to desert the play it was supposed to support and pursued its own emancipation. The Rockettes, daughters of the multiple sunset, are a democratic chorus line that has finally left its background role and gone to flex its muscles at center stage.

The Rockettes = the chorus line as main protagonist, the *lead,* a single personage made up of 64 individuals, filling the gigantic stage, dressed in Suprematist costumes: flesh-colored bodystockings marked with a series of black rectangles that shrink toward the waist to end in a small black triangle — living abstract art that denies the human body.

With the development of its own race, its own mythology, its own time, its own rituals, the container of Radio City Music Hall has finally generated a worthy content.

Its architecture has provoked, and is now supporting, a new culture which, preserved in its own artificial time, will remain forever fresh.

ARK

From the moment of his sunset Revelation, Roxy has become a Noah: the chosen recipient of a quasi-divine "message" who — oblivious to its apparent implausibility — imposes its reality on the world.

Radio City Music Hall is his Ark; it now contains ultrasophisticated accommodation for selected wild animals and the apparatus to dispatch them throughout the structure.

In the Rockettes, it has its own race, luxuriating in its mirror-clad dorm whose regular rows of unglamorous hospital beds suggest a maternity ward, but without babies. Beyond sex, strictly through the effects of architecture, the virgins reproduce themselves.

Rockettes in crisis: their permanent — useless — availability led to routine based on concept of lack of inspiration.

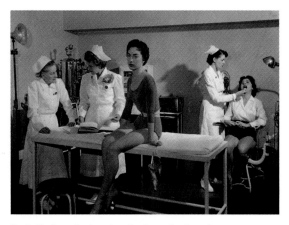

Rockettes' medical center: fresh awakening of a new race.

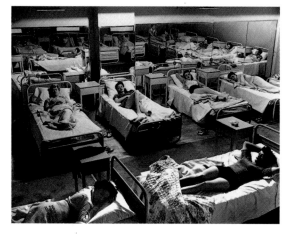

"Dormitory for dancers is located backstage. Girls can rest between shows, stay overnight...."

In Roxy, finally, the Music Hall has its own helmsman, a planner with a vision who has built a self-contained cosmos on the allotment of his block. But unlike Noah, Roxy does not depend on a cataclysmic event in the real world to vindicate his Revelation; in the universe of the human imagination he is right as long as the "fun never sets."

In the completeness of its facilities and mechanical equipment, in the selection of its human and animal menagerie — in its *cosmogony,* in other words — each of Manhattan's 2,028 blocks potentially harbors such an Ark — or Ship of Fools, perhaps — recruiting its own crew with competing claims and promises of redemption through further hedonism.

Existing in such abundance, their cumulative impact is one of *optimism;* together, these arks *ridicule* the possibility of apocalypse.

Kremlin on Fifth Avenue

MOSCOW

In 1927 Diego Rivera, famous Mexican muralist, "member of the Communist Party in good standing, delegate of the Mexican Section of the International Red Aid, representative of the Mexican Peasant League, General Secretary of the Anti-Imperialist League, editor of El Libertador," visits Moscow as a member of a delegation of "workers and peasants" that is invited to help celebrate the tenth anniversary of the October Revolution.

From the reviewing stand on Lenin's Tomb, he watches "with greedy eyes, notebook in hand, but mostly sketching on the tablets of his tenacious brain" the Red pageantry.

Delighted, the radical artist records the full panoply of totalitarian *mise en scène:* "Moscow's toiling millions celebrating their greatest holiday ... the surging sea of crimson banners, the swift straining movement of cavalry ... the cubic pattern of trucks loaded with riflemen ... the solid squares of marching infantry ... the vast, banner-plumed, float-bearing serpentine of the slow, joyous singing masses of men and women of the city marching all day long and far into the night through the great square," all impressions from "which he hoped one day to build murals for Russian Walls."

As his biographer writes, "It is not merely that [Rivera] apprehended [the Russian Revolution] intellectually — too many radical artists have found to their cost that in art bare intellect may prove a straight-jacket. Rather did it possess him wholly, stir him till thought and feeling were integrated into the unity from which art alone can issue."[36]

1927

In this year the collision between the Russian Modernists and the Soviet regime reaches an ominous phase: the Modernists are accused of being elitists whose production is literally use-less: the Soviet government is determined to define once and for all the principles of an art that will energize and inspire the masses.

The potential of Rivera's narrative style — he is one of the few convincing visual demagogues in the world — is not lost on his hosts. After interviewing Rivera, the head of the Department of Agitation and Propaganda of the Communist International attacks the Russian avant-garde with arguments borrowed from the Mexican. "The gap between the most advanced artistic expression and the elementary tastes of the masses

Rivera's unfinished mural in RCA Building. Diagonal from lower left to upper right: cosmos seen through telescope. Second diagonal: bacteria seen through microscope. Upper left: "chemical warfare typified by hordes of masked soldiers in the uniforms of Hitlerized Germany." In metal cocoon: "the degeneration and persistent pleasures of the rich in the midst of the atrocious sufferings of the exploited toilers." At center — seemingly bewildered by this ideological conflict — "man controls vital energy through the machine." Upper right: "expressed without demagogy or fantasy ... the organized Soviet masses ... are marching towards the development of a new social order, trusting in the light of history, in the clear, rational, omnipotent method of dialectical materialism...." Just off center: Lenin and subversive pact between soldier, black farmer and white worker. "The attack on the portrait of Lenin was merely a pretext.... In reality, the whole mural was displeasing to the bourgeoisie...." (Rivera, *Portrait of America*.)

can be bridged only by following a course which will improve the cultural level of the masses and capacitate them for artistic perception of the new ways developed by the dictatorship of the proletariat. Nevertheless, it may be possible to begin at once the rapprochement between the masses and art. The road is simple: Paint! Paint murals in the clubs and public buildings."[37]

Rivera adds a personal reproach that undermines the position of his Modernist colleagues still further: "They should have given an art simple and clear and transparent as *crystal,* hard as *steel,* cohesive as *concrete,* the trinity of the great architecture of the new historical stage of the world."[38]

The proto–Socialist Realism of Rivera's work fits exactly the ideological profile that guides the Soviets' search for the correct art.

Barely a month in Moscow, Rivera is asked to do a portrait of Stalin. He also signs a contract with Fine Arts Commissar Lunacharsky to do a fresco in the Red Army Club "and to prepare serious work for the new library V. I. Lenin, at present under construction in Moscow."

But through the professional jealousy of local artists, the Red Army project — the projection of Rivera's mental notes onto Russian walls — is aborted; Rivera leaves the USSR abruptly, taking with him only his notebooks and, inevitably, the sketches "on the tablets of his tenacious brain."

NEW YORK

Back in Mexico, Rivera decorates walls in the National Palace with, among other images, the *Billionaires' Banquet:* Rockefeller, Morgan and Henry Ford dining on ticker tape.

To feed his output, Rivera has to consume fresh iconographies continuously. Like a demented oil well, the America of the thirties gushes myth, from the assembly line to the bread line — both equally useful to Rivera.

In 1931 the Museum of Modern Art — the Rockefellers' connection to the latest developments in the avant-garde — offers Rivera a retrospective. Five weeks before the opening, on November 13, 1931, Rivera arrives in Manhattan to produce a series of seven mobile frescoes — portable as a precaution "in a land where buildings do not stand long."[39]

As in Moscow, he immediately starts to harvest iconography. Three of the new frescoes interpret New York: *Pneumatic Drilling, Electric Welding* and *Frozen Assets.* "The third depicted New York on three levels, at the base a guarded bank vault with immobilized wealth, in the middle a municipal lodging with immobilized men lying on the floor like corpses in a morgue and, above, the immobilized skyscrapers of New York like monuments on a tomb of business."[40] (The two "tombs" chosen to occupy the foreground are Raymond Hood's Daily News and McGraw-Hill buildings.) The explicit politics of *Frozen Assets* create controversy; the show breaks all MoMA records.

Sponsored by the Ford dynasty, Rivera spends 1932 largely in the mechanical entrails of Detroit, where he is asked to decorate the Ford-financed Institute for Fine Arts.

More fascinated than critical, his mural is a sensual apotheosis of the assembly line, a glorification of the industrial mystique, the sacred conveyor belt that delivers, at its end, a liberated mankind.

CROSSROADS

Like the Soviets, the Rockefellers are planning to incorporate appropriate works of art in their colossal complex to substantiate its cultural claims. Through the attraction of a peculiar economic-artistic gravity the Red Square notebooks — 48 watercolors and innumerable penciled notes — end up in the possession of Mrs. John D. Rockefeller, Jr. Other Rockefellers too buy Rivera's work.

Later in 1932, Nelson Rockefeller invites Rivera to decorate the main lobby of the RCA Building.

With Matisse and Picasso, Rivera is invited to submit sketches on the theme "man at the crossroads looking with hope and high vision to the choosing of a new and better future."[41]

The architects are anxious about art invading their domain; on Hood's insistence, the murals are to be in three colors: *white, black* and *gray.*

Matisse is not interested in the subject, Picasso refuses to see the Rockefeller delegation and Rivera is insulted that, although world-famous, he is still expected to submit for a competition. He refuses, but insists at the same time on using color, warning Hood that otherwise "we would accentuate the *funereal* feeling which is fatally aroused in the public by the juxtaposition of black and white.... In the lower parts of a building one always has the feeling of a crypt.... Suppose some ill-disposed persons should chance upon a nickname such as 'Undertakers' Palace.'"[42] "Sorry you can't accept," Hood wires hastily; but Nelson Rockefeller negotiates a settlement, and a more specific subject is formulated.

"The philosophical or spiritual quality should dominate the mural. We want the paintings to make people pause and think and to turn their

Diego Rivera, *Frozen Assets: A Cross-Section Through the City*, "mobile" fresco, 1931. For its exhibition, the Museum of Modern Art invited Rivera "to paint seven frescos ... in the style of his Mexican work with the possibility that two might be on United States subjects." They were painted with such speed and so late that they could not be included in the catalogue. The critical, subversive nature of his "United States subjects" was discovered when it was too late.

minds inward and upward ... [to] stimulate a not only material but above all spiritual awakening....

"Our theme is NEW FRONTIERS!

"Man cannot pass up his pressing and vital problems by 'moving on.' He has to solve them on his own lot. The development of civilization is no longer lateral; it is inward and upward. It is the cultivation of man's soul and mind, a fuller comprehension of the meaning and mystery of life. For the development of the paintings in this hallway, these frontiers are —

"1. Man's New Relation to Matter. That is man's new possibilities from his new understanding of material things; and

"2. Man's New Relation to Man. That is man's new and more complete understanding of the real meaning of the Sermon on the Mount."[43]

CONFUSION

1932 is a time of iconographic convergence between the USSR and the USA. The style of Communism and the style of Capitalism — two parallel lines that might be expected to meet in infinity, if ever — suddenly intersect.

This approximation of visual vocabularies is misread by many as actual ideological confluence: "Communism is the Twentieth-Century Americanism" is the slogan of the American Communists.

So it can be that Rivera's Red Square sketches — now in the possession of Mrs. Rockefeller — can surface in the pages of *Cosmopolitan* and even appear on the cover of *Fortune,* itself a Capitalist-realist pamphlet devoted to the glorification of management.

FATA MORGANA

The story of the RCA mural is that of two parties who start digging a tunnel from both ends, having arranged to connect in the middle, only to find that when they reach the intended spot there is no one on the other side. For Rivera, the virgin surface of the Manhattan lobby becomes a displaced Russian wall on which he will finally project the Red Army fresco. At the service of the Rockefellers, he will fix for eternity a Communist Fata Morgana in Manhattan — if not a "Kremlin on the banks of the Hudson," at least a Red Square on Fifth Avenue.

The fortuitous meeting of a layer of Communist paint and a Manhattan elevator bank represents a political version of the Murray's Roman Gardens strategy: the appropriation by individuals or groups of ideologically unclaimed territories inside Manhattan's architecture through special forms of decoration.

Just as before this strategy could produce flashbacks to *nonexistent*
pasts, it can now generate political flash-forwards, the establishment of
desirable futures: Rockefeller Center, headquarters of the Union of
American Socialist Soviets.

At the same time, consciously or not, Rivera is acting exactly within
Nelson Rockefeller's concept of "New Frontiers": "the development of
civilization is no longer lateral but inward and upward." For Rivera,
the ideological settler, the RCA lobby becomes an interior, metropolitan Wild West; in the best tradition of the frontier, he is staking a
claim.

DIAGONALS

The fresco is organized by two diagonals, elongated ellipses that for
Rivera create "dynamic symmetry."

On the left of this cross is an itemized quilt of capitalist abuse:
policemen victimizing workers in a bread line; images of war, "the result of
technical power unaccompanied by ethical development"; a nightclub
scene, in which a group of latter-day Marie Antoinettes — representatives
of the bourgeoisie — play cards in the armored isolation of a metallic
cocoon.

On the right, at last, the walls of the Kremlin.

The silhouette of Lenin's Tomb.

The "slow, joyous, singing masses of men and women marching all day
long and far into the night."

Underneath Red Square, materialized through the lenses of television,
"a group of young women in the enjoyment of health-giving sports." Then
another cocoon, in which (in Rivera's synopsis) "the Leader unites in a
gesture of permanent peace the hands of the Soldier, the Negro farmer
and the white worker, while in the background the mass of workers with
their fists held high affirms the will to sustain this fact."

In the foreground, "a pair of young lovers and a mother nursing her
newborn child see in the realization of the Leader's vision the sole possibility of living, growing and reproducing in love and peace."

Groups of students and workers are arranged on each side of the main
panel, made up of "international types" who will "realize in the future
the synthetic human compound divested of racial hates, jealousies and
antagonisms...." The first ellipse is a view through a microscope,
the cosmos of "infinitesimal living organisms." A tactless close-up of the
germs responsible for venereal disease forms an ominous, if colorful,
cloud over the heads of the card-playing women.

The second ellipse brings the vision of man to the most distant celestial bodies.

At the intersection of the ellipses, "the cosmic energy received by two antennae is conducted to the machinery controlled by the worker, where it is transformed into productive energy."[44] But this energy is rerouted from the formal center of the composition to an off-center point that is the fresco's real center of gravity: the multiple handshake, engineered by the Leader.

Looked at strictly in terms of square footage, by far the largest part of the image is occupied by a colossal machine that is to perform the miracle for which the entire mural is an incantation: the amalgamation of Communist ethos with American know-how.

Its enormous size is a measure of Rivera's subconscious pessimism as to whether the synthesis USSR/USA can ever be sparked into life.

ANXIETY

From the beginning, Rivera's juxtaposition of the two ideologies causes anxiety in his patrons, but they ignore its implications until, weeks before the May 1 opening, Rivera paints out the large cap that has so far obscured the Leader's face, and reveals a portrait of the bald-headed Lenin, staring the viewer straight in the face.

"Rivera paints scenes of Communist Activity, and John D. Jr. Foots Bill," screams a *World-Telegram* headline.

Nelson Rockefeller, willing to put up with Red Square, writes Rivera a note: "While I was in the #1 building yesterday viewing the progress of your thrilling mural, I noticed that in the most recent portion of the painting you had included a portrait of Lenin.

"This piece is beautifully painted, but it seems to me that his portrait appearing in this mural might very easily offend a great many people.... As much as I dislike to do so I am afraid we must ask you to substitute the face of some man where Lenin's head now appears."[45]

Rivera responds by offering to replace the card-playing women under their venereal cloud with a group of American heroes — such as Lincoln, Nat Turner, Harriet Beecher Stowe, Wendell Phillips — that might restore the balance.

Two weeks later, the lobby is sealed off. Rivera is asked to come down from the scaffolding, given a check for his full fee and asked to leave the scene with his assistants. Outside, another vision awaits Rivera: "The streets surrounding the Center were patrolled by mounted policemen and the upper air was filled with the roar of airplanes flying

Lenin in Manhattan.

Left side of Rivera's mural. Below right: the
crisis-ridden masses, barely controlled by
mounted police, threaten the rich in their
protective cocoon. Above: "progress" of the
armaments industry. Around the corner:
benevolent deity spins electricity.

round the skyscraper menaced by the portrait of Lenin....

"The proletariat reacted rapidly. Half an hour after we had evacuated the fort, a demonstration composed of the most belligerent section of the city's workers arrived before the scene of battle. At once the mounted police made a show of their heroic and incomparable prowess, charging upon the demonstrators and injuring the back of a seven-year-old girl with a brutal blow of a club.

"Thus was won the glorious victory of Capitalism against the portrait of Lenin in the Battle of Rockefeller Center...."[46]

It was the only Rivera mural ever to come alive.

Six months later the fresco is forever destroyed.

The Kremlin becomes elevator bank again.

2 Postscripts

ECSTASY

Atop the RCA Building is the Rainbow Room.

"Viewing New York through the 24 large windows of the Rainbow Room, or watching a floor show in the Rainbow Room's sparkling splendor, visitors taste the ultimate in 20th century entertainment."[47]

The planners of the Center want to call the space the "Stratosphere," but John D. Rockefeller vetoes the name, because it is not correct. The best orchestras play in the room; "Jack Holland and June Hart dance ... maybe fly is a better word."[48] The diners are arranged in curved terraces around a remnant of the Globe symbolism: a circular dance floor that slowly revolves.

The window recesses are clad with mirrors so that the view of the Metropolis is equal parts real and mirror-image Manhattan.

The room is the culmination of a perfect creation.

Only the lingering imperfection of the human race itself casts a shadow in this arena of ecstasy; the architecture is superior to its occupants. But even that may be corrected. "Now let's streamline Men and Women,"[49] suggests Count Alexis de Sakhnoffsky, designer, "tilting back his chair at the luncheon table in the Rainbow Room." The count has designed cars, watches and clothes. Now he unveils his plan for the remodeling of the human race.

"Improvement is in the air, let us apply it to ourselves. The scientists would tell us what the body lacks for things it is called on to do today. They would point out what it has that it no longer needs. The artists would then design the perfect human being for the life of today and tomorrow. The toes would be eliminated. They were given to us to climb trees, and we do not climb trees anymore. This would permit inter-changeable shoes, beautifully streamlined. The ears would be turned around, slotted and streamlined to the head. Hair would be used only for accent and decoration. The nose would be streamlined. Certain changes would be made in the contours of both men and women to make them more graceful.

"What poets and philosophers have called the eternal fitness of things is the objective of streamlining."

In a culture that creates congestion on all possible levels, streamlining equals progress.

Manhattan needs not decongestion but smooth congestion.

New human race unveiled, elevation and plan.
"Count Sakhnoffsky's idea of future men and
women. Ears and noses Sakhnoffsky-streamlined...
Hair would be used for decoration only...."

Reality of the RCA slab. "Americans are the
materialists of the Abstract...."

ILL

Hood has never been ill, but in 1933, when the first installment of Rockefeller Center is complete, his health collapses. Friends think that the frantic work on Rockefeller Center has exhausted him, but in fact he suffers from rheumatoid arthritis.

"His energy never left him" in the hospital; "even when he was sick to death he was tingling to go back to his office and do the buildings he felt he had in him."[50]

But in the Great Depression there is no work, not even for Hood. Rockefeller Center, first fragment of the final Manhattan, is, for the foreseeable future, also the last.

Hood, seemingly recovered, returns to the office. The RCA Building now completely dominates the view from his window in the Radiator Building. An old friend visits, reminding him that he left the provincial office "to become the greatest architect in New York."

"The greatest architect in New York?" Hood repeats, focusing on the RCA slab, fiery in a sunset. "By God, I am."

He dies in 1934.

Corbett, fellow theoretician of Manhattan, co-promoter and designer of the Culture of Congestion, writes: "His friends all knew him as 'Ray' Hood, dynamic, brilliant yet affable 'Ray.'

"I have never known a man in any walk of life with a more vivid imagination or more vital energy, and all without a trace of 'pose.'"[51]

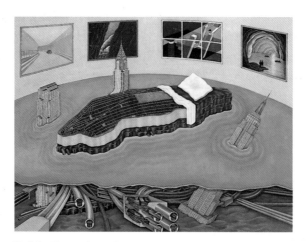

Madelon Vriesendorp, *Freud Unlimited.*

Europeans: Biuer!
Dalí and Le Corbusier
Conquer New York

For New York is the Futurist city, the Baden Baden of that dying stench called Europe, the ironic gargantuan offspring of the senility, the debilitating spirituality and black breath of the European succubus.
— Benjamin de Casseres, *Mirrors of New York*

BIUER! AI BRING OU SURREALISM.
AULREDI MENI PIPOUL IN NIU YORK JOVE BIN INFECTID BAI ZI LAIFQUIVING AND MARVELOS SORS OF SURREALISM.
— Salvador Dalí

Manhattan, great unfilleted sole spread out on a rock ...
— Le Corbusier

CONQUEST
In the mid-thirties both Salvador Dalí and Le Corbusier — they hate each other — visit New York for the first time.
Both conquer it, Dalí conceptually through interpretative appropriation ("New York: why, why did you create my statue long ago, long before I was born?"),[1] Le ("its skyscrapers are too small")[2] Corbusier by proposing literally to destroy it.
Their reactions — diametrically opposite — are episodes (fueled by equal parts jealousy and admiration) in the long history of European attempts to "reclaim" Manhattan.

METHOD
"I believe that the moment is at hand when by a paranoid and active advance of the mind, it will be possible to systematize confusion and thus help to discredit completely the world of reality":[3] in the late

Reinforcement-therapy patients at hospital party:
"sustained and potent challenge to Freud."
A plastic token for each convention remembered —
smile, lipstick, small talk, etc. Such "incentives
proved very effective in motivating the patients
to look after themselves...." (Note large number
of Polaroid cameras in foreground, ready to
"record" this triumph of simulated normality.)

Diagram of the inner workings of the Paranoid-
Critical Method: limp, unprovable conjectures
generated through the deliberate simulation of
paranoiac thought processes, supported
(made critical) by the "crutches" of Cartesian
rationality.

twenties Salvador Dalí injects his *Paranoid-Critical Method* into the
bloodstream of Surrealism.

"It was in 1929 that Salvador Dalí turned his attention to the internal
mechanism of paranoid phenomena, envisaging the possibility of an
experimental method based on the power that dominates the systematic
associations peculiar to paranoia; subsequently this method was to
become the frenzied critical synthesis that bears the name of 'paranoid
critical activity.'"

The motto of the Paranoid-Critical Method (PCM) is *"The Conquest of the
Irrational."*

Instead of the passive and deliberately uncritical surrender to the subconscious of the early Surrealist automatisms in writing, painting,
sculpture, Dalí proposes a second-phase Surrealism: the conscious
exploitation of the unconscious through the PCM.

The PCM is defined by Dalí mostly in tantalizing formulas: "the spontaneous method of irrational knowledge based on the critical and
systematic objectifications of delirious associations and interpretations...."[4]

It is easiest to explain the PCM by describing its exact opposite.

In the sixties two American behaviorists — Ayllon and Azrin — invent a
"reinforcement therapy" which they call *Token Economy*. Through the
generous distribution of colored plastic tokens, inmates of a particular
insane asylum are encouraged to behave like normal people whenever
possible.

The two experimenters "posted a list of desired behaviors on the wall
and then gave bonus points (tokens) to those patients who made
their beds, swept their rooms, worked in the kitchen, etc. These tokens
were redeemable for canteen items or for amenities such as a color TV,
staying up later at night or a private room. These incentives proved
very effective in motivating the patients to look after themselves and
take care of the ward."[5]

The hope that underlies such therapy is that, sooner or later, such
systematic simulation of normality will turn into real normality, that the
sick mind will insinuate itself successfully into some form of sanity like
a hermit crab into an empty shell.

TOURISM

Dalí's PCM is a form of reinforcement therapy, *but in the opposite
direction.* Instead of the diseased performing the rituals of health, Dalí
proposes a *tourism* of sanity into the realm of paranoia.

When Dalí invents the PCM, paranoia is fashionable in Paris. Through medical research, its definition has been amplified beyond simple persecution mania, which is only one fragment of a much larger tapestry of delusion.[6] In fact, paranoia is a *delirium of interpretation.* Each fact, event, force, observation is caught in one system of speculation and "understood" by the afflicted individual in such a way that it absolutely confirms and reinforces his thesis — that is, the initial delusion that is his point of departure. *The paranoiac always hits the nail on the head, no matter where the hammer blows fall.*

Just as in a magnetic field metal molecules align themselves to exert a collective, cumulative pull, so, through unstoppable, systematic and *in themselves strictly rational* associations, the paranoiac turns the whole world into a magnetic field of facts, all pointing in the same direction: the one he is going in.

The essence of paranoia is this intense — if distorted — relationship with the real world: "The reality of the external world is used for illustration and proof … to serve the reality of our mind…."[7]

Paranoia is a shock of recognition that never ends.

SOUVENIRS

As the name suggests, Dalí's Paranoid-Critical Method is a sequence of two consecutive but discrete operations:

1. the synthetic reproduction of the paranoiac's way of seeing the world in a new light — with its rich harvest of unsuspected correspondences, analogies and patterns; and

2. the compression of these gaseous speculations to a critical point where they achieve the density of fact: the critical part of the method consists of the fabrication of objectifying "souvenirs" of the paranoid tourism, of concrete evidence that brings the "discoveries" of those excursions back to the rest of mankind, ideally in forms as obvious and undeniable as snapshots.

As a didactic model of such a critical operation — in this case, to prove the paranoiac (i.e., essentially unprovable) thesis of Mary's Ascension — Dalí describes one of his dreams.

"Now that I am awake I still find this dream as masterly as when I slept. This is my method: take five bags of green peas, collect all of them in a single large bag and then drop them from an altitude of 50 feet; now project an image of the Holy Virgin on the falling peas; each pea, separated from the next one only by space, just like the particles of an atom, will reflect a small part of the total image; now one projects the image upside down and takes a photograph.

Salvador Dalí, c. 1929, before embarking on his
career as a Surrealist in Paris.

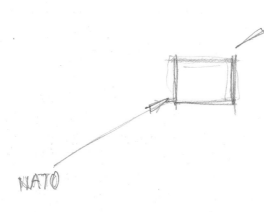

SITU

NATO

London Bridge rebuilt in original form at Lake Havasu, Arizona, perhaps the most blatant Paranoid-Critical journey in recent memory: dismantled stone by stone, it now spans an artificial lake, with fragments of London life — the red phone booths, the double-decker buses, the guards — adding authenticity at both ends. "London Bridge Racquet Club in foreground is part of the park complex at the West End of the bridge. Broad promenade under the east arch of the bridge leads to English Village at upper left...." "Nearly a century and a half after its inauguration, three years after its demolition in England, a quarter of a world away from Scotland where its stones were quarried, London Bridge stood again, a triumph of engineering skill and determination by English and American Builders five generations apart" — and incidentally solving the Reality Shortage at Lake Havasu.

"Due to the acceleration, conform to the laws of gravity, the upside-down fall of the peas will produce the effect of the Ascension. To refine the effect even more one can coat each pea with a reflective film, which will give it the quality of a screen...."[8]

Here, the conjecture of the Ascension is the initial paranoiac propellant; by recording it in a medium that cannot lie, that postulate is made *critical* — objectified, made undeniable, put into the real world where it can become active.

Paranoid-Critical activity is the fabrication of evidence for unprovable speculations and the subsequent grafting of this evidence on the world, so that a "false" fact takes its unlawful place among the "real" facts.

These false facts relate to the real world as spies to a given society: the more conventional and unnoted their existence, the better they can devote themselves to that society's destruction.

détournement

TOE

Facts wear, reality is consumed.

The Acropolis disintegrates, the Parthenon is collapsing due to the ever-escalating frequency of tourists' visits.

As the big toe of a saint's statue gradually disappears under the onslaught of his devotees' kisses, so the Big Toe of reality dissolves slowly but inexorably under perpetual exposure to the continuous Kiss of mankind. The higher the density of a civilization — the more metropolitan it is — the higher the frequency of the Kiss, the faster the process of consumption of the reality of nature and artifacts. They are worn out so rapidly that the supply is depleted.

That is the cause of the Reality Shortage.

This process intensifies in the 20th century and is accompanied by a parallel malaise:

the fact that all facts, ingredients, phenomena, etc., of the world have been categorized and catalogued, that the definitive stock of the world has been taken. Everything is known, including that which is still unknown.

The PCM is both the product of and the remedy against that anxiety: it promises that, through conceptual recycling, the worn, consumed contents of the world can be recharged or enriched like uranium, and that ever-new generations of false facts and fabricated evidences can be generated simply through the act of interpretation.

The PCM proposes to destroy, or at least upset, the definitive catalogue, to short-circuit all existing categorizations, to make a fresh start — as if

François Millet, *L'Angélus*. As a child, Dalí could see a reproduction of this painting from his school bench. It "produced a vague anxiety in me ... so intense that the memory of these two immobile silhouettes never left me...."

Dalí's permutations of Millet's *Angélus*. Illustration for *Les Chants de Maldoror*, 1934–35: here, Millet's original protagonists have disappeared, but their accessories — the pitchfork, the wheelbarrow and its enigmatic bags — have been reconstructed as paranoiac "substitutes."

Meditation on the Harp, 1932–33: Millet's couple now confronted with the accusatory offspring of their scandalous relationship.

the world can be reshuffled like a pack of cards whose original sequence is a disappointment.

PC activity is like cheating with the last moves of a game of solitaire that refuses to come out, or like banging a piece into a jigsaw puzzle so that it sticks, if not fits.

PC activity ties the loose ends left by the rationalism of the Enlightenment finally together.

DESIRE

As an example of recycling the used contents of the globe, Dalí himself attacks Millet's *Angélus*.

At first sight it is one of the most banal of 19th-century clichés: a couple on a barren field, saying prayers in front of a wheelbarrow loaded with two bags of unspecified contents; the scene is completed by a pitchfork stuck firmly in the earth, a basket and a church spire on the horizon.

Through the systematic reshuffling of these worn-out contents, through the fabrication of flashbacks and flash-forwards — the tableaux preceding and following the known image — Dalí reveals that the *Angélus* is an ambiguous freeze-frame and discovers hidden meanings: the couple is petrified in a moment of sexual desire that will animate them in the next instant; the man's hat, ostensibly taken off in a gesture of piety, hides an erection; the two enigmatic bags slumped together on the wheelbarrow only announce the imminent intimacy of the still-separated couple; the pitchfork is the force of sexual attraction made concrete; the woman's red hat glowing in the sunset is a close-up of the impatient tip of the man's member; and so on.

Through interpretation, Dalí explodes the *Angélus* and gives it a new lease on life.[9]

INDIANS 1

PC activity existed long before its formal invention. When Columbus sailed west, he wanted to prove two distinct hypotheses:

1. that the world was round, and
2. that he would reach India by sailing westward.

The first conjecture was right, the second wrong.

Yet when he printed his footstep on the New World, he proved both theses to his own satisfaction.

From that moment, the natives became "Indians" — fabricated evidence that their discoverer had indeed reached India, fingerprints of a

Dalí, *The Discovery of America by Christopher Columbus,* 1959. Columbus depicted a split second before his two theses — the correct one that the world is round and the incorrect one that he had reached India — were established as "facts" by the imprint of his footstep on the shore.

Jollain's "bird's-eye view of New Amsterdam," 1672, the only true representation of New York *as project:* the result of a never-ending flow of paranoid projections firmly established on the soil of Manhattan.

speculative error.

(A PC race, they were doomed to extinction when the mistake was discovered — wiped out as embarrassing evidence.)

GRAFT

Any process of colonization — the graft of a particular culture onto an alien site — is in itself a PC process, the more so if it occurs in the void left by the extirpation of the previous culture.

Amsterdam to New Amsterdam = from mud to bedrock; but this new foundation makes no difference. New Amsterdam is settled in an operation of conceptual *cloning:* the transplantation of Amsterdam's urban model onto an Indian island, including gabled roofs and a canal that has to be excavated with superhuman effort.

In a more conscious way, Murray's Roman Gardens — Antiquity on 42nd Street — is also an operation of paranoiac transposition. Erkins knows that the situation he claims to reproduce never really existed except as a hypothesis in his own mind. Therefore, to impose the "reality" of his analogy between the Romans and Manhattan's inhabitants — the past reshuffled as modern message — he depends on maximum authenticity of his stolen goods, on the most conventional, imitative, undeniable souvenirs of a journey that never was — to the extent of using actual plaster casts of the objects of antiquity to impose his own form of Modernity.

PROJECT

In the artificial light of the PCM, the 1672 "map" of New York — island accommodating a complete catalogue of European precedents — becomes the only true representation of New York *as project.*

From its discovery, Manhattan has been an urban canvas, exposed to a constant bombardment of projections, misrepresentations, transplantations and grafts. Many "took," but even those that were rejected left traces or scars. Through the strategies of the Grid (with its fabulous incremental receptivity), the inexhaustible *Lebensraum* of the synthetic Wild West of the Skyscrapers and the Great Lobotomies (with their invisible interior architectures), the 1672 map becomes in retrospect a more and more accurate prediction: portrait of a paranoiac Venice, archipelago of colossal souvenirs, avatars and simulacrums that testify to all the accumulated "tourisms" — both literal and mental — of Western culture.

COMBAT

Le Corbusier is ten years older than Dalí.

Coming from Switzerland, he shares with Dalí that Paris that is the breeding ground not only of Surrealism but also of Cubism (and Le Corbusier's private Protestant version: Purism).

Dalí abhors Modernism, Le Corbusier despises Surrealism. But Le Corbusier's persona and method of operation show many parallels with Dalí's PCM.

Some of these must be the involuntary signs of a truly paranoiac streak in his character, but there is no doubt that this streak has been systematically exploited, and with relish, by its proud owner. In a classic paranoid self-portrait, he claims: "I live like a monk and hate to show myself, but I carry the idea of combat in my person. I have been called to all countries to do battle. In times of danger, the chief must be where others aren't. He must always find the hole, as in traffic where there are no red or green lights!"[10]

OTHERWORLDLINESS

Architecture = the imposition on the world of structures it never asked for and that existed previously only as clouds of conjectures in the minds of their creators.

Architecture is *inevitably* a form of PC activity.

The transformation of the speculative into the undeniably "there" is traumatic for modern architecture. Like a lone actor who enacts an absolutely different play from that of other actors on the same stage, modern architecture wants to perform without belonging to the scheduled performance: even in its most aggressive campaigns of realization it insists on its otherworldliness.

For this subversive play within a play it has cultivated a rhetorical justification modeled on Noah's Paranoid-Critical episode in the Bible. Modern architecture is invariably presented as a last-minute opportunity for redemption, an urgent invitation to share the paranoiac thesis that a calamity will wipe out that unwise part of mankind that clings to old forms of habitation and urban coexistence.

"While everybody else foolishly pretends that nothing is wrong, we construct our Arks so that mankind may survive the coming flood...."

CONCRETE

Le Corbusier's favorite method of objectification — of making his structures *critical* — is reinforced concrete. The successive steps — from

"In times of danger, the chief must go where others aren't...."

Dali's diagram of the Paranoid-Critical Method at work doubles as diagram of reinforced-concrete construction: a mouse-gray liquid with the substance of vomit, held up by steel reinforcements calculated according to the strictest Newtonian physics; infinitely malleable at first, then suddenly hard as rock.

the speculative to the real — of this construction method constitute a transposition of Dalí's dream of photographing Mary's Ascension that, for all its commonness in everyday life, is no less dreamlike.

Broken down in sequence, reinforced-concrete construction proceeds as follows.

First, the conjectural structure of shuttering is erected — the negative of the initial thesis.

Then steel reinforcements — dimensioned strictly according to the rational principles of Newtonian physics — are inserted: the reinforcing process of paranoiac calculation.

Then a mouse-gray liquid is poured into the empty speculative counter-forms to give them permanent life on earth, an undeniable reality, especially after the signs of the initial madness — the shuttering — have been removed, leaving only the fingerprints of the wood's grain.

Infinitely malleable at first, then suddenly hard as rock, reinforced concrete can objectify vacuity and fullness with equal ease: it is the architects' plastic.

(It is no coincidence that each reinforced-concrete building site, with its mad clutter of shuttering, resembles Noah's project: an inexplicably land-locked shipyard.)

What Noah needed was reinforced concrete.

What Modern Architecture needs is a flood.

BUMS

In 1929 Le Corbusier realizes a Floating Asylum for the Parisian Salvation Army, an object that establishes all these metaphors on a literal plane.

His barge offers accommodation for up to 160 *clochards*.

(Bums are the ideal clients of modern architecture: in perpetual need of shelter and hygiene, real lovers of sun and the great outdoors, indifferent to architectural doctrine and to formal layout.) They are arranged in pairs of double-decker beds along the length of the barge, which is made of *reinforced concrete*.

(Remnant of World War I military experimentation. Like architecture, all paraphernalia of warfare are PC objects: the most rational possible instruments at the service of the most irrational possible pursuit.)

CITY

But these are mere finger exercises.

It is Le Corbusier's all-consuming ambition to invent and build the New City commensurate with the demands and potential glories

"Identikit" portrait of Le Corbusier's imaginary
New York. *"Living in order to work!* This means
breaking our backs, driving ourselves mad,
moral bewilderment, a prodigious hiatus between
us and the *realities of nature* [italics added],
plunging into a black abyss of artificiality. So
men have grouped themselves together. Why?
In order to struggle for improvement in their
lives? In order to suffer! To have gone so far, to
have allowed ourselves to drift so far in our cities
— all our cities — that the human mechanism
has run off the rails, so that we are mere hunted
animals!... Flowers! We must live surrounded
by flowers!" Illustration and caption for the
Radiant City.

of the machine civilization.

It is his tragic bad luck that such a city already exists when he develops this ambition, namely Manhattan.

Le Corbusier's task is clear: before he can deliver the city with which he is pregnant, he has to prove that it does not yet exist. To establish the birthright of his brainchild, he has to destroy New York's credibility, kill the glamorous sparkle of its modernity. From 1920 he fights on two fronts simultaneously: waging a systemic campaign of ridicule and defamation against the American Skyscraper and its natural habitat, Manhattan, while carrying out a parallel operation of actually designing the anti-Skyscraper and the anti-Manhattan.

For Le Corbusier New York's Skyscrapers are "child's play,"[11] "an architectural accident.... Imagine a man undergoing a mysterious disturbance of his organic life; the torso remains normal, but his legs become ten or twenty times too long...."[12] Skyscrapers are misshapen "adolescents of the machine age," "handled nonsensically as the result of a deplorably romantic city ordinance"[13] — the 1916 Zoning Law.

They represent not the second (real) Machine Age but "tumult, hairgrowth, first explosive stage of the new middle ages...."[14]

They are immature, *not yet* modern.

For the inhabitants of this grotesque congregation of architectural cripples, Le Corbusier feels only pity. "In the age of speed, the skyscraper has petrified the city. The skyscraper has reestablished the pedestrian, him alone.... He moves anxiously near the bottom of the skyscraper, louse at the foot of the tower. The louse hoists himself up in the tower; it is night in the tower oppressed by the other towers: sadness, depression.... But on top of those skyscrapers taller than the others, the louse becomes radiant. He sees the ocean and boats; he is above the other lice...."

That the louse is exhilarated, not by nature, but because he is eye to eye with other Skyscrapers, is inconceivable to Le Corbusier for "there, at the top, these strange skyscrapers are usually crowned by some academic contraption.

"The louse is flattered. The louse loves it.

"The louse approves of these expenses to decorate the cork of his skyscraper...."[15]

IDENTIKIT

Le Corbusier's campaign of denigration is made possible only by the fact that its strategist has never beheld the object of his aggression — an

The secret formula of Le Corbusier's Radiant City:
the "City of Panic [Manhattan] ... in the jungle."

ignorance that he carefully preserves for the duration of his attacks —
and that for his European audience, too, his imputations are unverifiable.
If an identikit portrait of an alleged criminal — assembled by the police
from photographic fragments on the strength of more or less accurate
descriptions by his victims — is a Paranoid-Critical product par excellence,
then Le Corbusier's portrait of New York is an identikit: a purely speculative collage of its "criminal" urbanistic features.

In book after book, Manhattan's guilt is illustrated in a series of hasty
paste-ups of grainy images — fabricated mug shots — that show no
resemblance whatsoever to his supposed adversary.

Le Corbusier is a paranoid detective who invents the victims (the
lice), forges the likeness of the perpetrator and avoids the scene of
the crime.

TOP HAT

Le Corbusier's passionate involvement with New York is, in fact, a 15-year-
long attempt to cut an umbilical cord. In spite of his angry obliterations
he is secretly nourished by its reservoir of precedents and models.
When he finally "introduces" his anti-Skyscraper, he is like a prestidigi-
tator who accidentally gives his trick away: he makes the American
Skyscraper disappear in the black velvet pouch of his speculative universe, adds jungle (nature in its purest possible form), then shakes up the
incompatible elements in his Paranoid-Critical top hat and — surprise! —
pulls out the *Horizontal* Skyscraper, Le Corbusier's Cartesian rabbit.

In this performance both the Manhattan Skyscraper and the jungle
become unrecognizable: the Skyscraper turns into a Cartesian (= French
= rational) abstraction, the jungle into a carpet of green vegetation that
is supposed to hold the Cartesian Skyscrapers together.

Usually after such PC kidnappings of models from their natural contexts,
the victims are forced to spend the rest of their lives in disguise. But the
essence of New York's Skyscrapers is that they already wear costumes.
Before, European architects have tried to design superior costumes.
But Le Corbusier understands that the only way to make the Skyscraper
unrecognizable is to *undress* it. (This form of forcible undress is of
course also a well-known police tactic to prevent further misbehavior
by a suspect.)

OVEREXPOSURE

The Cartesian Skyscraper is naked.
Top and base have been amputated from the original Manhattan model;

Presto! The Cartesian Rabbit; or, the Horizontal Skyscraper.

The Cartesian/Horizontal Skyscraper in all its splendor.

Section through the Cartesian Skyscraper: metro in the basement, surrounding park with elevated highways, 60 floors of offices and, at the top, "armored platform against aerial bombardments." (The "best" modern architecture is that which is prepared for the "worst" catastrophe.)

the part in between is stripped of its "old-fashioned" stone cladding, dressed in glass and stretched to 220 meters.

It is exactly the rational Skyscraper that Manhattan's official thinkers always *pretended* they wanted to realize, while in practice they steered as far away from it as possible. The make-believe of Manhattan's architects — pragmatism, efficiency, rationality — has colonized the mind of a European.

"To say skyscraper is to say offices, that is businessmen and automobiles...."[16]

Le Corbusier's Skyscraper means business only. Its lack of a base (no place for a Murray's) and a top (no seductive claims of competing realities), the merciless overexposure to the sun implied by the thin cruciform of its plan, all preclude occupation by any of the forms of social intercourse that have begun to invade Manhattan, floor by floor. By stripping off the reassuring exterior architecture that allowed the ideological hysteria of the interior architecture to flourish, Le Corbusier even undoes the Great Lobotomy.

He introduces honesty on such a scale that it exists only at the price of total banality. (Some desirable social activity is allergic to daylight.) There is no place here for Manhattan's Technology of the Fantastic. For Le Corbusier, *use* of technology as instrument and extension of the imagination equals *abuse*. True believer in the *myth* of technology from the distance of Europe, for him technology itself is fantastic. It has to remain virginal, can only be displayed in its purest form, a strictly totemic presence.

The glass walls of his Horizontal Skyscraper enclose a complete cultural void.

NON-EVENT

Le Corbusier names the grouping of these Cartesian Skyscrapers implanted in their park — the remnants of the jungle — the *Radiant City*. If the Cartesian Skyscraper is the antipode of Manhattan's primitive, infantile Towers, then the Radiant City is finally Le Corbusier's anti-Manhattan.

No trace here of New York's soul-destroying metropolitan wilderness.

"You are under the shade of trees.

"Vast lawns spread all around you. The air is clean and pure; there is hardly any noise....

"What? You cannot see where the buildings are?

"Look through the charmingly diapered arabesques of branches out into

Le Corbusier's Radiant City as a pedestrian would see — or not see — it. "A Battle of Giants? No! The miracle of trees and parks reaffirms the human scale...."

Further tricks of a Paranoid-Critical magician. The Cartesian Rabbit multiplies itself to constitute the Radiant City: Le Corbusier's anti-Manhattan unveiled.

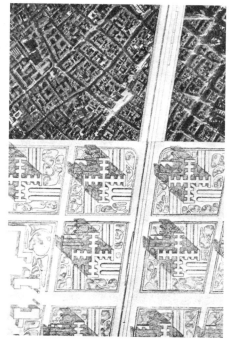

The Voisin Plan imposed on Paris as if according to the Surrealist formula of "Le Cadavre Exquis," whereby fragments are grafted onto an organism in deliberate ignorance of its further anatomy. "Since 1922 I have continued to work, in general and in detail, on the problem of Paris. Everything has been made public. The City Council has never contacted me. It called me 'Barbarian'!..."

Anti-Manhattan in the heart of Paris. "It is in the name of the beauty of Paris that you say 'No!'" "It is in the name of the beauty and destiny of Paris that I insist 'Yes!'"

the sky toward those widely spaced crystal towers that soar higher than any pinnacle on earth.

"Those translucent prisms that seem to float in the air without anchorage to the ground, flashing in summer sunshine, softly gleaming under gray winter skies, magically glittering at nightfall, are huge blocks of offices...."[17]

In designing the Cartesian Skyscraper as universal accommodation for business, to the exclusion of those indefinable emotional services that have been built into the Ferrissian Mountain, Le Corbusier has been the credulous victim of the pragmatic fairy tales of Manhattan's builders.

But his real intention in the Radiant City is even more destructive: to *really* solve the problems of congestion. Marooned in grass, his Cartesian convicts are lined up 400 meters apart (i.e., eight Manhattan blocks — about the distance between Hood's super-peaks *but with nothing in between*). They are spaced out beyond any possible association.

Le Corbusier has correctly perceived that Manhattan has "reestablished the pedestrian, him alone." The essence of Manhattan is exactly that it is an ultra-modern Mega-Village *enlarged to the scale of a Metropolis,* a collection of Super-"Houses" where traditional and mutant lifestyles are simultaneously provoked and sustained by the most fantastic infrastructure ever devised.

When he first strips, then isolates the Skyscrapers and finally connects them with a network of elevated highways so that automobiles (= businessmen = modern) instead of pedestrians (medieval) can shuttle freely from tower to tower over a carpet of chlorophyll-producing agents, he solves the Problem but kills the Culture of Congestion.

He creates the urban non-event that New York's own planners have always avoided (despite their lip service to it): Decongested Congestion.

AFTERBIRTH

Through the twenties, as Manhattan is "removing stone by stone the Alhambra, the Kremlin and the Louvre" to "build them anew on the banks of the Hudson," Le Corbusier dismantles New York, smuggles it back to Europe, makes it unrecognizable and stores it for future reconstruction.

Both operations are pure PC processes — cities of forged fabric — but if Manhattan is a phantom pregnancy, the Radiant City is its afterbirth, a theoretical Metropolis in search of a location.

In 1925 the first attempt to graft it onto the face of the earth is made "in the name of the beauty and destiny of Paris."[18] The Plan Voisin is

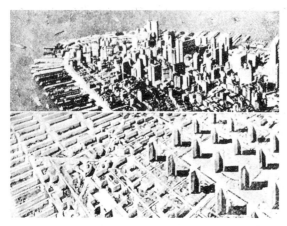

New York/Ville Radieuse: "opposites" that have
become inseparable; illustration for the Radiant
City. "The two theses face to face. New York is
countered by the Cartesian City, harmonious
and lyrical...."

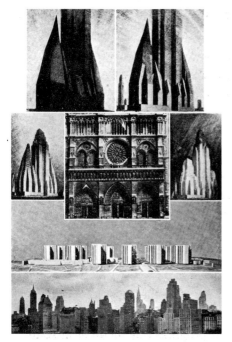

Further steps in a campaign of denigration:
Le Corbusier's juxtaposition Paris–New York, or,
birth of a Siamese Twin; illustration for the
Radiant City. "Two spirits confront each other:
the French tradition of the Nôtre Dame, the
Voisin Plan (with its Horizontal Skyscrapers) and
the American tradition (tumult, hair standing on
end, first explosive stage of a new middle age)."

planned, it seems, according to the early Surrealist theorem "Le Cadavre Exquis" — adaptation of the child's game in which a piece of paper is folded, the first participant draws a head and folds the paper, the second draws a body and folds, etc., so that a poetic hybrid is "released" from the subconscious.

As if Paris' surface were folded, Le Corbusier draws a torso that deliberately ignores the further anatomy of the "exquisite corpse."

Lower housing blocks meander around Cartesian Skyscrapers that are arranged on a plain in central Paris where all traces of history have been scraped away to be replaced by "jungle": the so-called *mobilization of the Ground,* from which even the Louvre barely escapes.

In spite of Le Corbusier's dedication to Paris' future, this plan is clearly a pretext. The transplantation is intended to generate not a new Paris but a first anti-Manhattan.

"Our invention, from its beginnings, was directed against the purely formalist and romantic conceptions of the American Skyscraper....

"Against New York's skyscraper we erect the Cartesian skyscraper, limpid, precise, elegantly shining in the sky of France....

"Against New York, turbulent clamor of the giant adolescent of the machine age — I counteract with horizontal skyscrapers. Paris, city of the straight line and the horizontal, will tame the vertical...."[19]

Manhattan will be destroyed *in Paris.*

TWINS

The Radiant City is intended as the apotheosis of an experiment in architectural alchemy — one element turned into another. But despite Le Corbusier's frantic efforts to outdistance Manhattan, the only way to describe his new city — verbally and even visually — is *in terms of its differences from Manhattan.*

The only way his city can be understood is by comparison and juxtaposition of the "negative" of Manhattan and the "positive" of the Ville Radieuse.

The two are like Siamese twins that grow progressively together in spite of a surgeon's desperate efforts to separate them.

SLIPPER

The Parisian authorities do not take the Radiant proposal seriously. Their rejection forces Le Corbusier to become a Cartesian carpetbagger, peddling his horizontal glass Skyscraper like a furious prince dragging a colossal glass slipper on an Odyssey from Metropolis to Metropolis.

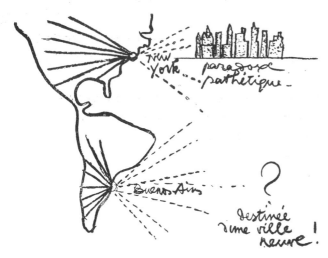

Illustration for the Radiant City: Buenos Aires,
Argentina, last stopover for the Cartesian
carpetbagger on his way to New York.
"New York: pathetic paradox ... Buenos Aires?
destination of a New City!"

In the best traditions of paranoia — natural or self-induced — it is a worldwide journey.

"Last spring he pulled out a pad and drew a map of the world, shading the areas where he felt his books [i.e., his wares] would sell. The only unshaded part was a negligible strip of Africa."[20]

Barcelona, Rome, Algiers, Rio de Janeiro, Buenos Aires, everywhere he offers his towers, offers the most chaotic cities the chance to be the opposite of the "pathetic paradox,"[21] Manhattan.

Nobody wants even to try the slipper on.

That only reinforces his thesis.

"I am kicked out.

"Doors slam behind me.

"But deep inside me I know:

"I am right,

"I am right,

"I am right...."[22]

ARRIVAL 1

In 1935 the attraction of the New World becomes irresistible for Dalí.

"Each image that came from America I would sniff, so to speak, with the voluptuousness with which one welcomes the first whiffs of the inaugural fragrances of a sensational meal of which one is about to partake.

"I want to go to America, I want to go to America....

"This was assuming the form of a childish caprice."[23]

He sails for New York.

For shock effect on arrival, Dalí decides to realize — retroactively — a Surrealist project originally intended to upset Paris, the baking of "a fifteen-meter loaf of bread."

The baker on board offers to bake a version 2½ meters long (the maximum capacity of the ship's oven) with "a wood armature inside it so that it would not break in two the moment it began to dry...." But when Dalí disembarks an "utterly disconcerting thing" happens: "Not one of the reporters [of a waiting group] asked me a single question about the loaf of bread which I held conspicuously during the whole interview either in my arm or resting on the ground as if it had been a large cane...."

The disconcerter disconcerted: Dalí's first discovery is that in Manhattan Surrealism is invisible. His Reinforced Dough is just another false fact among the multitudes.

PC activity counts for its impact on a solid background of convention.

Just as the success of Robin Hood's activity depends on the continuous supply of rich people traversing his forest, so all plots to "discredit completely the world of reality" rely on a reality that is, or seems to be, on solid ground and even in good health.

If a 2½-meter loaf of French bread becomes unnoticeable, it means that, in Manhattan, there is no such scale against which its intended shock waves can register.

SHOCK 1

Dalí cannot shock New York, but New York can shock Dalí.

On his first day in Manhattan he experiences three revelations that disclose to him the essential cultural mutations that make this Metropolis fundamentally different from any other.

1. On Park Avenue "fierce anti-modernism manifested itself in the most spectacular fashion, beginning with the very facade. A crew of workers armed with implements projecting black smoke that whistled like apocalyptic dragons was in the act of patining the outer walls of the building in order to 'age' this excessively new skyscraper by means of that blackish smoke characteristic of the old houses of Paris.

"In Paris, on the other hand, the modern architects à la Le Corbusier were racking their brains to find new and flashy, utterly anti-Parisian materials, so as to imitate the supposed 'modern sparkle' of New York...."

2. Dalí enters the Skyscraper; a second revelation occurs as he ascends in an elevator. "I was surprised by the fact that instead of electricity it was lighted by a large candle. On the wall of the elevator there was a copy of a painting by El Greco hung from heavily ornamented Spanish red velvet strips — the velvet was authentic and probably of the fifteenth century...."

3. That same night Dalí has a dream involving "eroticism and lions. After I was fully awake, I was surprised by the persistence of the lions' roars that I had just heard in my sleep. These roars were mingled with the cries of ducks and other animals more difficult to differentiate. This was followed by complete silence. This silence, broken only by roars and savage cries, was so unlike the din that I had expected — that of an immense 'modern and mechanical' city — that I felt completely lost...." But the lions' roar is real.

Directly under Dalí's window are the lions of the Central Park Zoo, Paranoid-Critical "souvenir" of a "jungle" that never existed there. Three revisions and the European myth of Manhattan disintegrates.

REDESIGN 1

To acquire the right to invent his own New York, Le Corbusier has spent 15 years proving that Manhattan is *not yet modern.* Dalí invents his own New York on his first day in town: a Manhattan that does not even want to be modern.

"No, New York was not a modern city.

"For having been so at the beginning, before any other city, it now... already had a horror of this...."

He maps his discovery through association and metaphor, a Paranoid-Critical redesign: New York is a field where all histories, doctrines, ideologies, once carefully separated by space and time, appear simultaneously. The linearity of history is short-circuited to celebrate a final spasm of Western culture.

"New York, you are an Egypt! But the Egypt turned inside out... She erected pyramids of slavery to death, and you erect pyramids of democracy with the vertical organ pipes of your skyscrapers all meeting at the point of infinity of liberty!

"New York... resurrection of the Atlantic Dream, Atlantis of the sub-conscious. New York, the stark folly of whose historical wardrobes gnaws away at the earth around the foundations and swells the inverted cupolas of your thousand new religions.

"What Piranesi invented the ornamental rites of your Roxy Theatre? And what Gustave Moreau apoplectic with Prometheus lighted the venomous colors that flutter at the summit of the Chrysler Building?"

EFFICIENCY 1

In his blind rage, Le Corbusier has stripped Manhattan's towers, expecting to find the rational core of the true Machine Age. Dalí looks only at their surface, but it is just this superficial inspection that exposes, with a jolt, the thinness of Manhattan's pragmatic dissimulations, its mimicry of philistinism, its ambivalent pursuit of efficiency.

New York's only efficiency is its poetic efficiency.

"The poetry of New York is not serene esthetics; it is seething biology.... The poetry of New York is organ, organ, organ... organ of calves' lungs, organ of Babel, organ of bad taste, organ of actuality; organ of virginal and history-less abyss....

"The poetry of New York is not that of a practical concrete building that scrapes the sky; the poetry of New York is that of a giant many-piped organ of red ivory — it does not scrape the sky, it resounds in it with the compass of the systole and diastole of the visceral canticle of elementary biology...."

"Each evening the skyscrapers of New York assume the anthropomorphic shapes of multiple gigantic Millet's *Angéluses* ... motionless, and ready to perform the sexual act...."

Dalí prepares this Manhattanist poetry as truculent antidote to the puritanical "apologists of the aseptic beauty of functionalism" who have tried to impose New York "as an example of anti-artistic virginity...." They have all made a terrible mistake. "New York is not prismatic; New York is not white. New York is all round; New York is vivid red. "New York is a round pyramid!"

MONUMENT

Dalí's Paranoid-Critical conquest of Manhattan is a model of economy, especially when, with one final gesture, he turns the whole city into a spectacle, performed for his sole pleasure.

"Each evening the skyscrapers of New York assume the anthropo-morphic shapes of multiple gigantic Millet's *Angéluses*... motionless, and ready to perform the sexual act and to devour one another....

It is the sanguinary desire that illuminates them and makes all the central heating and the central poetry circulate within their ferruginous bone structure...."

For a moment, his interpretation suspends all other functions of the city. It is there for him alone.

"New York: why, why did you erect my statue long ago, long before I was born, higher than another, more desperate than another?"[24]

ARRIVAL 2

Also in 1935 — 12 years pregnant with the Radiant City, glass slipper spurned by worldwide consensus — Le Corbusier sails for New York with the accumulated bitterness of an unwed mother, threatening, after the failure of all attempts to arrange an adoption, to lay the phantom found-ling on the doorstep of its natural father and instigate a paternity suit. For him no reporters.

"'Jacobs,' said Le Corbusier [to the interpreter engaged for him by MoMA, sponsor of his crossing, in its campaign to impose real Modernism on the USA], 'where are the photographers?' Jacobs... found that the press cameramen on board were busy taking pictures of other celebrities. He slipped a newspaperman five dollars and implored him to take a picture of Le Corbusier. 'I've used up all my film,' said the photographer, returning the money. Being an obliging fellow, however, he snapped his empty camera at Le Corbusier who looked mollified...." PC activity records facts that do not exist. Le Corbusier exists but cannot be recorded. As if under a curse, Le Corbusier is as invisible in New York as Dalí's bread.

"'Jacobs,' he said several times, as he riffled through the newspapers,... 'where is the picture they took of me on the boat?'"[25]

SHOCK 2
At a press conference in Rockefeller Center a few hours after his arrival, Le Corbusier stuns New York's hard-boiled reporters with his Parisian diagnosis and remedy, which have survived the first confrontation with Manhattan intact.

"After a cursory inspection of the New Babylon, he gave a simple recipe for its improvement.

"'The trouble with New York is that its skyscrapers are too small. And there are too many of them.'"

Or, as New York's tabloids headline in disbelief, he finds "CITY ALL RIGHT AS FAR AS IT GOES ... but it is utterly lacking in order and harmony and the comforts of the spirit which must surround humanity. The skyscrapers are little needles all crowded together. They should be great obelisks, far apart, so that the city would have space and light and air and order....

"These are the things that my town of Happy Light will have!

"I believe within myself that the ideas I bring here and that I present under the phrase Radiant City will find in this country their natural ground...."[26]

INDIANS 2
But that natural ground has to be fertilized by more Paranoid-Critical tautology.

"To reconstruct American cities and especially Manhattan, it is first necessary to know a place where the reconstruction can take place. *It is Manhattan, which is large enough to hold six million people....*"[27]

Manhattan itself is now one of the last remaining areas of the globe not yet exposed to Le Corbusier's Cartesian *hard sell*.

It is his last candidate.

But beyond this opportunistic urgency, there is a second, still more desperate motive: the real Manhattan confronts Le Corbusier — like the real America Columbus — with the fragility of his lifelong speculations.

To secure the Paranoid-Critical reinforcements underlying his urbanism and prevent the collapse of his "system," he is forced (in spite of his almost irrepressible admiration) to persist in his earlier casting of the American Skyscrapers as innocent, even childish natives and of his own horizontal Cartesian towers as the true settlers of the machine civilization.

LE CORBUSIER SCANS GOTHAM'S TOWERS

The French Architect, on a Tour, Finds the City Violently Alive, a Wilderness of Experiment Toward a New Order

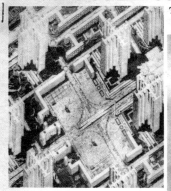

The City of the Future as Le Corbusier Envisions It.

By H. I. BROCK

THE citizen of the French Republic who is known as Le Corbusier—he was born Jeanneret and his given name is Charles-Edouard—is just now paying his first visit to America and has had his first eyeful of the man-made miracle which is New York. In circles where disputing about art is a major sport, Le Corbusier is identified as the founder and public exponent of the mood in architecture which has been labeled the International Style and which certain stiff conservatives insist does not look like architecture at all.

The basic principle of this style is to regard the architect's function as primarily one of household efficiency engineering. His job is to furnish human creatures with a convenient "machine for living in." As stated, the principle applies specifically to the family dwelling. But it applies also to the multiple arrangement of buildings which takes care of the composite employments and the complex human activities of a city where great numbers of people must live and most of them attend to business.

Since the modern dwelling and the modern city have each new demands to meet, since each has at command a service of machinery and materials which no dwelling and no city has ever had before, Le Corbusier and his school begin by discarding traditions and dismissing prejudices which would perpetuate formulas of building evolved from conditions of life that have ceased to exist.

* * *

THE rough idea is that the machine age, with its vast concentrations of population and its prodigious accumulation of mechanical devices for quantity production and for mass movement of goods and men, has created problems which the older architecture is incompetent to solve. The new architecture must face these problems squarely and find a solution on a sound mechanical basis, let the chips of academic estheticism fall where they may.

New York City, for example, is planted thick with skyscrapers—filing cases of millions of human beings at work or stowed away for the night. The streets of New York are jammed with automotive vehicles engaged in distributing the quantity-production output or moving these millions of people about, back and forth between home and business, and generally where they want to go, creating in the process no end of traffic tangles and even seriously endangering in life and limb those who still have to get about on their own feet.

Le Corbusier has built in France and other European countries machines for living in—machines also for doing business in. Whether these machines are, in fact, more efficient than the houses other architects build is a question which will not be argued here. But it is true that, at three years and more famous as the articulate

New York Times Studios.

Too Small?—Yes, Says Le Corbusier; Too Narrow for Free, Efficient Circulation.

voice of the new architecture than as the executant of its projects. He represents a vision of the future rather than a proved practice of the present.

* * *

MODERN architecture—that is, machine-made architecture—was born, as even its most ardent European advocates admit, in this country. The Europeans who have taken it up have made it much more "modern" than we have dared or cared to make it. Nevertheless, New York—the part of it, at least, which enjoys high visibility—is the creation on the greatest scale that the world knows of the new architecture which is our own. That architecture pierces the sky with pinnacles that lift the level of our rocky little island (which in a state of nature could not boast a really respectable hill) into rivalry with the lesser mountains.

Le Corbusier, from the deck of the giant liner Normandie, looked up the harbor and saw (as he says) afar off a dream city hanging in the blue sky above the horizon of the water—a vision of enchantment. He went below for déjeuner and came up again with the solid substance of the vision right on top of him. He was appalled by the brutality of the great masses—the "sauvagerie"—the wild barbarity of the stupendous, disorderly accumulation of towers, tramping the living city under their heavy feet, like a herd of mastodons.

As the ship moved up the river and he got the city broadside on, as the clutter of bunched towers of the stronghold of finance thinned out and other towers began to stand out separate, gleaming in the sunlight in the open space above their lowlier neighbors, his dispondency abated. Hope revived for the future which the first bright vision had seemed to embody. That vision might not, after all, be a mirage.

* * *

LATER, while touring the city in the company of the writer, he stood at the base of the steep sheer cliff of Raymond Hood's slat in Rockefeller Center and said that it was good, then began ruefully to rub the crick out of the back of his neck that was the result of trying to look up to the very top of anything so tall and uncompromisingly perpendicular.

He found the smaller buildings on the Fifth Avenue front—dedicated to France and the British Empire—out of scale, both with the upreared mass and the human beings walking about the central plaza. That plaza itself, all bare (as it is apt to be when the tourist season is on the wane), struck him as decidedly dull—in spite of Prometheus and his fountain.

Then he was shot in an elevator (at the rate of 1,300 feet a minute) to the very top of the big slat—the deck under which lurks the Rainbow Room—and looked out upon the map of the city, by that time half veiled, in a soft gray mist, which cut off the horizons far short of the two extremes of our narrow island but revealed the bounding ribbons of water on either side.

North, south, east and west, the skyscrapers nevertheless stood out boldly. Now and again the sun thrust through the thin clouds and bathed their faces in a brief glory of high light or gilded the fancy tops which some of them have borrowed from all the styles—unimportant to M. Le Corbusier—that came before the steel skeleton revolutionized large-scale building. It was excellent theatre—spectacular drama.

* * *

BUT the modern architect was not particularly impressed. He was looking for architecture, not theatre, and shy, besides, of succumbing to drama so melodramatic. Moreover, he was looking for architecture in his own sense of the word—in this case, the city that is a machine for living in—not merely frightfully expensive scenery built to knock the beholder's eye out.

"They are too small," he said, looking straight at the Empire State Building, tallest in all the world of filing cases for men and women devoted to that purpose in the city.

Somebody pointed out a building with "modern" horizontal lines, belting continuous windows about it, down by the Hudson, and a building with "modern" vertical lines, stacking up windows in parallel slits, over toward the East River.

"I am not interested," said Le Corbusier, "in that sort of thing—both sets of lines are all right as expressing the idea of horizontal and vertical circulation respectively. But what counts is the actual existence in the building of the two kinds of circulation and their efficient coordination. That is the combination which creates adequate machines for business for swarms of people—human beehives—if it is joined, of course, with free circulation among the buildings."

The skyscrapers that thrust up

(Continued on Page 23)

"Le Corbusier Looks, Critically...." Shock waves of the architect's arrival as recorded in New York's press. "Too small? — Yes, Says Le Corbusier; Too Narrow for Free, Efficient Circulation...." (*New York Times Magazine*, November 3, 1935.)

© *Andre Steiner*

Le Corbusier Looks—Critically

So obsessed was Le Corbusier with the "exterminating principles" of his urbanism and its
object, the massacre of the Indians/Skyscrapers,
that even the Christmas cards he sends from
New York show a grotesque Radiant City on
Manhattan, with no traces left of any previous
culture/architecture.

Manhattan's Skyscrapers are Le Corbusier's Indians.

By substituting his anti-Manhattan for the real Manhattan, Le Corbusier would not only assure himself of an inexhaustible supply of work, but destroy in the process all remaining evidence of his Paranoid-Critical transformations — wipe out, once and for all, the traces of his conceptual forgeries; he could finally become Manhattan's inventor.

The intransigence of this double motivation prepares the ground for a reenactment — architectural this time — of the New World's primordial tragedy, the massacre of the Indians. Le Corbusier's urbanism unleashes "exterminating principles which, with constantly augmenting force, would never cease to act until the whole aboriginal race" — the Skyscrapers — "should be extirpated and their memory ... be almost blotted out from under heaven."

When Le Corbusier ominously condescends to his American audiences that "you are strong, we have reflected,"[28] he warns them in effect that, once again, "North American barbarism" will "give place to European refinement."

In his ongoing surgery to separate the Siamese twins, Manhattan/ Ville Radieuse, Le Corbusier is now ready for the final solution: to kill the firstborn.

REDESIGN 2

Dalí's "discovery" of an antimodern Manhattan has been strictly verbal, its conquest therefore complete. Without tampering with its physique, he has recast the Metropolis as an antifunctional accumulation of atavistic monuments engaged in a process of continuous poetic reproduction. Cerebral as this project is, it immediately takes its rightful place as one of the "layers" that constitute Manhattan. Le Corbusier too acts under the influence of Manhattan's speculative delirium. "Night or day, at each step in New York I find pretexts for reflection, for mental construction, for dreams of extraordinary, cheering tomorrows near at hand...."[29] But *his* design for New York is literal, architectural and therefore more implausible than Dalí's: the Grid — "perfect ... in the age of the horse" — is to be scraped off the surface of the island and replaced by grass and a much wider network of elevated highways;

Central Park — "too large" — is to be shrunk, "its verdure distributed and multiplied throughout Manhattan";

the Skyscrapers — "too small" — are to be razed and superseded by about a hundred identical Cartesian settlers implanted in grass and framed by the new highways.

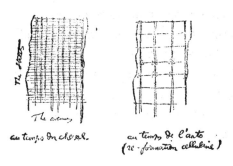

au temps du cheval.

au temps de l'auto
(re-formation cellulaire)

"The age of the horse" vs. "the age of the car."

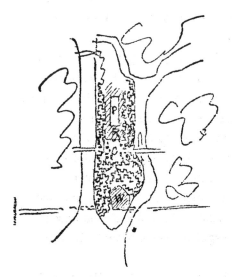

une nouvelle ville efficace sur manhattan:
six million d'habitants

"A new efficient city on Manhattan: six million
inhabitants ..."

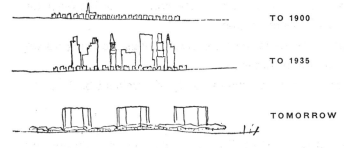

TO 1900

TO 1935

TOMORROW

Provisional timetable for the definitive Cartesian
settlement.

So redesigned, Manhattan will be fit for six million inhabitants; Le Corbusier "will restore an immense area of ground ... pay for the ruined properties ... give the city verdure and excellent circulation; all the ground in parks for pedestrians and cars up in the air, on elevated roads, a *few roads* (one way) permitting a speed of ninety miles an hour and going ... *simply from one skyscraper to another.*"[30] Le Corbusier's "solution" drains Manhattan of its lifeblood, congestion.

EFFICIENCY 2

Sometimes a tourist returns from foreign lands unrecognizable. This has happened to the Skyscraper on its Paranoid-Critical transatlantic excursion.

It left as hedonistic instrument of the Culture of Congestion; it returns from Europe brainwashed, instrument of an implacable Puritanism. Through a bizarre cross-fertilization of misunderstood rhetoric, American pragmatism and European idealism have exchanged ethos: the materialistic philistines of New York had invented and built an oneiric field devoted to the pursuit of fantasy, synthetic emotion and pleasure, its ultimate configuration both unpredictable and uncontrollable.

To the European humanist/artist this creation is only a chaos, an invitation to *problem solving:* Le Corbusier responds with a majestic flow of humanist non sequiturs that fails to disguise the sentimentality at the core of his vision of Modernity.

The European's program for the true Machine Age is the efficiency of banality: "to be able to open your eyes on a patch of sky, to live near a tree, beside a lawn," "to go simply from one skyscraper to another."

Everyday life will regain its eternal immutability amid the "essential joys" of sun, space and vegetation. To be born, to die, with an extended period of breathing in between: in spite of the optimism of the Machine Age, the Old World vision remains *tragic.*

Le Corbusier has patience. As for all paranoiacs, things are going his way.

"Reality, that is the lesson of America.

"It gives your boldest speculation the certainty of imminent birth...."[31]

EXPOSURE

Meanwhile, throughout the thirties, Dalí commutes between Europe and Manhattan. The natural affinity between the Metropolis and Surrealism is translated into astronomical fame, astronomical prices, a *Time* cover story. But this popularity also leads to a proliferation of fake Dalinian gestures, images, poetry.

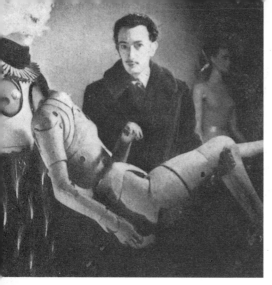

Retreat via the interior of Bonwit Teller or leap
through the window?

Ever since the non-event of the french bread, Dalí has pondered a *visible* Surrealist performance in NIU YORK to act as a "public demonstration of the difference between the true and the false Dalí manner" and, at the same time, to celebrate and impose his own poetic redesign of Manhattan.[32] When Bonwit Teller invites him to dress a display window on Fifth Avenue, Dalí conceives a "manifesto of elementary surrealist poetry right out in the street" that "would inevitably arrest the anguished attention of passersby with stupor when the morrow, amid so much Surrealist decorativism, lifted the curtain on an authentic Dalinian vision...."

His theme is "Day and Night."

In "Day" a manikin "marvelously covered with several years' dust and cobwebs" steps into a "hairy bathtub lined with astrakhan ... filled with water to the edge."

For "Night" a second figure reclines on a bed "whose canopy was a buffalo head carrying a bloody pigeon in its mouth." The black satin sheets are burnt and the "pillow on which the manikin rested her dreamy head was composed entirely of live coals...."

If Manhattan is an archipelago of Paranoid-Critical islands insulated by the neutralizing lagoon of the Grid, then to spill their hidden contents into the objective space of the street is a subversive action: exposure of the interior hothouse tips the balance between rational and irrational domains. Manhattanism acts in self-defense to restore the integrity of its formula: when Dalí returns — the morning after its midnight completion — to test the shock value of his manifesto in broad daylight, the fiery bed has been removed altogether, the naked manikins covered, the lasciviousness of the interior hysteria suppressed.

"Everything, but absolutely everything" has been changed by the store management so that the serenity of the Great Lobotomy is restored.

For once, Salvador Dalí turns into a European puritan to defend the rights of the artist.

From inside the store, he enters the window, attempts to lift and topple the bath. "Before I could raise one side it slipped right up against the window so that at the moment when in a supreme effort I finally succeeded in turning it over it crashed into the plate glass, shattering it into a thousand pieces."

A choice: Dalí can retreat via the interior of the store or leap "through the window bristling with the stalactites and stalagmites of my anger."

He jumps. The escapee from the interior prison enters no-man's-land.

A violation of Manhattan's formula.

As he walks back to his hotel, gaped at by a silent crowd, "an extremely

New York World's Fair, 1939, bird's-eye view with Manhattan skyline in background: *the exiled interiors of Manhattan's Skyscrapers.*

Dali's *Dream of Venus* at 1939 World's Fair. "The outside of the building vaguely resembles an exaggerated shellfish and is ornamented with plaster females, spikes and other oddities. All this is most interesting and amusing...." (*Life*, March 17, 1939.)

polite plainclothesman delicately placed his hand on my shoulder and explained apologetically that he had to arrest me...."

A Paranoid-Critical act has been "booked" in Manhattan.

BLOBS

Deep into the thirties, the Board of Design for the 1939 World's Fair works on the top floor of the Empire State Building. The object of its considerations is not on, but near Manhattan, in Flushing Meadows, Queens.

But no matter: "A set of telescopes on the roof of the drafting room brought the grounds into clear view, and one could check what one was drawing against actual site conditions...."[33]

The Fair itself is conceived as an anti-Manhattan: "By way of contrast with the Skyscrapers of adjacent New York, Fair Buildings consist largely of windowless, one-story structures artificially illuminated and ventilated. The barren aspect of blank surfaces was overcome through the application of sculpture, murals and shadows cast by vines and trees...."[34]

The pavilions, molluscs without shells, look like the *exiled* interiors of Manhattan's Skyscrapers, a collection of architectural jellyfish beached before they could reach their distant destination: the needles.

PLASTER

Among these jellyfish Dalí establishes his first architectural project, a plaster pavilion that contains the *Dream of Venus*. Unofficially, it is named "20,000 Legs Under the Sea."

Essentially, it is a basin inhabited by representatives of American womanhood—lean, athletic, strong, yet feminine and seductive.

Its exterior—a relentless assemblage of the Strange—only demonstrates Manhattanism's wisdom in isolating the unspeakable behind the facade of the common.

In trading his claim on the whole of Manhattan through words for the building of a specific fragment of actual Dalinian architecture, Dalí risks going from the sublime to the ridiculous.

PERISPHERE

The central feature of the Fair is the theme exhibit—Trylon and Perisphere—conceived by Wallace Harrison. It is a stark reappearance of the two formal poles that have defined Manhattan's architecture: Globe and Needle. Unconsciously, the exhibit marks the end of Manhattanism: after 50 years of relative engagement, the forms are now completely separated.

Revelation at interior of the Perisphere:
Democracity, the Metropolis of the Machine Age.
"This city is the result of all the research by
urbanists all over the world. It consists of a
single 100-story skyscraper at its center that will
accommodate all the services of the future city.
Vast avenues will originate from this central
building toward the gardens, parks and sporting
fields...." (*France-Soir*, August 25, 1938.)
After years of relentless Modernist propaganda,
orchestrated by the Museum of Modern Art,
Democracity represents the collapse of Manhattanism, the exact moment when Manhattan's
architects surrender their own version of the
Skyscraper as sublime instrument of controlled
irrationality — and therewith their own vision of
the Metropolis as headquarters of a Culture of
Congestion — to trade it for a vision of Towers in
a Park inspired mostly by Le Corbusier. Only the
fact that the central Skyscraper has 100 floors
betrays a lingering trace of Manhattanism.

The Needle of the Trylon — a *triangular pylon* — is empty.

The Globe is the largest ever built in the history of mankind: its diameter is 200 feet, exactly the width of a Manhattan block.

The Perisphere is nothing but the pure archetype of Manhattan's Skyscraper: a Globe tall enough to be a Tower. "Eighteen stories high, it is as broad as a city block, its interior more than twice the size of Radio City Music Hall...."

The Perisphere's location at the Fair, in Flushing Meadows, should be regarded as provisional, or at least displaced. It should be rolled over to Manhattan to assume its definitive position.

Unlike the Globe Tower, the Perisphere is not subdivided into floors. Its interior is hollow and contains an elaborate model of the elusive *City of the Machine Age:* "Democracity."

At its center stands a single 100-story Tower, implanted not in the Grid but in a meadow. It is flanked by rows of subordinate towers — all identical — and surrounded by a "perfectly integrated 'garden city of tommorrow,' not a dream city but a practical suggestion of how we should be living today, a city of light and air and green space as it would appear from 7,000 feet...."[35]

The center of the city accommodates the arts, business administration, the higher schools of learning and the amusement and sports centers. The population lives in satellite towns connected with the center by efficient public transport.

"This is not a city of canyons and gasoline fumes, it is one of simple functional buildings — most of them low — all of them surrounded by green vegetation and clean air...."

Through intermediaries, Le Corbusier has won. The city in the first and last Globe Tower is the Radiant City. From his monitoring position in Paris, he proudly claims credit. "By the way, even American architects realize that the unguided Skyscraper is a *nonsens.*

"For those who see far, New York is no longer the city of the Future, but of the past.

"New York, with its random, unspaced towers without sufficient air, that New York will, from 1939 onward, enter the middle ages...."[36]

DENOUEMENT

World War II postpones the denouement.

After the holocaust, the concept of a United Nations revives with a new urgency. America offers to finance its home base.

An international design committee is set up to advise Wallace Harrison, who is to build the new headquarters; Le Corbusier represents France.

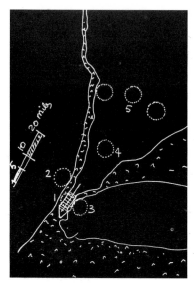

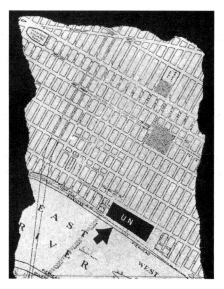

Search that is no search: Le Corbusier investigating suitable sites for UN head-quarters in Greater New York Metropolitan Region — the UN in Jersey City?

UN site torn off the map: Le Corbusier's prey in his grasp.

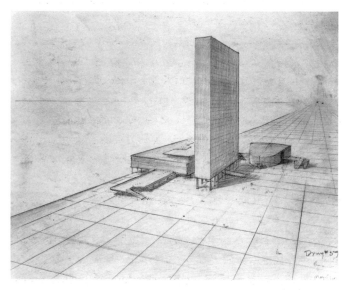

Last critical intervention of Manhattan's *automatic pilot:* Hugh Ferriss' rendering of Le Corbusier's proposal on East River site.

Like a posse, a search party — it includes the Swiss — travels across the USA to find a suitable site. Starting as far away from New York as possible — in San Francisco — it gravitates slowly toward the East Coast.
In September 1946 New York City formally invites the United Nations to make New York its permanent home.
Now sites in the New York area are considered: Jersey City, Westchester County, Flushing Meadows.... All this research is pretense: the real target is Manhattan itself, as it always has been. Like a vulture, Le Corbusier swoops down on his prey. He tears a piece of Manhattan off the map: the Site.
It is promptly donated by the Rockefellers.
For Le Corbusier this small strip of six blocks on the East River is as close as he will ever get to realizing his designs on Manhattan.
Follows a period that is traumatic for all parties involved.
Each day the UN design committee meets in Rockefeller Center (its elevators are the only part Le Corbusier ever admits liking). Frantic now to make the UN the delayed beginning of a Radiant Manhattan, Le Corbusier monopolizes all discussions. Though he is officially only an adviser, it is soon apparent that he expects to become the UN's sole architect on the strength of his urbanistic theories.
He does not know that in Manhattan theories are only diversionary tactics, mere decorative dressing for the essential founding metaphors. And Le Corbusier's urbanism contains no metaphor, except that of the *Anti-Manhattan,* which is, in New York, unseductive.
In Le Corbusier's UN, the office slab is placed exactly in the middle of a street. The auditorium, although lower, blocks a second street, one more reinforced-concrete Ark. The rest of the site is scraped clean like an old painting too drastically restored, all its layers of real or phantom architecture removed: the metropolitan surface replaced by a green Band-Aid of grass.
To Le Corbusier, this building is a medicine, bitter perhaps, but ultimately beneficial. "New York will not after all crush the UN in receiving it. On the contrary, the UN will bring to a head New York's long expected crisis, through which New York will find the ways and means to resolve its urbanistic deadlock, thus effecting upon itself a startling metamorphosis, though in this case it is a providential one. Life has spoken...."[37]
That conclusion — it follows the true paranoiac like celestial inner music wherever he goes — is premature. Harrison, imperturbable in the face of the French torrent of articulation, is and remains in control of the UN project *as architecture,* not theory.
Le Corbusier is not invited to administer Manhattan its final medicine.

"The UN will bring to a head New York's long expected crisis...."

The Master of Darkness trying to absorb Le Corbusier's Modernism in the Ferrissian Void: "The UN Building at Night." "He insisted that buildings float...."

Before any design is finalized, he goes home, once more disgusted with the world's ungratefulness — and perhaps also daunted by the "critical" difficulties posed by his vision.

"I just couldn't imagine him detailing that curtain wall," Wallace Harrison remembers, still anxious at the thought 30 years later.[38]

INNOCENCE

The design of the UN marks the last significant reappearance of the Master of Darkness, Hugh Ferriss, who is called in to make quick renderings of the various alternatives proposed by the advisers. He is now more than ever a believer in Modern Architecture. But in spite of this conscious engagement, Ferriss' art remains, subconsciously, critical. The dullness of Le Corbusier's urbanism has never been more ruthlessly exposed than in the modest renderings of Manhattanism's automatic pilot.

At the same time — like the healthy schizophrenic the Manhattan architect has to be — he desperately tries to imbue the new forms with romanticism and even mystery. His ultimate ambition is to absorb even modern urbanism in the Ferrissian Void.

He draws Le Corbusier's project in the gloom of his perpetual American night as an enigmatic quantity of concrete, suspended in the air:

"As nearly as I could understand things through the interpreter (I do not speak French), he insisted that buildings float...."[39]

Harrison is an admirer and friend of the Swiss architect. Like that of Ferriss, his attitude is ambiguous: he sincerely considers the merits of Le Corbusier's proposal, but discovers that what is intended as explosive fragment of an anti-Manhattan has no detonation charge. Le Corbusier's UN is, after all, nothing but a part of a redesigned Manhattan, laundered of its metaphoric and irrational contaminants through Le Corbusier's equally irrational interpretations. Harrison restores its innocence. In his elaboration of the UN — transforming it from theory to object — he carefully removes its apocalyptic urgencies — "build me or else!" — and undoes the paranoia.

As Le Corbusier tried to drain Manhattan of congestion, so Harrison now drains Le Corbusier's Ville Radieuse of ideology.

In his sensitive and professional hands, its abstract abrasiveness mellows to the point where the entire complex becomes merely one of Manhattan's enclaves, a block like the others, one isolated island of Manhattan's archipelago.

Le Corbusier has after all not swallowed Manhattan.

Manhattanism has choked on, but finally digested, Le Corbusier.

City of Light, pavilion for Consolidated Edison
at 1939 New York World's Fair, interior
(Wallace K. Harrison, architect). "Under the spell
of the voice from the sky and the ever-changing
pageant of color, light and sound, this miniature
city, staged on a heroic scale, suddenly comes to
life to give you a new picture of New York as
it actually exists — not just a mass of lifeless
masonry and steel — but a living, breathing city
with a network of iron and copper arteries and
veins under the surface to supply vital heat and
energy — a city with electrical nerves to control
its movements and transmit its thoughts...."
Manhattanism concluded with a climax in
cardboard.

Postmortem

CLIMAX

Consolidated Edison — Manhattan's electricity generator — has its own pavilion at the 1939 World's Fair, *City of Light*. Like the Perisphere, this contains a miniature Metropolis, but without the predictive pretensions of Democracity.

The City of Light is a model of Manhattan — "from skyline to subway" — that compresses the Metropolis' 24-hour cycle of day and night into 24 minutes. Its ballpark shows only highlights of famous games, the weather changes from sunshine to thunderstorm in seconds, sections through buildings and the earth reveal the subconscious of the infrastructure: the frenzied shuttling of elevators between ground and top, the speeding of trains underground.

But beyond this 1,000-percent intensification of life in the Metropolis, the model exhibits an even more disturbing innovation.

Manhattan has been bent.

The spine of the Grid has been forced into a slight curve, so that its streets converge at a point somewhere in the dense crowd that has rushed to witness the spectacle. The curved island describes the initial section of a circle that, if completed, would hold the audience captive. Among the multiple anxieties of the late thirties, Manhattanism runs out of time; the definitive Manhattan can only be realized *as a model;* Manhattanism can be concluded only with a climax in cardboard. This model is a simulacrum of the Culture of Congestion *completed;* its presence at the Fair suggests that Manhattan itself is doomed to remain an imperfect approximation of its theoretical model — this exhibit — which presents Manhattan as a city not of matter but of light, traveling along the cosmic curve of relativity.

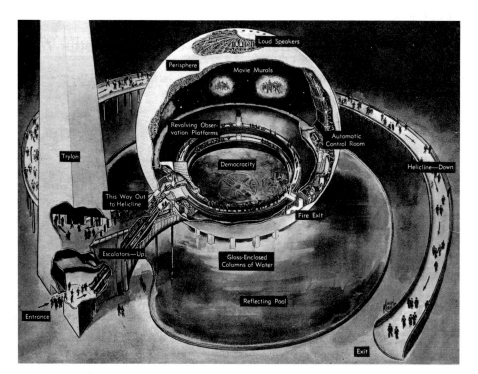

Cutaway of Trylon and Perisphere, showing circulation and mechanical apparatus. "Entrance to the exhibit is through the lobby of the Trylon, from which enclosed escalators, one 96 feet long, the other 120, the longest moving staircases ever built in this country, carry the visitor to the two entrances in the side of the Perisphere.... There he steps onto one of two circular balconies, one above the other, set away from the walls of the Globe and revolving in opposite directions, seemingly unsupported in space.... Below lies *Democracity*... not a dream city but a practical suggestion of how we should be living today, a city of light and air and green space as it would appear from 7,000 feet.... During the daylight cycle, the voice of a commentator describes the physical plan of Democracity while a special symphony is synchronized with the entire show.... After two minutes of daylight the lights in the Perisphere slowly dim, stars appear in the dome above and the city's lights go on. Night has fallen.... Far in the distance a chorus of a thousand voices is heard singing the Theme Song of the Fair. From ten equidistant points in the sky come groups of marching persons, farmers, miners, factory workers, educators — wave upon wave of men and women representing the various groups in modern society.... Starting as pinpoints, the figures attain a size of fifteen feet, a living mural in the sky..... Democracity may be in morning, mid-afternoon or night as the spectator steps upon the revolving balcony. By the time the six-minute cycle is completed and he steps off, the show will have come around again to the hour at which he entered...." (*New York Herald Tribune,* World's Fair Section, April 30, 1939.)

HERITAGE

Democracity — a Metropolis of the Future — and City of Light have a single architect: Wallace Harrison.

The fact that one man is responsible for two such wildly divergent spectacles — whose incompatible implications deny each other — illuminates the acute crisis of Manhattanism like a fake thunderbolt. Trained and nourished on the purest architecture of Manhattan ever since the design of Rockefeller Center, Harrison, with City of Light, conceives the apotheosis of Manhattanism — be it in cardboard — while with Democracity he seems to have forgotten all its doctrines and even started to believe those rhetorical conversions to Modern Architecture that were merely intended as tactical diversions.

It is probably inevitable that a doctrine based on the continual simulation of pragmatism, on a self-imposed amnesia that allows the continuous reenactment of the same subconscious themes in ever new reincarnations and on inarticulateness systematically cultivated in order to operate more effectively can never last longer than a single generation. Manhattan's knowledge was stored in the brains of architects who made the businessmen foot the bill — ostensibly for their own myths of hyper-efficiency, but in fact for the creation of a Culture of Congestion, distilled by the architects from the desires of the population.

As long as its tribal secrets were preserved by a cabal of sophisticated architects posing as philistines, they were safe, safer than they would have been as explicit formulas. But such a method of preservation ensures its own extinction: never revealing their true intentions — not even to themselves — Manhattan's architects took them with them to the grave.

They left all their masterpieces with no testament.

Manhattan had become, by the late thirties, an enigmatic heritage that the next generation could no longer decipher.

That made Manhattan's architecture susceptible to the ravages of European *idealism*, as the Indians had been to measles; Manhattanism had no defense mechanism against the virulence of any explicit ideology.

HAMLET

Harrison is Manhattan's last genius of the *possible.* It is his tragedy that after World War II the possible coincides no longer with the sublime.

No longer can architects count on the businessmen's phantom calculations that make the impossible inevitable. The postwar architecture is the accountants' revenge on the prewar businessmen's dreams.

The revolutionary formula of Coney Island — technology + cardboard =

Wallace K. Harrison, Manhattan's Hamlet.

X-City (rendering by Hugh Ferriss). On site of present UN building, two curved slabs straddle a colossal, luminous "blob" surrounded by office towers. X-City was conceived by Harrison simultaneously as the retroactive realization of the "dream" of Rockefeller Center — the "blob" would finally contain, among other theaters, accommodation for the Metropolitan Opera and the New York Philharmonic — *and* as a modernistic "revision" of Rockefeller Center's urbanistic ideology. Where Radio City is a series of superimposed projects in which each "layer" enriches the others, functions in X-City are rigorously separated and each given its own specific location. Discipline of the Grid is rejected in favor of free play of Towers implanted in a riverside park. Big apron cantilevered over East River was to be heliport. When site was subsequently considered for UN headquarters, Harrison "converted" scheme to accommodate the new program. Theaters were turned into the main public assembly rooms, slabs into Secretariat (on the south) and a hotel (north slab). But for a body that wanted to symbolize World Unity, relationship between the two slabs — and within that, the inexplicable bifurcation of the north slab into two towers — remained problematic.

X-City is the missing link between Radio City/Rockefeller Center and Lincoln Center, an in-between stage in the gradual loss of Manhattan's density. On the same site, Harrison would later realize a fragment of his proposal — the two-tower slab, now unbent — with his United Nations Apartments on the exact location of Le Corbusier's unrealized second slab. Lincoln Center is a partial realization of the "blob." In the sequence Radio City — X-City — Lincoln Center, the collapse of a Culture of Congestion stands most starkly revealed.

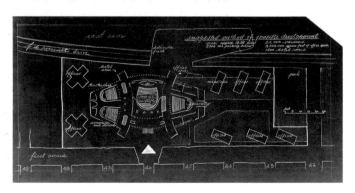

X-City "converted" for the United Nations, plan (Harrison, assisted by George Dudley).

reality — has returned to haunt Manhattan. The result is not "peeling white paint" but the disintegrating curtain walls of the *cheap Skyscraper:* that is, unfortunately, the last contradiction in terms Manhattan resolves.

Harrison's career is marked by this waning of Manhattanism. He becomes Manhattan's Hamlet: sometimes he acts as if he still knows the inner secrets, at other times as if he has lost them or never even heard of them. In the name of Modernity, Harrison — like a reluctant liquidator — seems to strip Manhattan, step by step, of its architectural assets; but at the same time — in the name of Manhattanism — he preserves always some of its essence and resuscitates its most persistent echoes.

CURVE

Harrison's trajectory from Rockefeller Center via the Perisphere and the City of Light to (after the war) X-City, the UN, the Alcoa and Corning buildings, La Guardia Airport and Lincoln Center describes the tangible stages of his ambivalence.

At first sight X-City (1946) is a straightforward version of Le Corbusier's Ville Radieuse, a collection of Towers in a park on the East River site of the later UN. But its centerpiece, as revealed once again in Ferriss renderings, is an impossible coupling of elements that any European would surely have kept separate: an idiosyncratic composition of two slabs — curved in plan — straddling an auditorium that is curved in *both* plan and section.

Those curves — since City of Light the secret symbols of a bent, definitive Manhattan — become Harrison's trademark.

After X-City they recur obsessively in the UN; not only is the roof of the auditorium curved, but inside there is a dizzying collection of curved balconies that stun the visitor with the impact of their unexpected sensuality. The park around the slabs is landscaped on a single theme: the curve. The line of flagpoles flying all the nations' flags along First Avenue inflects suddenly in the middle toward the main slab to form Harrison's longest curve in Manhattan.

The most spectacular curve is described by the plan of La Guardia Airport. The building's guiding concept is a curve that runs its full length. Its suspense (where does it end?) is reinforced by blocking out the airplane traffic behind plates of frosted glass, so that even through the "Modern" curtain wall, Manhattan is perpetually shrouded in mist.

The same curve returns in his Alcoa Building (the entrances are formed as if the curtain wall is lifted like a veil to form a curve) and the Corning Glass Building (where the interior "escapes" from the main volume in the form of a curved extension of the mirrored lobby ceiling).

"A secret — and perhaps even agonized — dialectic between the rectangle and the kidney shape": initial concept for Lincoln Center was a circular court that would connect all component theaters and facilities through a system of curvilinear lobbies, a bent version of the "Radio Forum" once planned for Rockefeller Center (Hugh Ferriss, worksheet, December 5, 1955).

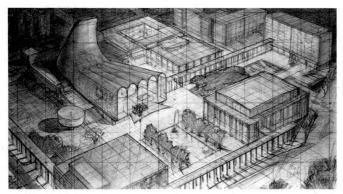

Lincoln Center as "island": sloping plaza replaced by steps; elevations echo Corbett's pergolas.

Harrison's oeuvre is a secret — and perhaps even agonized — dialectic between the rectangle and the kidney shape, between rigidity and freedom. His first architectural impulse, derived from the Modernism of, for instance, Calder, Léger, Arp — all his friends — is always to propose some curvilinear antithesis to the rigidity of Manhattan — the most glorious example being of course the Perisphere. But then that liberating impulse surrenders to the implacable logic of the Grid; the free form is forced back uncomfortably to the conformity of the rectangle.

Only his curve remains as a fossil of the freer language.

That curve is Harrison's theme, the discreet signature of his loyalties divided between the old and the new. Always juxtaposed against the inhumanity of the Grid, he posits his own *limp curve of humanism.*

ISLAND

The pathos of Harrison's ambiguity is most touchingly evident in his Lincoln Center project.

At first sight it is a triumph of monumental Modernism. But on close inspection it can also be understood as the resurfacing and retroactive realization of one of the original designs for Rockefeller Center's ground floor, that *"three block ocean of red velvet chairs, acres of stage and backstage"* that shrank in the end to the size of Radio City Music Hall.

But the genius of Rockefeller Center is that it is at least five projects at the same time. In postwar Manhattan, Lincoln Center is doomed to be one project only. It has no Beaux-Arts basement, no parks on the tenth floor — no tenth floor — and missing most of all are the commercial superstructures of the Skyscrapers.

The munificence of its culture-loving patrons has finally made possible the subsidized existence of an opera *only,* a theater *only,* a philharmonic *only.* Culture lovers have paid for the dissolution of Manhattanism's poetic density. Through its amnesia, Manhattan no longer supports an infinite number of superimposed and unpredictable activities on a single site; it has regressed back to the clarity and predictability of univalence — to the known.

That is a development Harrison cannot resist. But even in Lincoln Center the remnants of his old faith are apparent.

Lincoln Center's raised podium — echo of Corbett's "Venetian" version of Rockefeller Center — is nothing but that elusive "island" that none of Harrison's earlier colleagues managed to build.

ALPHABET

The X, Y and Z buildings of Rockefeller Center are Wallace Harrison's last contribution to Manhattan.

The Skyscraper has come full circle; once again, it is a simple extrusion of the site that stops somewhere arbitrarily. Harrison has finally unlearned Manhattanism; X, Y and Z are the last letters of the alphabet. But on the other hand, after the Z follows A again. The implosion of these universes is like that of the original 100-story building and perhaps merely the beginning of a new alphabet.

GLOBE

World's Fair, 1964.

Theme exhibit: the Unisphere.

The Globe again, but ghostlike and transparent, with no contents.

Like charred pork chops, the continents cling desperately to the carcass of Manhattanism.

X, Y and Z buildings — postwar addition to
Rockefeller Center: Manhattanism unlearned.

World's Fair, 1964: the Unisphere. "The Globe is
120 feet in diameter with an open grid of
latitudes and longitudes supporting the land
masses.... It dramatizes the interrelation of the
peoples in the world and their yearning for
'peace through understanding.'"

Appendix:
A Fictional Conclusion

The Metropolis strives to reach a mythical point where the world is completely fabricated by man, so that it absolutely coincides with his desires. The Metropolis is an addictive machine, from which there is no escape, unless it offers that, too....

Through this pervasiveness, its existence has become like the Nature it has replaced: taken for granted, almost invisible, certainly indescribable. This book was written to show that Manhattan had generated its own metropolitan Urbanism — a *Culture of Congestion.*

More obliquely, it contains a hidden second argument: that the Metropolis needs/deserves its own specialized architecture, one that can vindicate the original promise of the metropolitan condition and develop the fresh traditions of the Culture of Congestion further.

Manhattan's architects performed their miracles luxuriating in a self-imposed unconsciousness; it is the arduous task of the final part of this century to deal with the extravagant and megalomaniac claims, ambitions and possibilities of the Metropolis *openly.*

After the chronicle in "Postmortem" of the shriveling of Manhattanism — as if it had been too suddenly exposed to daylight — the Appendix should be regarded as a *fictional conclusion,* an interpretation of the same material, not through words, but in a series of architectural projects. These proposals are the provisional product of Manhattanism as a conscious doctrine whose pertinence is no longer limited to the island of its invention.

The City of the Captive Globe (1972)

The City of the Captive Globe is devoted to the artificial conception and accelerated birth of theories, interpretations, mental constructions, proposals and their infliction on the World. It is the capital of Ego, where science, art, poetry and forms of madness compete under ideal conditions to invent, destroy and restore the world of phenomenal Reality.
Each Science or Mania has its own plot. On each plot stands an identical base, built from heavy polished stone. To facilitate and provoke speculative activity, these bases — ideological laboratories — are equipped to suspend unwelcome laws, undeniable truths, to create nonexistent, physical conditions. From these solid blocks of granite, each philosophy has the right to expand indefinitely toward heaven. Some of these blocks present limbs of complete certainty and serenity; others display soft structures of tentative conjectures and hypnotic suggestions.
The changes in this ideological skyline will be rapid and continuous: a rich spectacle of ethical joy, moral fever or intellectual masturbation. The collapse of one of the towers can mean two things: failure, giving up, or a visual Eureka, a speculative ejaculation:
A theory that works.
A mania that sticks.
A lie that has become a truth.
A dream from which there is no waking up.
At these moments the purpose of the Captive Globe, suspended at the center of the City, becomes apparent: all these Institutes together form an enormous incubator of the World itself; they are breeding on the Globe.
Through our feverish thinking in the Towers, the Globe gains weight. Its temperature rises slowly. In spite of the most humiliating setbacks, its ageless pregnancy survives.

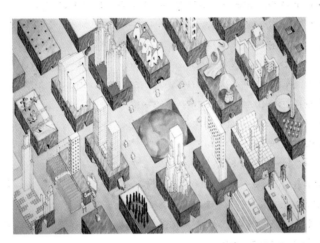

The City of the Captive Globe.

The City of the Captive Globe was a first, intuitive exploration of Manhattan's architecture, drawn before research would substantiate its conjectures.

If the essence of metropolitan culture is change — a state of perpetual animation — and the essence of the concept "city" is a legible sequence of various permanences, then only the three fundamental axioms on which the City of the Captive Globe is based — Grid, lobotomy and schism — can regain the terrain of the Metropolis for architecture.

The *Grid* — or any other subdivision of the metropolitan territory into maximum increments of control — describes an archipelago of "Cities within Cities." The more each "island" celebrates different values, the more the unity of the archipelago as system is reinforced. Because "change" is contained on the component "islands," such a system will never have to be revised.

In the metropolitan archipelago each Skyscraper — in the absence of real history — develops its own instantaneous "folklore." Through the double disconnection of *lobotomy* and *schism* — by separating exterior and interior architecture and developing the latter in small autonomous installments — such structures can devote their exteriors *only* to formalism and their interiors *only* to functionalism.

In this way, they not only resolve forever the conflict between form and function, but create a city where permanent monoliths celebrate metropolitan instability.

Alone in this century, the three axioms have allowed Manhattan's buildings to be both architecture *and* hyper-efficient machines, both modern and eternal.

The projects that follow are interpretations and modifications of these axioms.

Hotel Sphinx (1975–76)

Hotel Sphinx straddles two blocks at the intersection of Broadway and Seventh Avenue, a site condition of Manhattan that (with few exceptions) has failed to generate its own typology of urban form.

It sits facing Times Square, its claws on the southern block, its twin tails to the north and its wings spreading across 48th Street, which dissects it. The Sphinx is a luxury hotel as a model for mass housing.

The ground and mezzanine floors contain functions that are extensions and additions of the questionable facilities that give the Times Square area its character. They are designed to accommodate the luxuriant demand of sidewalk activities along Broadway and Seventh Avenue.

The Hotel's main entrance lobby on 47th Street, facing Times Square (and the Times Building) contains an international information center. This lobby also connects with the existing infrastructural facilities.

A new subway station — complicated as a spider's web — will link all the subway stations that now serve the Times Square area. The legs of the Sphinx contain escalators ascending to a large foyer serving theaters, auditoriums, ballrooms, conference and banquet rooms. Over this zone, a restaurant forms the wings of the Sphinx. On one side it enjoys the view of a typical midtown street, on the other side of Nature, or at least New Jersey.

The roof of this restaurant is an outdoor playground and garden for the surrounding residential accommodation in the flanks of the structure. This accommodation consists of a collection of any imaginable number of units: hotel bedrooms and serviced suites for transient population alternate with apartments and culminate in villas with private gardens on the terraced steps that descend in opposite directions to avoid the over-shadowing that would result from the narrowness of the site, and to achieve better east-west views. The twin towers that form the tail of the Sphinx contain north-facing double-height studio apartments, while the connecting middle section is an office block for the residents.

The neck of the Sphinx facing Times Square contains the residents' clubs and social facilities: this is the section over the entrance lobby and main auditorium, and below the circular head of the Sphinx. This section is divided by the number of clubs that occupy it. These are headquarters for the various trades and professions to which the residents belong, each displaying its identity and proclaiming its messages by means of the ideological billboard construction that clads the face of the tower, competing with the existing signs and symbols of Times Square.

Hotel Sphinx facing onto Times Square.

The head of the Sphinx is dedicated to physical culture and relaxation. Its main feature is the swimming pool. A glazed screen divides the pool into two parts: indoor and outdoor. Swimmers can dive under the screen from one part to the other. The indoor section is surrounded by four stories of locker rooms and showers. A glass-brick wall separates these from the pool space. A spectacular view of the city can be enjoyed from the small open-air beach. Waves made in the outdoor part of the pool crash directly onto the pavement. The ceiling over the pool is a planetarium with suspended galleries for the audience and a semi-circular bar that forms the crown of the Sphinx; its patrons can influence the planetarium's programming, improvising new trajectories for the heavenly bodies.

Below the pool is a floor for games and gymnastics. A staircase and ladders connect the diving island in the pool to this floor and continue to the floor below, which contains steambaths, saunas and massage parlor. In the beauty parlor and hairdresser (the lowest floor of the head of the Sphinx), residents relax. The chairs face the perimeter wall, which is clad in mirror glass. Below the part reflecting the face from a sitting position, a small porthole affords a view out toward the city below.

Finally a lounge, indoor/outdoor restaurant and garden form the section that separates the head of the Sphinx from the clubs. This is the location of the jacking and twisting mechanisms of the head of Hotel Sphinx: in response to certain important events, the face of the Sphinx can be directed to "stare" at various points in the city. In response to the level of nervous energy in the Metropolis as a whole, the whole head can be jacked up or down.

New Welfare Island (1975–76)

Welfare (now Roosevelt) Island is a long (about three kilometers), narrow (200 meters on average) island in the East River, more or less parallel to Manhattan. Originally the island was the site of hospitals and asylums — generally a storehouse for "undesirables."

Since 1965, it has been undergoing a half-hearted "urbanization." The question is: is it to be a true part of New York — with all the agonies that implies — or is it to be a civilized escape zone, a kind of *resort* that offers, from a safe distance, the spectacle of Manhattan burning?

The island's planners have so far chosen the latter alternative — although no more than 150 meters from Manhattan, it is now connected to the mother island merely by a cable car (colored in a cheerful "holiday" purple) whose service could easily be suspended in case of urban emergencies.

For over a century, Welfare Island's dominant architectural incident had been the crossing of the monumental Queensboro Bridge that connects Manhattan to Queens (without an exit to the smaller island) and casually cuts Welfare Island into two parts. The area north of the bridge has now been developed by the Urban Development Corporation, a New York State agency, with a series of blocks that terrace down with equal enthusiasm to both Manhattan *and* Queens (why?), and which are arranged on both sides of a picturesquely kinked Main Street. New Welfare Island, on the contrary, is a *metropolitan* settlement on the sector *south* of Queensboro Bridge, a stretch that coincides with the area between 50th and 59th streets in Manhattan.

The project is intended as a resuscitation of some of the features that made Manhattan's architecture unique: its ability to fuse the popular with the metaphysical, the commercial with the sublime, the refined with the primitive — which together explain Manhattan's former capacity to seduce a mass audience for itself. It also revives Manhattan's tradition of "testing" certain themes and intentions on smaller, experimental "laboratory" islands (such as Coney Island at the beginning of the century).

For this demonstration, the Manhattan Grid is extended across the East River to create eight new blocks on the island. These sites will be used as a "parking lot" for formally, programmatically and ideologically competing architectures — which would confront each other from their identical parking spaces.

All the blocks are connected by an elevated travelator (moving pavement) that runs from the bridge southward down the center of the island: an accelerated architectural promenade. At the tip of the island it becomes amphibious, leaving the land to turn into a *trottoir* on the river, connecting floating attractions too ephemeral to establish themselves on land. Those blocks that are not occupied are left vacant for future generations of builders.

From north to south, New Welfare Island so far accommodates the following structures:

1. Built around Queensboro Bridge without actually touching it is the Entrance Convention Center — a formal entrance porch to Manhattan that is, at the same time, a colossal "roadblock" separating the southern half of the island from the northern. An auditorium for mass meetings is slotted underneath the bridge; two marble slabs contain cellular office accommodation. Between them, above the bridge, they support a suspended glass object — whose steps reflect the curve of the bridge — that contains a stacked sports and entertainment center for the Conventioneers.

2. Buildings that were once proposed for New York, but for whatever reason aborted, will be built "retroactively" and parked on the blocks to complete the history of Manhattanism. One such building is a Suprematist Architecton stuck by Malevich on a postcard of the Manhattan skyline — sometime in the early twenties in Moscow — but never received. Due to an unspecified scientific process that would be able to suspend gravity, the involvement of Malevich's Architectons with the surface of the earth was tenuous: they could assume, at any moment, the status of artificial planets visiting the earth only occasionally — if at all. The Architectons had no program: "Built without purpose, [they] may be used by man for his own purposes...." They were supposed to be "conquered" programmatically by a future civilization that deserved them. Without function, Architectons simply exist, built from "opaque glass, concrete, tarred felt, heated by electricity, a planet without pipes.... The planet is as simple as a tiny speck, everywhere accessible to the man living inside it who, in fine weather, may sit on its surface...."

3. In the middle of the New Welfare Island development is the harbor, carved out of the rock to receive floating structures such as boats — in this case Norman Bel Geddes' "special streamlined yacht" (1932).

New Welfare Island, axonometric. Manhattan is
on the left, Queens on the right, New Welfare
Island in the middle. From top to bottom:
Entrance Convention Center penetrated by
Queensboro Bridge; Suprematist Architecton;
harbor with streamlined yacht; "Chinese" swimming pool; Welfare Palace Hotel with raft; plaza;
river-*trottoir*. Opposite the UN Building on
Manhattan Island is the Counter-UN standing on
a small island. On Manhattan itself can be seen
the "separation" of Hotel Sphinx and the RCA
Building. In Queens is "desperation park" with
its modern housing; the suburb; the Pepsi-Cola
sign; the Power Station. Approaching in the
river is the floating pool.

4. South of the harbor is a park with a "Chinese" swimming pool in the form of a square, part of which is carved out of the island, while the complementary part is built out on the river. The original coastline has become three-dimensional — an aluminum Chinese bridge that follows in plan the line of the natural coastline. Two revolving doors at either end lead to locker rooms inside the two halves of the bridge (one for men, the other for women). Undressed, the sexes emerge from the middle of the bridge, from where they can swim to the recessed beach.

5. The tip of the island is occupied by Welfare Palace Hotel and a semicircular plaza.

6. The travelator continues on the water to a point just south of 42nd Street. Along its way, it passes a small island opposite the United Nations Building, to which the Counter-UN has been attached: a slab that repeats the silhouette of the original, with an attached auditorium. The open space of this small island serves the recreational needs of the office workers of this Counter-UN.

Welfare Palace Hotel (1976)

The Welfare Palace Hotel — a "City within a City" — occupies the block
near the tip of the island. It accommodates 10,000 guests, and each day
as many visitors again. It is a composition of seven towers and two slabs.
The ten-story slabs are placed on the edges of the block to define the
"field" of the Hotel. Since the island tapers toward the tip, the block of the
Hotel is incomplete, but the two slabs still run the full width of the island
into the water so that the shore runs through the Hotel as a geological
fault. On the field between the slabs, six towers are arranged in a V formation, pointing at Manhattan. A seventh tower on the Queens side does not
"fit" on the island; it has become a horizontal water-scraper with a roof-
garden on its former facade.
The towers increase in height as they move away from Manhattan; the
tops are so designed that they "stare" at Manhattan, especially at the
RCA Building, which steps down toward the Hotel.
The Hotel has four facades, designed individually to respond to the
different formal and symbolic demands of their respective situations.
The southern facade, along the semicircular plaza, is the dominant
elevation. Three-dimensional fragments have dissociated themselves from
the main slab to lead their own lives. The fragments have a double
function: together, they form a decorative relief with an explicit figurative
message — a city collapsing; separately, they provide differentiation of the
Hotel's accommodation — small palatial skyscrapers that can be reserved
for private functions. The materials of the fragments are as diverse
as possible — marble, steel, plastic, glass — providing the Hotel with the
history it would otherwise lack.
The ground floor of the Hotel is subdivided into a series of independent
zones, each with its own particular function:
The first zone — the sector closest to Manhattan — is a theater and night-
club-restaurant on the twin themes of *shipwreck* and *uninhabited island*. It
holds 2,000 people — only a small percentage of the Hotel's visitors. Its
floor is inundated. A stage is carved out of the steel hull of an overturned,
sinking ship. Columns are disguised as lighthouses, frantically piercing the
darkness with their beams. Guests can sit, eat and watch performances on
the terraces along the water or they may board the lifeboats — luxuriously
equipped with velvet benches and marble tabletops — that emerge from a
hole in the sinking ship to move slowly through the interior on submerged
tracks. Opposite the sinking ship is a sandy island, symbolizing Manhattan
in its virgin state. It can be used for dancing. Outside the Hotel, exactly

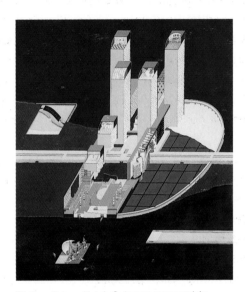

Welfare Palace Hotel. Cutaway axonometric
shows, consecutively on the ground floor:
inundated theater/restaurant/nightclub (with
uninhabited island, overturned ship, lighthouse
columns, dining terraces, lifeboats); island-as-
found-plaza with shopping; reception area of
Hotel; access to the horizontal water-scraper
(concealed between the rear four skyscrapers
with park on top).
On each side of the Hotel's transverse axis is
a long low slab — one overlooks the "Chinese"
pool, the other the semicircular plaza. The
facade of this latter slab has been fragmented
into a three-dimensional mural which functions
as luxury accommodation.
In V formation are six skyscrapers — each with
its own club (whose respective themes are
related to the mythology established on the
ground floor of each tower).
Tower 1: locker rooms, square beach surrounded
by circumferential pool; tower 2: ship's bridge
as bar; tower 3: Expressionist club as climax of
the mural; tower 4: vacant; tower 5: waterfall/
restaurant; tower 6: Freud Unlimited Club.
The light blue in front of the Hotel is an artificial
skating rink; to the left of the Hotel is a park
with the "Chinese" swimming pool; in front of
the Hotel is a gigantic three-dimensional *Raft of
the Medusa* executed in plastic (with a small
area equipped for dancing).

between Manhattan and Welfare Island, floats a gigantic reproduction of Géricault's *Raft of the Medusa;* it is a symbol of Manhattan's metropolitan agonies — proving both the need and the impossibility of "escape." It is an equivalent of 19th-century public sculpture. When the weather permits it, the lifeboats leave the interior of the Hotel to go out on the river. They circle around the raft, compare the monumental suffering of its occupants to their own petty anxieties, watch the moonlit sky and even board the sculpture. A section is equipped as dance floor, relaying the music that is produced inside the Hotel through hidden microphones.

The second zone of the Hotel — open to the air — represents the island *as found,* and is lined with shops.

The third zone — where the course of the travelator is interrupted — is the reception area of the Hotel.

Beyond that is the fourth zone — the horizontal water-scraper with a park on top and conference facilities inside.

There is a different club at the top of each skyscraper. Their glass visors can retract to expose the club's activities to sunlight.

The themes of the clubs relate to the themes established directly below them on the ground floor, so that elevators shuttle between two interpretations of the same "story."

The first tower — above the uninhabited island on the ground floor — has a square beach and a circumferential swimming pool. A glass plate separates locker rooms for men and women.

The second tower — the only office building — is equipped, with the "displaced" bridge of the sinking ship. Guests feel like captains here, drinking their cocktails in the euphoria of apparent control, oblivious to the disaster that occurs 30 floors below them.

The third tower is an Expressionistic environment, concluding the agitation of the south facade in a paroxysm of decorative arbitrariness. The top of the fourth tower is vacant and awaits future, unspecified occupancies.

The top of the fifth tower, which stands in water, is a waterfall whose unpredictable reflections will be visible from the city.

The top of the sixth tower, the one furthest removed from Manhattan, is terminated by a three-dimensional allegorical interior that extrapolates and "predicts" the real destinies of the RCA, Chrysler and Empire State buildings, of whose tortured relationships the Hotel is the "postponed" offspring.

That part of the semicircular plaza in front of the Hotel which is not on the island is turned into ice. North of the Hotel is the "Chinese" swimming pool.

The Story of the Pool (1977)

MOSCOW, 1923

At school one day, a student designed a floating swimming pool. Nobody remembered who it was. The idea had been in the air. Others were designing flying cities, spherical theaters, whole artificial planets. Someone *had* to invent the floating swimming pool. The floating pool — an enclave of purity in contaminated surroundings — seemed a first step, modest yet radical, in a gradual program of improving the world through architecture. To prove the strength of the idea, the architecture students decided to build a prototype in their spare time. The pool was a long rectangle of metal sheets bolted onto a steel frame. Two seemingly endless linear locker rooms formed its long sides — one for men, the other for women. At either end was a glass lobby with two transparent walls; one wall exposed the healthy, sometimes exciting underwater activities in the pool, and the other, fish agonizing in polluted water. It was thus a truly *dialectical* room, used for physical exercise, artificial sunbathing and socializing between the almost naked swimmers.

The prototype became the most popular structure in the history of Modern Architecture. Due to the chronic Soviet labor shortage, the architects/ builders were also the lifeguards. One day they discovered that if they swam in unison — in regular synchronized laps from one end of the pool to the other — the pool would begin to move slowly in the opposite direction. They were amazed at this involuntary locomotion; actually, it was explained by a simple law of physics: *action = reaction.*

In the early thirties, the political situation, which had once stimulated projects such as the pool, became rigid, even ominous. A few years later still (the pool was quite rusty now, but popular as ever), the ideology it represented became suspect. An idea such as the pool, its shiftiness, its almost invisible physical presence, the iceberg-like quality of its sub-merged social activity, all these became suddenly subversive.

In a secret meeting, the architects/lifeguards decided to use the pool as a vehicle for their escape to freedom. Through the by now well-rehearsed method of *auto-propulsion,* they could go anywhere in the world where there was water. It was only logical that they wanted to go to America, especially New York. In a way, the pool was a *Manhattan block* realized in Moscow, which would now reach its logical destination.

Early one morning in the Stalinist thirties, the architects directed the pool away from Moscow by swimming their relentless laps in the direction of the golden onions of the Kremlin.

NEW YORK, 1976

A rotating schedule gave each lifeguard/architect a turn at the command
of the "ship" (an opportunity rejected by some hard-core anarchists,
who preferred the anonymous integrity of continuous swimming to such
responsibilities).

After four decades of crossing the Atlantic, their swimsuits (front and
back panels were exactly the same, a standardization following a 1922
edict to simplify and accelerate production) had almost disintegrated.
Over the years, they had converted some sectors of the locker room/
corridor into "rooms" with improvised hammocks, etc. It was amazing how,
after 40 years at sea, relationships between the men had not stabilized
but continued to display a volatility familiar from Russian novels; just
before arriving in the New World, there had been a flare-up of hysteria
which the architects/swimmers had been unable to explain, except as
a delayed reaction to their collective middle age.

They cooked on a primitive stove, living on supplies of preserved cabbage
and tomatoes, and on the fish they found each daybreak washed into
the pool by the Atlantic's waves. (Although captive, these fish were hard
to catch due to the pool's immensity.)

When they finally arrived, they hardly noticed it — they had to swim away
from where they wanted to go, toward what they wanted to get away from.
It was strange how familiar Manhattan was to them. They had always
dreamed of stainless-steel Chryslers and flying Empire States. At school,
they had even had much bolder visions, of which, ironically, the pool
(almost invisible — practically submerged in the pollution of the East River)
was proof: with the clouds reflected in its surface, it was more than a
Skyscraper — it was a patch of heaven here on earth.

Only the Zeppelins they had seen crossing the Atlantic with infuriating
velocity 40 years before were missing. They had expected them to hover
over the Metropolis like a dense cloud drift of weightless whales.

When the pool docked near Wall Street, the architects/swimmers/
lifeguards were shocked at the uniformity (dress, behavior) of their visitors,
who swamped the craft in a brute rush through the lockers and showers,
completely ignoring the instructions of the superintendents.

Had Communism reached America while they were crossing the Atlantic?
they wondered in horror. This was exactly what they had swum all
this time to avoid, this crudeness, lack of individuality, which did not
even disappear when all the businessmen stepped out of their Brooks
Brothers suits. (Their unexpected circumcisions contributed to this
impression in the eyes of the provincial Russians.)

Arrival of the Floating Pool: after 40 years of
crossing the Atlantic, the architects/lifeguards
reach their destination. But they hardly notice
it: due to the particular form of locomotion of
the pool — its reaction to their own displacement in the water — they have to swim toward
what they want to get away from and away
from where they want to go.

They took off again in shock, directing the pool further upstream: a rusty salmon, ready — finally — to spawn?

3 MONTHS LATER

The architects of New York were uneasy about the sudden influx of Constructivists (some quite famous, others long thought to have been exiled to Siberia — if not executed — after Frank Lloyd Wright visited the USSR in 1937 and betrayed his Modern colleagues in the name of Architecture).

The New Yorkers did not hesitate to criticize the design of the pool. They were all against Modernism now; ignoring the spectacular decline of their profession, their own increasingly pathetic irrelevance, their desperate production of flaccid country mansions, the limp suspense of their trite complexities, the dry taste of their fabricated poetry, the agonies of their irrelevant sophistication, they complained that the pool was so bland, so rectilinear, so unadventurous, so boring; there were no historical allusions; there was no decoration; there was no ... shear, no tension, no *wit* — only straight lines, right angles and the drab color of rust.

(In its ruthless simplicity, the pool threatened them — like a thermometer that might be inserted in their projects to take the temperature of their decadence.)

Still, to have Constructivism over with, the New Yorkers decided to give their so-called colleagues a collective medal at a discreet waterside ceremony. Against the background of the skyline, the dapper spokesman of New York's architects gave a gracious speech. The medal had an old inscription from the thirties, he reminded the swimmers. It was by now irrelevant, he said, but none of Manhattan's present architects had been able to think of a new motto....

The Russians read it. It said, "THERE IS NO EASY WAY FROM THE EARTH TO THE STARS." Looking at the starry sky reflected in the narrow rectangle of their pool, one architect/lifeguard, still dripping wet from the last lap, answered for all of them: "We just went from Moscow to New York...."
Then they dove into the water to assume their familiar formation.

5 MINUTES LATER

In front of Welfare Palace Hotel, the raft of the Constructivists collides with the raft of the Medusa: optimism vs. pessimism.
The steel of the pool slices through the plastic of the sculpture like a knife through butter.

First tentative landings of pool: Wall Street. A moving "block" joins the blocks of Manhattan's Grid.

Notes

PREHISTORY

1. E. Porter Belden, *New York: Past, Present and Future* (New York: Putnam, 1849), p. 1.
2. John A. Kouwenhoven, *The Columbia Historical Portrait of New York* (New York: Doubleday, 1953), p. 43.
3. John W. Reps, *The Making of Urban America* (Princeton, N.J.: Princeton University Press, 1965), p. 148.
4. Ibid., pp. 297–98.
5. William Bridges, "Commissioners' Remarks," in *Map of the City of New York and Island of Manhattan* (New York, 1811), p. 24.
6. Text of advertisement in Belden, *New York: Past, Present and Future.*
7. Reps, *The Making of Urban America,* pp. 331–39.
8. Ibid.
9. William Richards, *A Day in the Crystal Palace and How to Make the Most of It* (New York, 1853).
10. *Official Guidebook, New York World's Fair* (New York: Exposition Publications, 1939).

CONEY ISLAND:
THE TECHNOLOGY OF THE FANTASTIC

1. Lindsay Denison, "The Biggest Playground in the World," *Munsey's Magazine,* August 1905.
2. Maxim Gorky, "Boredom," *The Independent,* August 8, 1907.
3. *History of Coney Island* (New York: Burroughs & Co., 1904), pp. 4–7.
4. Denison, "The Biggest Playground."
5. Edo McCullough, *Good Old Coney Island* (New York: Charles Scribner's Sons, 1957), p. 55.
6. *Guide to Coney Island* (Long Island Historical Society Library, n.d.).
7. McCullough, *Good Old Coney Island,* p. 291.
8. *Guide to Coney Island.*
9. "The Annual Awakening of the Only Coney Island," *New York Times,* May 6, 1906.
10. *Guide to Coney Island.*
11. Ibid.
12. "The Annual Awakening."
13. Oliver Pilat and Jo Ransom, *Sodom by the Sea* (New York: Doubleday, 1941), p. 161.
14. *History of Coney Island,* p. 10.
15. Ibid.
16. *Guide to Coney Island.*
17. *History of Coney Island,* pp. 24, 26.
18. Pilat and Ransom, *Sodom by the Sea,* p. 191.
19. *Guide to Coney Island.*
20. *Grandeur of the Universal Exhibition at St. Louis* (Official Photographic Company, 1904).
21. *History of Coney Island,* p. 22.
22. Ibid.
23. Ibid., p. 12.
24. Ibid., p. 15.
25. Ibid., p. 16.
26. *Guide to Coney Island.*
27. Pilat and Ransom, *Sodom by the Sea,* p. 168.
28. Denison, "The Biggest Playground."
29. James Huneker, *The New Cosmopolis* (New York, 1915).
30. Gorky, "Boredom."
31. Walter Creedmoor, "The Real Coney Island," *Munsey's Magazine,* August 1899.
32. Advertisement in *New York Herald,* May 6, 1906.
33. Quotes about Globe Tower are from *Brooklyn Union Standard,* May 27, 1906, and *Brooklyn Daily Eagle,* May 19, 1907.

34. Article, *New York Herald*, February 22, 1909.
35. Gorky, "Boredom."
36. Pilat and Ransom, *Sodom by the Sea*, p. 169.
37. Ibid., p. 172.
38. Text on back of postcard.
39. Pilat and Ransom, *Sodom by the Sea*, text on book jacket.
40. McCullough, *Good Old Coney Island*, p. 331.
41. Ibid., p. 333.

THE DOUBLE LIFE OF UTOPIA: THE SKYSCRAPER

1. *Life,* October 1909.
2. *King's Views of New York* (New York: Moses King, Inc., 1912), p. 1.
3. Benjamin de Casseres, *Mirrors of New York* (New York: Joseph Lawren, 1925), p. 219.
4. Text on back of postcard.
5. W. Parker Chase, *New York — The Wonder City* (New York: Wonder City Publishing Co., 1931), p. 185.
6. Louis Horowitz, as quoted in Earle Schultz and Walter Simmons, *Offices in the Sky* (Indianapolis and New York: Bobbs-Merrill Co., 1959), p. 80.
7. Ibid., p. 177.
8. All quotes about the 100-story building are from an article in the *New York Herald*, May 13, 1906, sec. 3, p. 8.
9. *Manna Hatin, The Story of New York* (New York: The Manhattan Company, 1929), p. xvi.
10. Chase, *New York — The Wonder City*, p. 184.
11. Andy Logan, *New Yorker,* February 27, 1965.
12. This section is based on various Hippodrome programs; on Murdock Pemberton, "Hippodrome Days — Case Notes for a Cornerstone," *New Yorker,* May 7, 1930; and on "Remember the Hippodrome?" *Cue,* April 9, 1949.
13. Henri Collins Brown, *Fifth Avenue Old and New — 1824–1924* (New York: Official Publication of the Fifth Avenue Association, 1924), pp. 72–73.
14. S. Parker Cadman et al., *The Cathedral of Commerce* (New York: Broadway Park Place Co., 1917).
15. All quotes about Murray's Roman Gardens from Chas. R. Bevington in *New York Plaisance — An Illustrated Series of New York Places of Amusement,* no. 1 (New York: New York Plaisance Co., 1908).
16. This building was first discovered by Robert Descharnes and published in his superb *Gaudí;* I am very grateful for his collaboration in securing the illustrations reproduced here.
17. Hugh Ferriss, *The Metropolis of Tomorrow* (New York: Ives Washburn, 1929).
18. Hugh Ferriss, *Power in Buildings* (New York: Columbia University Press, 1953), pp. 4–7.
19. Howard Robertson, as quoted on book jacket of Ferriss, *Power in Buildings*.
20. Ferriss, *The Metropolis of Tomorrow,* pp. 82, 109.
21. Ferriss, *Power in Buildings*.
22. Thomas Adams, assisted by Harold M. Lewis and Lawrence M. Orton, "Beauty and Reality in Civic Art," in *The Building of the City,* The Regional Plan of New York and Its Environs, vol. 2 (New York, 1931), pp. 99–117.
23. As quoted in ibid., pp. 308–10.
24. "Fête Moderne: A Fantasie in Flame and Silver," program for the Beaux-Arts Ball, 1931.
25. Article, *New York Herald Tribune,* January 18, 1931.
26. "Fête Moderne."
27. *Pencil Points,* February 1931, p. 145.
28. *Empire State, A History* (New York: Empire State, Inc., 1931).
29. Edward Hungerford, *The Story of the Waldorf-Astoria* (New York: G. P. Putnam & Sons, 1925), pp. 29–53, 128–30.
30. Frank Crowninshield, ed., *The Unofficial Palace of New York* (New York: Hotel Waldorf-Astoria Corp., 1939), p. x.
31. Hungerford, *The Story of the Waldorf-Astoria.*
32. *Empire State, A History.*
33. William F. Lamb, "The Empire State Building, VII: The General Design," *Architectural Forum,* January 1931.
34. *Empire State, A History.*
35. Paul Starrett, *Changing the Skyline: An Autobiography* (New York: Whittlesey House, 1938), pp. 284–308.
36. *Empire State, A History.*
37. *Architectural Forum,* 1931.
38. Lucius Boomer, "The Greatest Household in the World," in Crowninshield, *Unofficial Palace,* pp. 16–17.
39. Ibid.
40. Kenneth M. Murchison, "The Drawings for the New Waldorf-Astoria," *American Architect,* January 1931.
41. Ibid.
42. Texts on back of postcards.

43. Kenneth M. Murchison, "Architecture," in Crowninshield, *Unofficial Palace*, p. 23.

44. Francis H. Lenygon, "Furnishing and Decoration," in ibid., pp. 33–48.

45. Lucius Boomer, as quoted by Helen Worden in "Women and the Waldorf," in ibid., p. 53.

46. Clyde R. Place, "Wheels Behind the Scenes," in ibid., p. 63.

47. Boomer, "The Greatest Household."

48. B. C. Forbes, "Captains of Industry," in Crowninshield, *Unofficial Palace*.

49. Worden, "Women and the Waldorf," pp. 49–56.

50. Elsa Maxwell, "Hotel Pilgrim," in Crowninshield, *Unofficial Palace*, pp. 133–36.

51. See "The Downtown Athletic Club," *Architectural Forum*, February 1931, pp. 151–66, and "The Downtown Athletic Club," *Architecture and Building*, January 1931, pp. 5–17.

52. Arthur Tappan North, *Raymond Hood*, in the series Contemporary American Architects (New York: Whittlesey House, McGraw-Hill, 1931), p. 8.

53. Chase, *New York — The Wonder City*, p. 63.

HOW PERFECT PERFECTION CAN BE: THE CREATION OF ROCKEFELLER CENTER

1. For much of the biographical information on Raymond Hood, this chapter has relied on Walter Kilham, *Raymond Hood, Architect — Form Through Function in the American Skyscraper* (New York: Architectural Publishing Co., 1973), and on further details generously provided by Kilham in personal interviews.

2. Kilham, *Raymond Hood*, p. 41.

3. "Hood," *Architectural Forum*, February 1935, p. 133.

4. See Howard Robertson, "A City of Towers — Proposals Made by the Well-Known American Architect, Raymond Hood, for the Solution of New York's Problem of Overcrowding," *Architect and Building News*, October 21, 1927, pp. 639–42.

5. North, *Raymond Hood*, introduction.

6. Hugh Ferriss, *The Metropolis of Tomorrow*, p. 38.

7. Kilham, *Raymond Hood*, p. 174.

8. North, *Raymond Hood*, p. 14.

9. Kilham, *Raymond Hood*, p. 12.

10. "Hood," *Architectural Forum*, p. 133.

11. North, *Raymond Hood*, p. 7.

12. Ibid., p. 8.

13. Ibid., p. 12.

14. All quotations from Raymond Hood are in F. S. Tisdale, "A City Under a Single Roof," *Nation's Business*, November 1929.

15. Published in "New York of the Future," special issue of *Creative Art*, August 1931, pp. 160–61.

16. "Rockefeller Center," *Fortune*, December 1936, pp. 139–53.

17. Raymond Hood, "The Design of Rockefeller Center," *Architectural Forum*, January 1932, p. 1.

18. Merle Crowell, ed., *The Last Rivet* (New York: Columbia University Press, 1939), p. 42.

19. David Loth, *The City Within a City: The Romance of Rockefeller Center* (New York: William Morrow & Co., 1966), p. 50.

20. Hood, "The Design of Rockefeller Center," p. 1.

21. Wallace K. Harrison, "Drafting Room Practice," *Architectural Forum*, January 1932, pp. 81–84.

22. Hood, "The Design of Rockefeller Center," p. 4.

23. Kilham, *Raymond Hood*, p. 120.

24. *Rockefeller Center* (New York: Rockefeller Center Inc., 1932), p. 16.

25. Ibid., p. 7.

26. Text on back of postcard.

27. *Rockefeller Center*, p. 38.

28. Kilham, *Raymond Hood*, p. 139.

29. See Loth, *The City Within a City*, p. 27, and "Off the Record," *Fortune*, February 1933, p. 16.

30. *The Showplace of the Nation*, brochure published to celebrate the opening of Radio City Music Hall.

31. "Debut of a City," *Fortune*, January 1933, p. 66.

32. *Showplace of the Nation*.

33. Kilham, *Raymond Hood*, p. 193.

34. "Off the Record."

35. "Debut of a City," pp. 62–67.

36. Bertram D. Wolfe, *Diego Rivera — His Life and Times* (New York: Alfred A. Knopf, 1943), p. 237.

37. Alfred Kurella, as quoted in ibid., p. 240.

38. Diego Rivera, "The Position of the Artist in Russia Today," *Arts Weekly*, March 11, 1932.

39. Wolfe, *Diego Rivera*, p. 337.

40. Ibid., p. 338.

41. Ibid., p. 354.

42. Diego Rivera, as quoted in ibid., pp. 356–57.

43. Ibid., p. 357.

44. Ibid., p. 359, and Diego Rivera, *Portrait of America* (New York: Covici, Friede, Inc., 1934), pp. 28–29.

45. As quoted in Wolfe, *Diego Rivera*, p. 363.

46. Rivera, *Portrait of America*, pp. 26–27.

47. Caption in *The Story of Rockefeller Center* (brochure, New York: Rockefeller Center, Inc., 1932).

48. *Rockefeller Center Weekly,* October 22, 1937.

49. As quoted in "Now Let's Streamline Men and Women," *Rockefeller Center Weekly,* September 5, 1935.

50. Kilham, *Raymond Hood*, pp. 180–81.

51. Harvey Wiley Corbett, "Raymond Mathewson Hood, 1881–1934," *Architectural Forum,* September 1934.

EUROPEANS: BIUER!
DALI AND LE CORBUSIER
CONQUER NEW YORK

1. Salvador Dalí, "New York Salutes Me!," *Spain,* May 23, 1941.

2. Le Corbusier, as quoted in *New York Herald Tribune,* October 22, 1935.

3. Salvador Dalí, *La Femme visible* (Paris: Editions Surrealistes, 1930).

4. Salvador Dalí, "The Conquest of the Irrational," appendix of *Conversations with Dalí* (New York: Dutton, 1969), p. 115.

5. This "theory" was actually put into practice, as described in Robert Sommer, *The End of Imprisonment* (New York: Oxford University Press, 1976), p. 127.

6. Especially important reinforcement for Dalí's theses was provided by the dissertation of the psychiatrist Jacques Lacan, "De la psychose paranoïaque dans ses rapports avec la personalité."

7. Dalí, *La Femme visible.*

8. Salvador Dalí, *Journal d'un genie* (Paris: Editions de la Table Ronde), entry for July 12, 1952.

9. For a more complete record of all the permutations, see Salvador Dalí, *Le Mythe tragique de l'Angélus de Millet* (Paris: Jean Jacques Pauvert, 1963).

10. Geoffrey T. Hellman, "From Within to Without," parts 1 and 2, *New Yorker,* April 27 and May 3, 1947.

11. Le Corbusier, *La Ville radieuse* (Paris: Vincent Fréal, 1964), caption, p. 129.

12. Le Corbusier, *When the Cathedrals Were White — A Journey to the Country of Timid People* (New York: Reynal & Hitchcock, 1947), p. 89.

13. Ibid.

14. Le Corbusier, *La Ville radieuse*, p. 133.

15. Ibid., p. 127

16. As quoted in Hellman, "From Within to Without."

17. Ibid.

18. Le Corbusier, *La Ville radieuse*, p. 207.

19. Ibid., p. 134.

20. Hellman, "From Within to Without."

21. Le Corbusier, *La Ville radieuse*, p. 220.

22. Ibid., diary entry for Sunday, July 22, 1934, p. 260.

23. Quotations are from Salvador Dalí, *The Secret Life of Salvador Dalí* (New York: Dial Press, 1942), pp. 327–35.

24. Dalí, "New York Salutes Me!"

25. Hellman, "From Within to Without."

26. See *New York Herald Tribune,* October 22, 1935.

27. Le Corbusier, *When the Cathedrals Were White*, p. 197.

28. Ibid., p. 92.

29. Ibid.

30. Le Corbusier, "What is the American Problem?," article written for *The American Architect,* published as appendix to *When the Cathedrals Were White*, pp. 186–201.

31. Le Corbusier, *When the Cathedrals Were White*, p. 78.

32. Quotes from Dalí, *The Secret Life of Salvador Dalí*, pp. 372–75.

33. Hugh Ferriss, *Power in Buildings*, plate 30.

34. Frank Monagan, ed., *Official Souvenir Book, New York World's Fair* (New York: Exposition Publications, 1939), p. 4.

35. *Official Guidebook, New York World's Fair.*

36. *Paris Soir,* August 25, 1939.

37. For Le Corbusier's description of the UN design process, see Le Corbusier, *UN Headquarters* (New York: Reinhold, 1947).

38. Interview with author.

39. Ferriss, *Power in Buildings*, plate 41.

Acknowledgments

This book would not exist without the support of:

the *Harkness Fellowships,* which sponsored my first two years in the USA;

the *Institute for Architecture and Urban Studies,* which offered a base in Manhattan; and

the *Graham Foundation for Advanced Studies in the Fine Arts* in Chicago, which awarded a grant to complete it.

In ways known and unknown to them, Pierre Apraxine, Hubert Damisch, Peter Eisenman, Dick Frank, Philip Johnson, Andrew MacNair, Laurinda Spear, Fred Starr, James Stirling, Mathias Ungers, Teri Wehn and Elia Zenghelis have stimulated this book's progress without, in any way, being responsible for its contents.

James Raimes and Stephanie Golden have contributed to the book through their critical interventions in the text, but even more through their continuous moral support.

Without Georges Herscher, Jacques Maillot, Pascale Ogée and Sylviane Rey the book would never have become a physical reality.

Walter Kilham, Jr., has been exceptionally generous in sharing his original materials and his recollections.

Active collaborators at various stages of the work — all of them invaluable — have been Liviu Dimitriu, Jeremie Frank, Rachel Magrisso, German Martinez, Richard Perlmutter, Derrick Snare and Ellen Soroka.

The Appendix is a collective production of Madelon Vriesendorp, Elia and Zoe Zenghelis and myself, working together in the Office for Metropolitan Architecture.

Above all, *Delirious New York* owes a special debt of inspiration and reinforcement to Madelon Vriesendorp.

R.K., January 1978

Credits

Illustration Credits

Avery Architectural Library, Columbia University: 109, 111, 115, 121, 122, 124, 167 bottom, 186, 187, 196, 278 bottom, 280 top, 286 right top, 286 right middle, 286 right bottom, 288

Cooper-Hewitt Museum of Design, New York: 112

Robert Descharnes, Paris: 106, 239

Mrs. Jean Ferriss-Leich: 280 bottom

Herb Gehr, Life Picture Service: 209, 212, 218 top, 218 bottom

Mrs. Joseph Harriss: 116

Walter Kilham, Jr.: 167 top, 168, 175, 179, 180 top, 188, 189, 190

Library of Congress, Division of Maps and Charts: 12

Life Picture Service: 180 bottom

Museum of Modern Art, New York: 268

Museum of the City of New York: 14, 16, 18–19, 244 bottom

New York Public Library: 22 left

Regional Plan Association, New York: 118

Rockefeller Center, Inc.: 193, 202–3, 205, 206, 290

Salvador Dali Museum, Cleveland: 242 bottom right, 244 top

Eric Schall, Life Picture Service: 274 bottom

Waldorf-Astoria Hotel: 149

Appendix

City of the Captive Globe:
Rem Koolhaas with Zoe Zenghelis.
Hotel Sphinx:
Elia and Zoe Zenghelis.
New Welfare Island:
Rem Koolhaas with German Martinez, Richard Perlmutter; painting by Zoe Zenghelis.
Welfare Palace Hotel:
Rem Koolhaas with Derrick Snare, Richard Perlmutter; painting by Madelon Vriesendorp.

Between 1972 and 1976 much of the work on the Manhattan projects was produced at the Institute for Architecture and Urban Studies in New York, with the assistance of its interns and students.

Designed by Nigel Smith
with Donald Chong, Bob Gundu,
Chris Rowat and Nazik Tahri.

Typeset in Franklin and News Gothic.
Additional typesetting by Archetype.

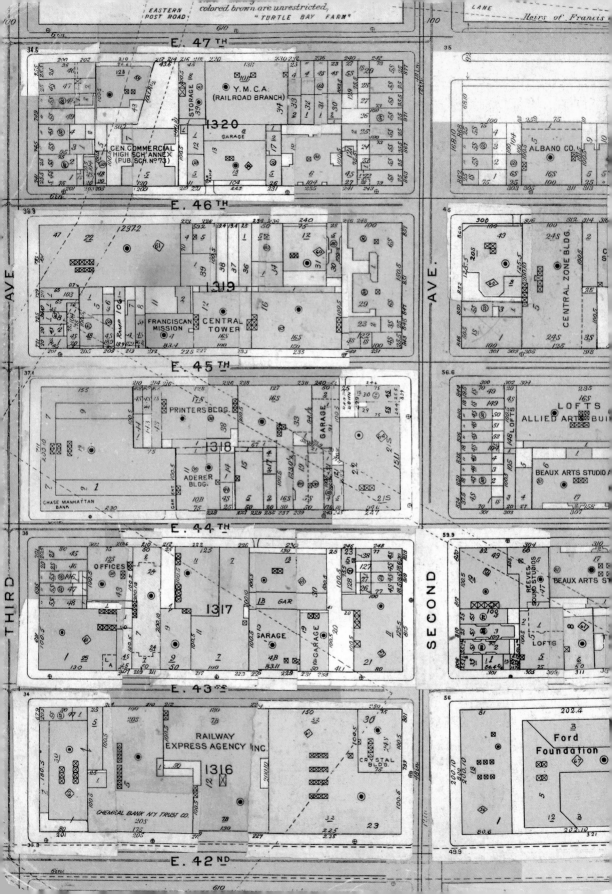